Postmodernism AND THE Enlightenment

Postmodernism AND THE Enlightenment

NEW PERSPECTIVES IN EIGHTEENTH-CENTURY FRENCH INTELLECTUAL HISTORY

EDITED BY DANIEL GORDON

ROUTLEDGE • NEW YORK • LONDON

Published in 2001 by
Routledge
29 West 35th Street
New York, NY 10001

Published in Great Britain by
Routledge
11 New Fetter Lane
London EC4P 4EE

Routledge is an imprint of the Taylor & Francis Group.

Printed in the United State of America on acid-free paper.

Most of the essays in this volume appeared in their current form in the journal *Historical Reflections*, vol. 25, no. 2 (summer 1999). The essays of Daniel Gordon and Alessa Johns have undergone revisions. The essay by Sophia Rosenfeld is published in this volume for the first time.

10 9 8 7 6 5 4 3 2 1

Library of Congress Cataloging-in-Publishing Data

Postmodernism and the Enlightenment : new perspectives in eighteenth-century French intellectual history / edited by Daniel Gordon.
    p. cm. —
Includes bibliographical references and index.
ISBN 0–415–92796–X — ISBN 0–415–92797–8 (pbk.)
    1. Enlightenment—France. 2. Postmodernism. I. Gordon, Daniel, 1961–

B1925 .E5 P65 2000
194—dc21   00–034475

CONTENTS

Postmodernism AND THE
Enlightenment

INTRODUCTION

Postmodernism and the French Enlightenment

DANIEL GORDON

A man does not show his greatness by being at one extremity,
but rather by touching both at once.
                                        —Pascal

Postmodernist thinkers and Enlightenment scholars ought to be in close communication, but in reality they have little to do with each other. On the one hand, we find postmodernist academics whose knowledge of the Enlightenment is limited to a series of derogatory cliches: the Enlightenment glorified "instrumental" reason; the Enlightenment set out to eliminate cultural diversity; the Enlightenment naively idealized history as infinite progress. The bias is acute because "Enlightenment" is to postmodernism what "Old Regime" was to the French Revolution. The Enlightenment, that is to say, symbolizes the modern that postmodernism revolts against. It is the other of postmodernism: not only that which preceded postmodernism but that in opposition to which postmodernism defines itself as a discovery and a new beginning.

On the other hand, the Enlightenment has often attracted scholars who regard *it* with admiration as a new and fortunate beginning. This admiration reached a high point in the period from the early 1930s to the early 1970s, and particularly among liberal intellectuals of German Jewish origin for whom the Enlightenment symbolized the alternative to racism and totalitarianism. For Viktor Klemperer, a professor of Romance languages in Dresden and a Jew who managed to survive the entire Nazi period in Germany, images of the French Enlightenment sustained the will to live in dark times.[1] Ernst Cassirer's *The Philosophy of the Enlightenment*, first published in 1932 and still the most thoughtful book on the subject, took shape as an act of resistance against the cult of the state and an effort to salvage the aesthetic and moral integrity of European culture.[2] The work of Peter Gay, who came to the United States as a young refugee from Hitler, represents one of the last great expressions of this effort to set up the Enlightenment as the positive face of modernity.[3] While postmodernism is critical of modernity *in toto*, these figures presented eighteenth-century thought as a redeeming path into the future.

Since the wide appeal of postmodernism began in the 1970s, when the great wave of pro-Enlightenment scholarship was coming to an end, the two conceptions of the Enlightenment, critical and ideal, did not directly confront each other. The lack of direct contact between theory and erudition continues to this day, for in recent years the central questions in eighteenth-century studies have been not about the structure of Enlightenment thought but about the origins of the French Revolution. This shift from the study of the Enlightenment as an intellectual effervescence in its own right to the study of ideas as a cause of revolutionary politics has powerfully changed the nature of the scholarly discourse. In the works of Robert Darnton, Keith Baker, Sarah Maza, Dale Van Kley, and other leading specialists, one can detect a broadening of the range of sources consulted but also a thinning out of the intellectual history of the period. By streamlining eighteenth-century culture to the point where it can be viewed in relation to a specific outcome, the Revolution, scholars have forged a kind of history that does not require dwelling on the exquisite sophistication of eighteenth-century writing. None of the books by the scholars named above includes extended discussion of the ideas of Voltaire, Montesquieu, Diderot, or Rousseau.[4] This is not to say that the Enlightenment is nothing other than the ideas of a few great authors. There is considerable room for play in the definition of the Enlightenment as a period in cultural history—considerable room to include institutions as well as texts, hack writers as well as canonical theorists, and impersonal processes of change as well as the intentions of individuals. But it would be meaningless to define the Enlightenment without some extended discussion of its greatest minds. The reluctance of so many prominent historians to dwell on the eighteenth century's most complex and nuanced thinkers clearly signifies that the very problem of how to interpret Enlightenment thought has dropped down to the bottom of the agenda for American scholars. A generation of historians in the United States (roughly speaking, those now in their 50s and 60s) has treated the eighteenth century as a studio for filming the process by which absolutism turned into democracy. The major thinkers of the Enlightenment play only cameo roles, or no role at all, in these moving pictures of the rise of a democratic public sphere, the process of desacralization that allegedly undermined kingship, and the formation of Jacobin ideology. Historians would rather discuss a popular pamphlet than a subtle play or a systematic treatise, for the simpler the message, the easier it can be inscribed in a story that must rapidly approach its denouement in 1789. Today, in fact, there are very few historians with an intimate knowledge of the writings of the major *philosophes.*

Tracing the straight genealogy of the Revolution and ignoring the subtle turns of Enlightenment thought made sense to a generation of scholars who were politically charged by the 1960s. Avoiding the liberal predicaments of Montesquieu, Voltaire, and Diderot and focusing instead on the stark terms of Revolutionary ideology ("virtue," "the people," and so forth) appealed to a generation of academics that was not only passionately political but also rigidly disciplined by the idea of progress through academic specialization—hence embarrassed by the literary quality of traditional intellectual history and unresponsive to the literary and unspecialized character of Enlightenment thought itself. In search of a determinate subject around which it could organize archival research while deploying the new methods of statistics and cultural anthropology, these historians found the subject they needed not in the philosophic depths of the period but in its interests, ideologies, mentalities, and discourses—these being terms used to reduce the intellectual field to a clear and simple structure that serves political narrative.

This approach is subject to one of the great pitfalls of historical scholarship—teleology. It is also unclear how our intellectual life has been enriched by historians who have set aside the French Enlightenment and conferred so much status on the problem of Revolutionary origins. Why do we need increasingly detailed accounts of the ideological battles that led to the Revolution? We are told that understanding everything about the Revolution is of vital importance because the Revolution was the beginning of "modern" politics. But it has reached the point where the term "modern" is used like a mantra to give prestige to a field of research and to avoid being precise about its reason for existing. François Furet brilliantly demonstrated the subject's importance for his generation by writing not only about the origins and course of the Revolution but also about its legacy to the radical French Left, of which he was initially a passionate member and later a passionate critic. American scholars, in contrast, have dug into the problem of the origins of the Revolution, but because the Revolution has no obvious legacy in this country, they have not been able to climb out of the hole of academic specialization. The field has become existentially vague: scholars working on the origins of the Revolution have not taken steps to relate their interpretations to the problems and passions of their readers.

Inevitably a reaction has occurred. The work of Dena Goodman seems to mark a generational turning point, a renewed enthusiasm for the ideals of the Enlightenment.[5] Among scholars who, like Goodman, have done their Ph.D.s since the 1980s, there is a rising interest in the nuances of Enlightenment thought as distinct from its ideological distillations. The stock precepts of 1960s and 1970s historiography, which included the denunciation of intellectual history as a type of "elitism," are no longer binding upon a generation that regards "history from below" as what older historians—members of the establishment—like to do. The prospect of spending decades studying the French Revolution has also proved less alluring for a generation not active in the 1960s and thus less intrigued by the idea of revolutionary change. There is, however, a serious interest in the permanent tensions of being a self-conscious person living in a complicated social order.

The *philosophes* were the first to make such tensions the continuous theme of their work, and the essays in this volume display a fascination with the problem of how to give public form to ambivalence. Nearly all the contributors to the volume belong to the post-'60s generation described above. (The exception is Arthur Goldhammer, a freelance writer and translator whose previous academic career was in mathematics and whose independent spirit, one could say, makes him part of every, or no, generation.) Here, I believe for the first time, is a set of essays by scholars who have done patient research about eighteenth-century thought but who are also theoretically astute and aware of the postmodernist tradition. Up to now, the accusations of postmodernist thinkers against the Enlightenment have been ignored, or have been dealt with only in a most superficial or contradictory way, by the older generation of scholars that shifted the historiography over to the question of Revolutionary origins and took little interest in the Enlightenment's own questions. Robert Darnton has taken on the postmodernist challenge in a broadly interpretive essay called "George Washington's False Teeth." But as Jeremy Popkin has observed, Darnton's hostility to postmodernism has little connection to his own scholarship, which is itself postmodernist in its effort to deconstruct the canon and explore marginal discourses. When facing postmodernism's critique of the Enlightenment, Darnton also falls back upon a view of the period that surprisingly resembles the interpretation of Peter Gay, whom Darnton otherwise repudiates in his scholarship.[6]

The discontinuities noted by Popkin, I would add, are symptomatic of an unconfronted contradiction in the older generation of French historians: a contradiction between its own scholarly agenda, which is hostile toward any form of cultural or intellectual history that shows veneration for classic authors and texts, and its discomfort with postmodernist philosophies that take this spirit of negativity to its most radical conclusions. Unable to articulate this discomfort without undermining their own scholarly agenda, many specialists of eighteenth-century French history have reinforced the prejudice of postmodernism against the Enlightenment instead of critically scrutinizing this bias.

The contributors to this volume, in contrast, face the postmodernist challenge to Western culture head-on, both theoretically and empirically. At some point in his or her essay, each author has identified how a leading postmodernist author has characterized a specific theme in Enlightenment thought (some examples are the sense of time in the Enlightenment, the attitude toward European colonies in the Enlightenment, conceptions of economic self-interest and the market in the Enlightenment). The author then dwells on the theme in question and compares the postmodernist account to his or her own scholarly account of how the theme really operated in Enlightenment thought.

In the area combining scholarship and theory arises interpretation, provocative and unorthodox. Unorthodox—because the point of this volume is not to reject skepticism, concern for difference, and everything else that the most conservative critics of postmodernism repudiate. The authors establish the limits of postmodernism's vision of the past, but they do not uncritically worship the Enlightenment. Most have themselves been affected by the postmodernist sensibility. But unlike so many practitioners of "cultural studies," they have not been affected *only* by postmodernism. They are open to the idea that past thinkers can supply as much insight as contemporary ones. They believe the dilemmas experienced in the Enlightenment were as profound as those experienced by Foucault, Lyotard, and de Man. Sometimes, in fact, the dilemmas were the same—but there is no doubt about who dramatized them more acutely and with greater literary flair!

The Enlightenment, then, has not been superseded. It is perhaps not sufficient, but it is not obsolete. While not providing solutions to all our problems, it does provide an introduction to sophistication and clarity, without which nothing can be solved. The essays in this volume, which cover a wide range of topics, reveal a common spirit. The authors sympathize with the honest anxieties of contemporary criticism, but they dispense with its habitual condescension toward the past. Instead of urging us to go beyond the Enlightenment, they encourage us to define our position within its legacy.

The idea for a volume on this subject came from Stuart L. Campbell, the editor of *Historical Reflections*. Most of the essays appeared in their current form in volume 25 (summer 1999) of this journal. Some of the contributors, I among them, have revised their contributions. The essay by Sophia Rosenfeld appears for the first time. I am very grateful to Professor Campbell for initiating this project and for his insightful suggestions and corrections along the way.

NOTES

1. Viktor Klemperer, *Ich will Zeugnis ablegen bis zum letzen: Tagebücher 1933–1945*, 2 vols. (Berlin, 1995). The diary is sprinkled with reflections on the French Enlightenment and notes toward a magnum opus on the subject. Klemperer did in fact publish several works on the Enlightenment after the war.

2. Ernst Cassirer, *The Philosophy of the Enlightenment* (Princeton, 1979; first pub. in German, 1932). For Cassirer's critique of the modern cult of politics, see his *The Myth of the State* (New Haven, 1961; first pub. in 1946). See also Daniel Gordon, "Ernst Cassirer," in *Oxford Encyclopedia of the Enlightenment*, ed. Alan Kors (New York, publication pending).

3. In addition to Gay's numerous books on the Enlightenment, see his *My German Question: Growing Up in Nazi Berlin* (New Haven, 1998).

4. One could claim that Darnton's essay, "Readers Respond to Rousseau" in *The Great Cat Massacre* (New York and London, 1984) is an exception. But this essay deals more with the popular impact of Rousseau's thought than with its internal structure. Darnton, the most influential American scholar of the Enlightenment, is well known for his critique of Peter Gay and for his argument that the previous generation of scholars spent too much time studying the "high" ideas of the Enlightenment. See *The Darnton Debate: Books and Revolution in the Eighteenth Century*, ed. Haydn T. Mason (Oxford, 1998), vol. 359 of *Studies on Voltaire and the Eighteenth Century*.

5. Dena Goodman, *Criticism in Action* (Ithaca, 1989); *The Republic of Letters* (Ithaca, 1994).

6. Robert Darnton, "George Washington's False Teeth," *New York Review of Books*, 27 March 1997, pp. 34–38. Jeremy Popkin, "Robert Darnton's Alternative (to the) Enlightenment" in *The Darnton Debate*, pp. 105–28.

MONTESQUIEU IN THE CARIBBEAN

The Colonial Enlightenment between
Code Noir and *Code Civil*

MALICK W. GHACHEM

The physiognomies of governments can be best detected in their colonies, for there their features are magnified, and rendered more conspicuous.[1]

—Alexis de Tocqueville, *The Old Regime and the Revolution* (1856)

[R]esistance is never in a position of exteriority in relation to power.[2]

—Michel Foucault, *The History of Sexuality: An Introduction* (1976)

For all the influence French thought has had in promoting innovative scholarship in the rest of the world, French historians have by and large neglected to cultivate their own garden insofar as colonial history is concerned. Tocqueville's suggestion that colonialism yields a magnified picture of the true tendencies of the state is just now beginning to bear fruit on the other side of the Atlantic. In France itself, however, an apparent failure to integrate the experience of empire into French history generally has deprived the profession of an important opportunity.[3] To the best of my knowledge, not a single major scholar of the French Revolution has produced important work on colonial history. The prognosis for postrevolutionary history is only slightly more encouraging. Conversely, those French historians who actually *have* spent time in the colonial archives display little evidence of sustained interest in the dynamics of metropolitan history. In some instances this lack of interest stems from a conscious decision to privilege the "agency" of subject populations who for long went without a written history of their own. Considered as a whole, the history of the French empire remains a classic example of a *dialogue des sourds*.

This neglect is both puzzling and deeply rooted in French culture. Empire and its attendant phenomena, including slavery, were a major concern of the philosophes and their nineteenth-century successors. This is to say nothing of such canonical modern intellectuals as Albert Camus, whose novels and short stories are at once unequaled models of colonial writing and acute explanations for the failure of such writing to take hold in French consciousness. In recent years a spate of successful novels and films about former French colonies from Martinique to Algeria to Vietnam has produced an unmistakable cultural efflorescence, fueled by immigration and the tensions associated with a rapidly changing demographic profile.[4] In the face of these contemporary reminders of a remarkably rich and endlessly fascinating heritage, French historical writing seems determined to preserve the insularity and lack of adventurousness that have consigned colonialism and the foreign to a distinctly marginal place.

THE POSTMODERN AND THE POSTCOLONIAL

The polarization between "domestic" and "overseas" history so characteristic of the French situation is only one manifestation of a more disquieting problem that transcends national boundaries. Anglo-American historians have also failed by and large to engage Tocqueville's argument about the relationship of colony to metropole. This failure has much to do with the influence of postmodern thought on the writing of colonial history in recent years, an influence that has tended to push in two closely related directions.

First, postmodern thought has directed attention away from the study of formal law and institutions in favor of constantly multiplying "sites" of nongovernmental, "immanent" authority. The paradigmatic thinker in this respect is of course Foucault, whose famous injunction to "conceive of sex without the law, and power without the king" has become a rallying cry of the burgeoning school of "postcolonial" studies in the United States and in Britain.[5] Foucault's unveiling of what he termed the "juridico-monarchic" image of power and its continuing stranglehold on postabsolutist understandings of society seemed to discredit an older historiography centered on the institutional and bureaucratic workings of the colonial state. "Our historical gradient," he wrote,

> carries us further and further away from a reign of law that had
> already begun to recede into the past at a time when the French

Revolution and the accompanying age of constitutions and codes seemed to destine it for a future that was at hand.[6]

The impulse to "expel" law from history resonated perfectly with the postcolonial determination to restore "agency" to the "subaltern" populations of the European empires.[7] But despite all the focus on indigenous resistance to the imposition of metropolitan authority, it is not at all clear that recent scholars of empire have listened to Foucault's warning that "there is no binary and all-encompassing opposition between rulers and ruled at the root of power relations."[8] Indeed, it may be precisely because of its categorical emphasis on resistance that postcolonial writing has largely failed to do justice to Foucault's nuanced but elusive thesis: "[R]esistance is never in a position of exteriority in relation to power."[9]

In an interview published after the first volume of *The History of Sexuality* appeared, Foucault sought to mollify the anti-institutional thrust of his theory, claiming that he did not mean to say the state is irrelevant.[10] This may be true, but it skirts the ways in which Foucault's essentialist concept of the "juridico-monarchic sphere" and his reduction of law to prohibition vastly oversimplified the legal history of the Old Regime.[11] The same could be said for a second direction in which postmodern thought has tended to push the study of law and colonialism in recent years. Less directly tied to Foucault, the view that "the Enlightenment project" consisted in the effort "to develop . . . universal morality and law . . . for the rational organization of everyday social life" has overtaken postmodern and postcolonial studies to an even greater degree than the "normalization of power" thesis.[12] The Enlightenment is said to have imposed a "homogeneous,"[13] "totalizing discourse"[14] of universalism and rationality on the rest of the world. This imperialist, abstract "fiction" is often contrasted with the "heterogeneities" of the local, the particular and the concrete, values at the expense of which the Enlightenment project is feared to have triumphed. "It is part of the embarrassment of [Enlightenment] bourgeois ideology," writes Terry Eagleton, "that it has never really been able to reconcile difference and identity, the particular and the universal."[15]

In the face of this barrage of accusations, the *philosophes* themselves appear more often than not as the disembodied, protomythic founders of modernity than as objects of local, particular, and concrete historical investigation. It would be unreasonable to expect scholars who are primarily interested in the technologies of power in the nineteenth and twentieth centuries to undertake detailed, archival investigations into the work of eighteenth-century intellectuals. But given all of the talk about Enlightenment universalism and rationalism, pm

it is striking that discussion about the *philosophes* and their legacy remains at such a high level of abstraction, as though epigrammatic assertions about the nature of eighteenth-century thought suffice to account for something mysteriously called the "project of modernity." A similarly detached posture has characterized treatments of what the Enlightenment may have had to say about the forms of colonialism it actually *did* know (as opposed to those it supposedly made possible, or at least helped to justify, in a later age).

In this context, Montesquieu's influence as a theorist of colonial law during the final decades of the Old Regime assumes an unexpected importance. If this is not a role historians often associate with Montesquieu, that may be partly because it provides a useful corrective to the postmodern vision of Enlightenment legal theory as antithetical to the principles of local custom and the particular. It is true that many of the philosophes and physiocrats saw in the more than 360 customary traditions of the Old Regime an ingrained recipe for legal archaism and political obstructionism. But for Montesquieu, those same traditions represented the wisdom of a society that had agreed to tailor its laws to satisfy the diverse interests of culturally autonomous regions.[16] Customary law appeared all the more significant against the backdrop of the "foreign" imports with which it was hopelessly entangled: Roman and canon law. In the *Persian Letters*, he asked:

> Who would think that the oldest and most powerful kingdom in Europe has been governed for more than ten centuries by laws which were not made for it? If the French had been conquered it would not be hard to understand, but it is they who have been the conquerors.[17]

With characteristic irony, Montesquieu thus advocated one particular strand of Enlightenment legal theory, the one that glorified local, homegrown law over both archaic and "superstitious" laws, in the face of a much more vocal strand of criticism that championed uniformity over custom.[18]

For reasons having as much to do with the iconic status of the Civil Code in French political culture as with postmodern images of the Enlightenment, codification and uniformity have been traditionally portrayed in Weberian terms as going hand in hand: "right reason" and the "logically abstract" vindicating the universalist values of a polity dedicated to the rights of individual persons rather than the interests of particular groups and regions.[19] But to a generation of legal reformers in prerevolutionary Saint-Domingue, the greatest of France's eighteenth-century colonies, the contradictions inherent in a code of customary laws were not quite so apparent. This was not a mere failure of insight, but rather a reflection of a peculiar legal sensibility that created and sustained its own canons of coherence and legitimacy. In the 1770s and 1780s a group of colonial jurists approached the daunting task of codifying French law *outre-mer* through the hallowed prism of Montesquieu's radically contextual legal sociology. Under the aegis of a project carried out in the name of universal applicability and conformity, timelessness and centralization, these jurists sought to create a space in which to carry out a politics of the local and the particular, the contingent and the historical.[20] In their writings, it is possible to detect the contours of a latent polarization *within* Enlightenment legal theory itself, a paradoxical synthesis of custom and uniformity that has been largely erased from legal-historical memory.

THE DIALECTIC OF THE COLONIAL ENLIGHTENMENT

Associated to varying degrees with the monarchy and its colonial bureaucracy, the jurists of Saint-Domingue also identified passionately with a "creole" *parlementaire* tradition that toyed repeatedly in the eighteenth-century with the possibility of autonomy from France.[21] This tradition found expression in a veritable deification of what the colonists typically called "local knowledge" (*connaissances locales*). Shorthand for a kind of secondhand, native legal sensibility to which only creole lawyers could stake claim, local knowledge was the centerpiece of the jurists' effort to construct a theory of colonial society that would underwrite their demands for autonomy from the metropole.[22] At its most basic level, the colonial Enlightenment consisted in the "crystallization of a fatal distinction between metropolitans and creoles."[23] The jurists of Saint-Domingue cultivated this distinction with a dedication bordering on the obsessive, knowing that it was their single most powerful weapon in the campaign to organize the legal life of the colony around the principle of local custom. If there was a "dialectic of Enlightenment" to be found in the eighteenth-century French colonies, then, its parameters must surely be located in the relationship between creole self-consciousness and the jurisprudence of the particular.

The language of colonial autonomy clearly bore a strong family resemblance to the judicial rhetoric of provincial resistance to the monarchy, a subject that has spawned a whole industry of secondary works on the Old Regime. Beginning well before the Fronde (1648–53) and extending even beyond Maupeou's ill-fated muzzling of the Parlement of Paris (1771–74), French magistrates repeatedly frustrated attempts to unify and standardize the laws of the metropole. Moreover, it is worth noting that many members of the colonial elite originally hailed from commercial centers, such as Bordeaux, that were also strongholds of *parlementaire* resistance in the early modern period.[24] But the possible connections in this regard, though tantalizing, take us beyond the subject at hand.[25] For however much metropolitan magistrates may have had in common with their colonial counterparts, the two groups were set apart by a complicated legal and political gap that transcended the issue of physical distance.

Montesquieu neatly symbolized this gap at a number of levels. To begin with, he bore witness to a traditional metropolitan distrust of the colonists, a skepticism especially evident among the ranks of the Bordeaux judiciary. In Montesquieu's view, France would never be able to rely on the loyalty of a population that felt victimized from all angles by the *exclusif*, that much despised metropolitan monopoly on trade with the colonies.[26] Montesquieu's notorious antislavery polemics furnished an even sharper thorn of contention, for the obvious reason that without slavery the entire system of colonial trade would amount to little more than a minor enterprise. The colonial magistrates were not necessarily ardent apologists for the Caribbean labor system, but as plantation owners they generally had enough of a financial stake in slavery to view *De l'esprit des lois* as an especially unwelcome form of interference.[27] Or did they? For somehow despite these formidable barriers, Montesquieu found an audience in the colonies that seemed utterly to dwarf his rather muted reception in France itself.

The paradox is a revealing one and serves, in its own right, as a concentrated repository of the contradictions of colonial law. From the perspective of the colonists, however, Montesquieu's overwhelming appeal is not very difficult to explain. Though they could hardly turn a blind eye to the chapters on slavery, the creole jurists were able to impose an adamantly selective reading on the book as a whole. And in this regard they were hardly the last exemplars of an approach to which *De l'esprit* has always been vulnerable, chopped up as it is into so many digestible sections, false starts, and half-baked ruminations. The book's manifest celebration of discontinuity and eclecticism helps to account in part for its ironic fate in the Caribbean, where Montesquieu's opening appeal— "not to judge, by a moment's reading, the labor of twenty years; to approve or to condemn the entire work, and not just individual sentences"—clearly fell on deaf ears.[28]

To say that the colonists' reading of *De l'esprit* was selective, of course, is not to imply that it lacked an internal coherence. Montesquieu's theory of *moeurs* furnished this coherence in all its needed quantities, and then some. Once translated into English as mores (which is derived from the Latin *mores*), the term is stripped of all the connotations that make it such a suggestive concept in the original language.[29] This is because the word *moeurs* bore an intimate connection to the Continental tradition of customary law. Roughly half of part 3 of *De l'esprit des lois* is an extended sermon about the perceived tendency of legislators to "confuse" law with either *moeurs* or manners. For Montesquieu, *moeurs* were prepolitical and hence immune to sudden changes and excessive tinkering by the science of legislation. Inescapably local in character, they were a function of the climate and terrain of a region.[30] "The difference between laws and *moeurs*," he wrote, "is that laws rule the actions of the citizen, [whereas] *moeurs* rule more over the actions of man."[31] In contrast to manners, which were external in nature, *moeurs* expressed the inner character of a person, that vaguely ineffable essence that seemed to elude all but the greatest of legislators.

On the other hand, while laws and *moeurs* were separate categories, they were not to be seen as unrelated.[32] Nor were the environmental *sources* of *moeurs* to be confused with mechanistic *causes*.[33] For if that were so, then legislators would have to give up all hope of influencing the customs of a nation in a positive direction, a hope Montesquieu was determined not to surrender. In a free country, where the laws necessarily bear a strong connection to *moeurs* and manners, it was sufficient for legislators to "inspire other *moeurs* and manners" if they wanted to bring about reform:

> In general, people are very attached to their customs; to deprive
> them forcefully of their customs is to make them unhappy; thus
> one must not change customs, but rather engage people in chang-
> ing their customs themselves. Any penalty that does not derive
> from necessity is tyrannical. The law is not a pure act of power;
> things indifferent by their nature are not part of its jurisdiction.[34]

Montesquieu rather glosses over the precise manner in which these incentives are to be generated, perhaps because he knew that the line between gentle inducement and coercive pressure was hard to distinguish. But he insisted that the line was real, and that any nation choosing to flout this distinction was a despotic one, its people no better than slaves.

Not surprisingly, the subject of slavery filled the other half of the same section that discussed *moeurs*. Sandwiched between the books on climate and the soil, Montesquieu's reflections on slavery formed an integral component of his theory of customary law, which is yet another reason for wondering how the colonists managed to exploit the latter without also stoking the fire of the former. Montesquieu's emphasis on the varieties of slavery clearly provided one way out of this dilemma: political servitude was not the same thing as civil or domestic slavery, though all three tended to reinforce each other in the state of despotism. More reassuringly, from the colonists' perspective, the ideology of custom *itself* generated a loophole by which to justify the New World labor regime. Slavery was contrary to both nature and civil law, but "there are countries where the heat weakens the body, and so impairs one's courage, that men are only brought to carry out onerous duties by the fear of punishment; in these countries slavery is less shocking to reason."[35] Where this was the case, however, political servitude was sure to follow.

The loophole in Montesquieu's theory of slavery was thus not entirely open. But it would suffice for a colonial audience that, after all, had more do with its time than think of ways to resolve the ambiguities of the Enlightenment. Faced with a choice between the letter and the spirit of Montesquieu's text, colonial jurists were quite happy to opt for the latter and to leave textual exegesis to the academy. In so doing, they were not only acting in accord with an ancient legal tradition—privileging the *mens* (spirit) rather than the particularity of the laws[36]—but also shifting the ground of political debate in the colonies. Familiarity with local *moeurs* became not simply the foundation of "good" law but a prerequisite for the very ability to speak about colonial law. In the process, law itself came to be defined not in terms of a set of doctrines, still less in terms of an aggregation of ordinances and decisions, but rather in terms of a legal sensibility, an *esprit.* To reflect this spirit was to display authentic proof of one's "*créolité.*"[37]

One of the first and most important creole jurists to take up this battle cry was Emilien Petit, a distinguished member of the Saint-Domingue judiciary.[38] In his *Droit public, ou Gouvernement des colonies françaises*, Petit described three "general principles for the government of the colonies." The second item on this list of cardinal virtues read: "a knowledge of local places and laws must be the basis of all administration." In Petit's view, the colonies were in the potentially despotic hands of unenlightened bureaucrats "chosen in Europe." For these officials, local knowledge was a kind of experience they "do not even suspect to be necessary, an experience that none of them brings to the place, and that they can only acquire by means of a period of residence they are not permitted."[39] Petit went on to suggest a number of policies, including the establishment of indigenous *conseils d'administration*, which would ensure the harmonious adjudication of colonial disputes. "These principles," he concluded, "are neither foreign nor contrary to the legislation of France for the government of its provinces, nor even [to the legislation] for the government of its colonies."[40]

As this last comment suggests, Petit was willing to go only so far with his criticisms of the existing order. A royalist at heart, he believed that "the choice of laws to transmit to the colonies, [and] their adaptation to the local, belong solely to the sovereign legislator." Moreover, said Petit, the king was fully cognizant of the peculiar conditions of colonial life, conditions that made his overseas possessions "so different from the objects of legislation in the ancient parts of the kingdom."[41] Other jurists were less certain that the scope of the problem was confined to ignorant agents chosen by the Ministère de la Marine. The unofficial leader of this motley band of radicals was Michel René Hilliard-d'Auberteuil, whose *Considérations sur l'état présent de la colonie française de Saint-Domingue* was published in 1776. D'Auberteuil was actually born in France where he was educated as a lawyer before moving to Saint-Domingue to ply his trade as a colonial *avocat*.[42] But his sometimes vituperative attacks on the royal bureaucracy and his passionate defense of colonial autonomy earned him a prominent place in the creole legal community of Saint-Domingue.

The *Considérations*, suppressed in both France and the colonies by an *arrêt du conseil* of 1777,[43] did more than any other single work of the colonial Enlightenment to advance a jurisprudence of *créolité*. It consisted of a series of polemics predictably centered on "the difference that exists between the climate of Saint-Domingue, the *moeurs* and undertakings of the colonists [on the one hand], and the climate of the interior of France [on the other]."[44] Like Petit, d'Auberteuil insisted that eliminating metropolitan "ignorance of the local" was a precondition of positive legal reform. But he went further in his analysis of the underlying problem, invoking language that was scarcely distinguishable from Montesquieu. Laws are legitimate only by virtue of an organic connection to the local community from which they spring.

> Usages and customs, which derive from [the law of nations] (*droit des gens*), are dictated by necessity: they owe their creation to the nature of climates; they are directed by local situations: thus it is absurd to try to establish Customs by means of fiction, and to seek the rule for one country's usages in the usages of another. . . .
> Only local knowledge, which is acquired solely by means of long observation, can lead to good laws.[45]

In a later age, this passage would have been vulnerable to charges of plagiarism.[46] In prerevolutionary Saint-Domingue, on the other hand, regurgitations of *De l'esprit des lois* ran little risk of saturating their market. Between the "*moeurs* of Creoles" and "those of Frenchmen transplanted in the Colony," in short, there was no room for negotiation: only polarization.[47]

To be fair to d'Auberteuil, he was not entirely uncritical of Montesquieu's formulation of custom, nor was he afraid to challenge the *philosophe's* theory of slavery. In a remarkable passage of the *Considérations*, he accused Montesquieu of confusing questions of "law" with questions of "fact" ("*il a presque toujours jugé le droit par le fait*").

Montesquieu turned his gaze to the "thrones of Asia," saw despotism and slavery enshrined in law, and concluded fallaciously that climate was the culprit. In fact, said d'Auberteuil, the regimes of such frosty northern countries as Sweden, Denmark, and Russia proved that political servitude and personal bondage were hardly the exclusive fates of the Southern Hemisphere.[48] But even while criticizing *De l'esprit des lois*, d'Auberteuil claimed fidelity to what he saw as the essential tenets of Montesquieu's system:

> One can oppose Montesquieu with the authority of his own principles, and use him to contradict himself: *the more one is struck in a forceful and lively manner* [by the influence of a hot climate], he says, *the more important it is that this impression be received in a suitable manner*. All that is needed to contain the passions is the eternal power of reason, and in countries where they are at their liveliest, it is all the more important to sustain the empire of the law (*loi*); thus these countries are not made for despotism.[49]

If this passage may not have inspired confidence in d'Auberteuil's capacities as a professional philosopher, it nonetheless serves as a good illustration of the inability of colonial jurists to articulate *créolité* independently of Montesquieu's overshadowing framework.

Even more refined critics of *De l'esprit des lois*, such as the Abbé Raynal and Malouet, were unable to break free from the spell of *moeurs*. Consider the case of the *Essai sur l'administration de Saint-Domingue*, a book first published in Paris in 1785 and then five years later in an extracted "creole" edition (in both cases under Raynal's name). Malouet, a lawyer who resided in the colony as an administrator in the 1770s, is suspected of having played an important role in producing this work, which incorporated scattered materials from the *Histoire philosophique et politique . . . des deux Indes*.[50] Raynal's famous *Histoire*, read the anonymous preface to the 1790 edition, lacked the "horde of local knowledge" that could be found in the present work.[51] Closely following the creole party line about the need for a "local jurisprudence"[52] in the colonies ("It is not possible that the laws and customs of France are all good in America"),[53] the *Essai* indirectly faulted Montesquieu for simplifying the character of creole society. Good and bad qualities were always found "mixed and confused," without either predominating over the other; thus it was foolish to suppose that the resident of Saint-Domingue is "happy or sad, intelligent or stupid, . . . lazy or active." Nonetheless, the *Essai* went on to say, "the climate, the style of life, of work, and of industry necessarily have general and uniform influences on this diversity of types." It was therefore legitimate to speak of the particular "habits of the Colonies."[54]

As this same book demonstrated, the adulation of Montesquieu in Saint-Domingue could go so far as to reach frankly racist levels. Expressing impatience with the sentiments of "philosophy and humanity" even while denouncing slavery as contrary to natural law, the *Essai* argued that blacks were better off under French control than as the "absurd victims" of African "despotism."

> Sugar, coffee, and indigo . . . can only be cultivated by negroes; and I believe that until these people can raise amongst themselves a Montesquieu, they will more closely approach the condition of rational men by becoming our laborers than by remaining subject in their country to the excesses of brigandage and ferocity.[55]

Though other colonial jurists were not nearly as inflammatory about the matter as this, the *Essai*'s approach to the Caribbean labor regime was typical of creole writings: first the condemnation of slavery in the name of *jus naturale*, then its qualified defense in the name of environmental "necessity" and local custom, and finally a closing statement or two about the need to restrain the more savage of the slaveholders.[56] In this sense the *Essai*'s invocation of Montesquieu had a perverse sort of logic to it, in that *De l'esprit des lois* seemed to have inaugurated the Enlightenment tradition of equivocating on the issue of black bondage.

THE CUNNING OF "LOCAL KNOWLEDGE"

Behind the deification of *connaissances locales*, of course, lay some very worldly interests. Those interests were affected by the application of Parisian customary law and royal legislation to the colonies, a policy that constituted the cornerstone of the monarchy's effort to "reduce" the Caribbean islands to manageable form. Before the assumption of full-scale control by the monarchy in 1685 (the year the *Code Noir* was promulgated), the colonies had been governed by a relatively anarchic mix of mercantilist and renegade elements. The colonial courts, it was said repeatedly, had failed to exercise care in the observation of the King's ordinances. Only a strict, "point-by-point" application of the laws of the monarchy could safeguard the principle of juridical certainty and stability.[57]

For the jurists of Saint-Domingue, on the other hand, this policy had to be seen as the source of all manner of troubles. Raynal's and Malouet's *Essai* provided a useful, occasionally sardonic laundry list of these complaints:

> Litigation [in the colonies] bears on objects of interest absolutely foreign to those that occupy us in France. Thus it seems that in

preserving the spirit of our Laws and customs, they should have been combined and modified according to the cases and types appropriate for a Colony; because a proprietor is not a *bourgeois*, a plantation is not a small farm, nor a fief; Negroes are hardly peasants, credits and mortgages no longer have the same character, partitions among direct or collateral inheritors can not be subjected to the same subdivisions. You annihilate manufacturing if you divide the land, Negroes, and buildings into four or five parts; the majority are not even susceptible to partition.[58]

Both Hilliard-d'Auberteuil's *Considérations* and Petit's *Droit public* set forth remarkably similar litanies of grievances.[59] This was far from coincidental, for the magistrates and lawyers of Saint-Domingue were the principal spokespersons for the colony's large plantation owners, most of whom were heavily indebted to metropolitan merchants for past supplies of slaves and luxury goods. Indeed, many of the *conseillers* who sat on the two high courts (*Conseils Supérieurs*) of Saint-Domingue were themselves proprietors of vast sugar, coffee, and indigo estates.

This background helps to explain why the jurists invested so much of their energy in devising particularized and technical legal arguments about the "contradictions" of colonial law. The laundry list of complaints in the *Essai* is only a terse allusion to these arguments, which filled the better part of d'Auberteuil's two-volume *Considérations* (recall that the latter work was subtitled "Ouvrage politique et législatif").[60] Behind the notion that "Negroes are hardly peasants," for example, lay a confusing jumble of customary landlord-tenant law and the doctrines of the Roman law of slavery.[61] It hardly needs saying that this comment reflected concerns about the ability of masters to control their slaves with an unfettered hand. The phrase "credits and mortgages no longer have the same character" was shorthand for a complicated set of distinctions between "mobile" and immobile" property and the conditions under which creditors could seize either kind from insolvent debtors. This was not a minor concern for colonial proprietors who often faced the possibility of losing their slaves in unrelated actions brought by metropolitan merchants for the recovery of overdue loans.[62] Finally, reference to the "annihilation" of "manufacturing" advertised profound anxieties about the application of the Parisian customary law of inheritance to large plantations. The *coutume de Paris*, argued the jurists, reduced profitable estates to irrational proportions, favored inexperienced, absentee landlords at the expense of creole proprietors, and generally disrupted the flow of the plantation economy.[63]

Little wonder, then, that colonists saw Parisian custom as "barbarous in America."[64] In a society "without laws"[65] it was only natural for legislators to derive their rules à la Montesquieu from "the sky and its influence, the soil and its products."[66] The colony's positive law seemed to offer nothing more than a hopeless mass of contradiction and confusion. But for all the resonance of *moeurs* in Saint-Domingue, localism was never the only reaction to this state of affairs. Nor could it be, for weighty interests required the mediation of legal institutions, and those institutions demanded clear and unambiguous rules upon which to base their decisions.[67] The metropolitan administration was clearly unwilling to indulge the party of local custom in these matters, but it was no more satisfied with the status quo than its feisty critics in the Caribbean. Indeed, the difficulty of drawing sharp lines between agents and opponents of the monarchy in the colonies was such that one pamphlet could address the king in the following terms: "Sire, your court is creole."[68] As in France, the royal administration *outre-mer* was never one unitary entity acting according to a set of coherent and consistent motives.

For these and other reasons, the impulse to systematize went hand in hand with the impulse to particularize. Perhaps even more than their counterparts in the metropole, the lawyers of prerevolutionary Saint-Domingue could sense the paradoxical nature of the impending age of codification. Among them was a savvy student of Montesquieu named Moreau de Saint-Méry, a creole jurist who would become the prophet of this new age and all of its unfolding contradictions.

FIXING THE COLONIAL CODE

Several attempts to syncretize custom and uniformity were made as far back as 1716, 1738, and 1758. Emilien Petit, author of the previously discussed *Droit public, ou Gouvernement des colonies françaises*, was hired in 1761 to "collect together" and "perfect" the laws of the colonies.[69] He produced several manuscript volumes for colonial codes in the fields of civil procedure and criminal law that were never published.[70] Petit was also involved with the establishment in 1761 of a "Commission for the Legislation of the French Colonies." The immediate goal of this commission seems to have been the compilation of a compendium *(recueil)* of colonial laws, not a code per se. Even so, the monarchy seems to have thought better of the idea after it had taken hold in the colonies: in 1768, another *arrêt* was issued suppressing the king's own commission.

What was it about the project of a colonial compendium, the prelude to a code, that might have resulted in such embarrassingly self-defeating policies? One possible answer is hinted at in the preface to Petit's *Projet d'ordonnance criminelle*, which lays the evils of colonial jurisprudence at the feet not simply of metropolitan law *per se* but also the colonial courts whose task it was to register and administer that law.[71]

"Codification," R. C. Van Caenegem observes, "was historically a weapon against the judiciary."[72] From this perspective, the monarchy's seeming inability to move forward with a colonial code owed as much to a power struggle between creole magistrates and bureaucratic agents as to the incoherence and contradictions of colonial laws. Only by going over the heads of the colonial magistrates altogether could the monarchy side-step this conflict, but such an approach must have seemed unrealistic so long as all the knowledge necessary to construct a code of laws was held by figures such as Petit. What was needed was a member of the judiciary who did not so identify with that institution that he would see in the idea of a colonial code nothing more than a plot to wrestle discre-tionary power away from the hands of local tribunals. A creole judge who also harbored ambitions to wield authority in metropolitan politics would be the perfect candidate.

Born in Martinique in 1750, Moreau de Saint-Méry was the heir to a long and proud tradition of family service in the colonial judiciary.[73] After leaving his native island in 1768 to pursue a law degree in Paris, he returned to the Antilles in 1774 fully expecting to become a barris-ter in Martinique. But a shortage of funds forced him to disembark instead at Cap Français, then the bustling commercial capital of Saint-Domingue. In 1776, as an *avocat* attached to the *Conseil Supérieur* for the colony's northern district, he started to put together a massive collec-tion of manuscript legal documents that an earlier creole jurist, dis-couraged by the effort's massive scope and unrelenting tedium, had left unfinished. When the Marquis de Castries became minister of the Marine in 1780, he retained Moreau to complete research on this pro-ject and to begin the task of transforming the compendium into a code. In short, Moreau was finally involved in redacting the great colonial panacea that had been the monarchy's goal for decades. The first of six volumes of the *Loix et constitutions des colonies françaises* was published in 1784 and distributed to an initial group of 30 illustrious subscribers, the first of whom was the king himself. The next year Moreau was appointed to a much-coveted seat on the colonial bench.

The *Loix et constitutions* was an enormous collection over five-thou-sand pages in length documenting in minute detail the legal and administrative history of French colonialism in the Caribbean from its inception down to the eve of the Revolution. For the monarchy Moreau's work must have seemed the final step on the road to "fixing" a colonial code and thereby containing creole discontent in Saint-Domingue.[74] But as in the debates over the French constitution, two very different meanings could be ascribed to the notion of "fixation": a massive aggre-gation of the extant laws of the colonies, or a thoroughgoing systematiz-ation resulting in the promulgation of entirely new, more general principles and rules.[75] The various attempts to codify French law *outre-mer* had always wavered between these poles without seeming to settle definitively on either one. To compound the problem, Moreau himself seems to have viewed the *Loix et constitutions* in terms of a somewhat broader range of purposes than the domestication of creole agitation. Like his benefactors, Moreau was determined to streamline and simplify colonial jurisprudence "by more certain principles."[76] But just what Moreau understood by these "principles" was another matter altogether. In the preliminary discourse to the *Loix et constitutions*, he would think through the problems of colonial law in such a way as to give the project of codification a distinctly unexpected twist.

Moreau's primary insight was to recognize that "a conscious and universal reorientation of legal life" in Saint-Domingue would not succeed unless it was accompanied by a theory of colonial society consistent with the political culture of *créolité*. The preliminary discourse thus gives every indication of having been written for the domestic consumption of two very different audiences. At the same time, it reads like something of a manifesto for the imperial future of France, delicately weighing the implications of any shift in the systemic balance of power between metropole and colony. Acknowledging that the "specific Administration of the colonies" was but "a branch of the Administration of the Kingdom," Moreau nonetheless asserted that

> it is not possible to link the colonies to this general system without their influencing that system in turn, and in a more or less appreciable manner at that. Thus, only the proper combination of this sort of action and reciprocal reaction can give rise to the greatest common good.[77]

The concept of "reciprocity" was central to Moreau's understanding of colonialism: it distinguished his approach from the polemics of creole publicists on the one hand and the "false ideas" of metropolitan administrators on the other.[78] By tempering metropolitan "actions" with creole "reactions," the government of Saint-Domingue would be able to transcend the most intractable obstacle in the way of colonial reform: interest. "How many special and opposing interests to combine and to reconcile!" Moreau lamented. "Even when one believes one has prepared and calculated for everything, an obstacle often remains in the execution, and the project wisest in appearance is blocked."[79]

Now that the colonial code was no longer a distant prospect on the horizon but a very real imperative, it was "more essential than ever that a deft hand guard the balance between the colonies and the metropole and allow it to tilt only in the direction of the State."[80] The key to maintaining this balance, Moreau argued, was to provide a set of principles that would "stabilize" the colonial system, a system "that has thus far resulted only in measures lacking a sense of interconnection."[81] Not surprisingly, these principles were to be found in the province of legislation. Departing from the traditional mantra of creole lawyers, Moreau avoided a head-on confrontation with the *coutume de Paris* and argued instead that the primary problem of colonial legislation was administrative instability. The successive governors and *intendants* of Saint-Domingue had issued an endless series of "contradictory and multiple" decrees, leaving colonial law in a state of "continuous fluctuation" and uncertainty.[88]

But Moreau did not take this confused state of affairs as a license to promulgate an entirely new body of laws for the colonies. Rather, it was necessary to proceed on the basis of already established policies that had been designed for "a People existing for more than a century." Then, reasoning by "relation" and "analogy," it would be possible to compare these laws with each other, examining them in light of colonial "*moeurs*" and "current events":

> It is not that the legislation of the colonies can be perfected without new laws, but rather that such laws must be kept to a minimum; the objects with which they may concern themselves being but an extension of previously promulgated laws, the new regulations, properly speaking, will consist only in the natural development of the old ones.[83]

With these words Moreau attempted to resolve the tension between the metropolitan and creole understandings of codification. Rather than an ambitious rationalization of law from the top down, Moreau's *code des colonies* would work from the colonial ground up, relying on those time-tested practices embodied in the "specific legislation of this superb province."[84]

This formulation of the matter still left a number of issues undecided, however. To begin with, if the corpus of colonial laws had *already* been corrupted by the contradictory influences of arbitrarily issued administrative decrees, it was unclear precisely what principles would be used in sorting out the good from the bad in this "specific legislation." Moreau's only remedy was to reassert the received creole wisdom about the virtues of local knowledge, and the preliminary discourse accordingly rambles on for several pages in a discussion of the necessary relationship between law and the "*moeurs*," "climate" and "character" of a people:

> Nothing can take the place of local knowledge. With the immortal Montesquieu, we submit that laws must always cater to the genius, *moeurs*, and essential needs of those for whom they are destined . . .

But is it not in the study of laws and of the history of this country that one must seek this prerequisite, absolutely necessary knowledge?[85]

The circularity of this all too familiar argument was exceeded only by its ineffectiveness in addressing the concrete dilemmas facing colonial legislators. To Moreau this may not have seemed as grave a problem as in fact it was, for he correctly saw the *code des colonies* as involving a fundamentally political conflict between largely incompatible goals. Just as it was the task of colonial administrators to balance metropolitan "actions" against local "reactions," Moreau would use his preliminary essay to temper the discourse of codification—and its emphasis on uniformity and conformity—with the more palatable language of customary law.

The result was a prescription that, in seeking to appease both the impulse to codify and the pressure to customize, ultimately satisfied neither. Moreau was able to avert this problem only by leaving an even larger matter unresolved: the precise contours of the colonial code itself. For even as he slighted an innovative jurisprudential scheme in favor of relying on the existing body of colonial laws, Moreau spoke of the massive *Loix et constitutions* as the mere

> base of the Edifice that we wish to raise. . . . It is this base that must serve as a repertory and as a prescription for the design of a new body of legislation; . . . it is a corpus of law anatomically presented . . . the careful study of which is made to precede all interpretation and reform.[86]

Moreau clearly had more in mind by the phrase "colonial code" than simply compiling in meticulous detail the totality of colonial laws from 1550 to 1784. He wished no less than to "perfect" the legal framework of colonial life, to set it on thoroughly determinate foundations. But it was precisely this that the traditions and tensions of colonial politics would not permit.

The *Loix et constitutions* thus remained a hybrid, more than a random compilation and less than a formal code but finally something in between. As both an intellectual abstraction and as a concrete political document, the colonial code was perhaps destined to acquire the permanent status of a work-in-progress. But however incomplete, the *Loix et constitutions* set Moreau's career on a radically new course. It also helped set in motion a political dynamic that was to end only with the irreversible divorce between colony and metropole Moreau struggled so hard to forestall, thereby bringing the dialectic of the colonial Enlightenment to a culmination. When that split began to appear imminent, even this most loyal and creole of colonial servants knew it was finally time to leave "an immense country populated with slaves, restrained by a handful of free men."[87]

The early years of the French Revolution would make clear just how far Moreau had succeeded in effectuating a reorientation in the legal consciousness of the colonies.[88] After returning to France for the last time in 1788, Moreau threw himself into the flurry of political agitation on behalf of the Third Estate of Paris, successfully running for president of that estate's Assembly of Electors. At the same time he preserved his bridge to the world of colonial affairs, serving as the outspoken leader of the Martinique delegation to the National Assembly while quietly lobbying for a royal nomination as *intendant* of Saint-Domingue. Only the stunning accusation that Moreau had called for emancipation of the slaves in a May 1789 speech before the Assembly of Electors kept him from rising even higher up the ladders of metropolitan and colonial politics. He was able to demonstrate the fabricated nature of the charge, but this did not prevent Moreau from becoming a pariah in the colonies.[89]

Saint-Domingue would finally get its code, but only after a full-scale slave rebellion culminated in the establishment of an independent Haiti in 1804. That same year the long struggle to systematize the civil laws of France was finally brought to a close. In 1828, a diminutive volume entitled *Les Six Codes d'Haiti* was published in the new capital of Port-au-Prince. Modeled on the various Napoleonic codes, the volume contained within its slender covers that "unambiguous fixation of the law" that had always seemed to elude the French monarchy.[90] As for the new nation rising slowly from the ashes of old Saint-Domingue, codification was only the beginning of its sorrows.

AFTER POSTCOLONIALISM

The notion of a colonial Enlightenment gnaws at the modern conscience. For those who see in eighteenth-century thought a kind of ethical compass, associating the term "Enlightenment" with the legal philosophy of a slaveholding society seems inconsistent at best and morally dubious at worst. Philosophes such as Montesquieu and Raynal, according to this line of thinking, were prophets of individual autonomy and critical humanism, heroic progenitors of the abolitionist movement, not the instruments of legitimation for a creole culture that was willing to maintain its racist privileges at almost any cost.[91]

The great achievement of postmodern thought has been to unsettle this warm and fuzzy view of things. However uncomfortable it may be for us to recognize, the transatlantic political culture of prerevolutionary France did indeed generate a "colonial Enlightenment," a movement of ideas that looked for inspiration to the very same thinker who is so often identified with modern liberalism: Montesquieu. The colonists' selective reading of him facilitated this paradox but does not fully explain it, since the dilemmas of colonial law were built into the logic of *De l'esprit des lois* itself. But postmodernism has triumphed in revising our picture of eighteenth-century thought only at the cost of imposing its own oversimplification, one that sees in the Enlightenment and its apostles so many dark harbingers of later tragedies. Often denounced as a hegemonic, totalizing effort to construct universal morality and law, the Enlightenment has been deprived of its complex character as "an event, or set of events . . . located at a certain point in the development of European knowledge."[92]

For this reason, the efforts of postmodern and postcolonial scholars to endow the particular and the peripheral with an inherently positive value—by way of reinforcing postmodernism's negative image of the Enlightenment—make little historical sense. If anything, the experience of French colonial law in its formative period should make these scholars wary of attempts to organize politics around the principle of local knowledge. But that is hardly the point of understanding the Enlightenment as a contingent complex of events whose meaning, said Foucault, must be sought in "a series of historical inquiries that are as precise as possible."[93] Perhaps, as more of this historicizing work registers with contemporary theory, the once harmonious chorus of "the Enlightenment" will give way to a cacophony of disparate voices. Foucault himself seems skeptical of this possibility; in his words, "[we] must try to proceed with the analysis of ourselves as beings who are historically determined, to a certain extent, by the Enlightenment."[94] Be that as it may, to the extent that concepts such as the colonial Enlightenment continue to clash with and thereby complicate our sense of the moral content of eighteenth-century thought, they will serve a useful role.

There is another reason why we should persist in wrestling with historical incongruities of the sort afforded by Montesquieu's posthumous Caribbean career. Though it remains a well-kept secret in France, colonial historians are the trustees of a valuable perspective on modernity. In Tocqueville's version of this inheritance, the history of empire is a stage on which the authentic tendencies of metropolitan politics reveal themselves. "When I want to discover the spirit and vices of the government of Louis XIV," he wrote, "I must go to Canada. Its deformities are seen there as through a microscope." Liberated by the absence of "feudal traditions" in the colonies, "nothing prevented the central power from abandoning itself to all its natural inclinations."[95] But Tocqueville was not the first person to exploit the colonies as both metaphor and laboratory for the Old Regime, nor did he fully exhaust their potential as a heuristic device. Three years before the Revolution a jurist named François de Neufchateau gave a speech before the high court for the northern district of Saint-Domingue in which he made the following claim: "It is a great advantage of the state of our colonies that they conduce more easily than the kingdom to the introduction of useful reforms."[96]

Thus, eighteenth-century writers themselves seemed attuned to the possibilities of empire as a privileged locus of analysis wherein no shadow falls between the act and the intention. Unlike Tocqueville, who was more interested in identifying the "vices" and "deformities" of absolutism than in teasing out its virtues, Neufchateau sought rather vainly to portray the New World as a streamlined version of the Old. For our purposes, though, the real excitement may lie in the space *between* these two complementary perspectives, a space in which the colonies can be seen to form islands of metropolitan history not quite real and yet not wholly imaginary either. And in that sense, scholars of the Enlightenment might do well to follow Montesquieu on a Caribbean voyage of their own.

NOTES

1. Alexis de Tocqueville, *The Old Regime and the French Revolution*, trans. Stuart Gilbert (Garden City, NY, 1955), p. 253. I would like to thank Daniel Gordon, Keith Baker, Peter Sahlins, James Whitman, Joe Zizek, Laurent Dubois, and Jonathan Schorsch for their comments on earlier versions of this essay.

2. Michel Foucault, *The History of Sexuality: An Introduction*, trans. Robert Hurley (New York, 1990), p. 95.

3. Two notable exceptions in the field of Enlightenment studies are Michelle Duchet, *Anthropologie et histoire au siècle des lumières: Buffon, Voltaire, Helvétius, Diderot* (Paris, 1971; reprinted Paris, 1995), and Tzetvan Todorov, *Nous et les autres: La Réflexion française sur la diversité humaine* (Paris, 1989).

4. One of the most prominent contributors to this phenomenon has been Patrick Chamoiseau, a writer from Martinique whose novel *Texaco* was awarded the Prix Goncourt, France's highest literary honor.

5. Foucault, *The History of Sexuality*, p. 91.

6. Ibid., p. 89.

7. The term "expulsion" is used by Alan Hunt and Gary Wickham, *Foucault and the Law: Towards a Sociology of Law as Governance* (London, 1994), pp. 59-71. "Subaltern studies" is the label for a school of largely Indian historians who have approached the history of the British Empire from the perspective of landless peasant populations joining together to resist the Raj.

8. Foucault, p. 94.

9. Ibid., p. 95.

10. Michel Foucault, *The Foucault Reader*, ed. Paul Rabinow (New York, 1984), p. 64.

11. This point is developed at length in Hunt and Wickham, *Foucault and Law*, pp. 39–71.

12. On the notion of an "Enlightenment project," see Jürgen Habermas, "Modernity—An Incomplete Project" in Patricia Waugh, ed., *Postmodernism: A Reader* (London, 1992), p. 165. While Habermas is not often thought of as belonging comfortably to the postmodernist camp, he is regularly invoked as authority for the "Enlightenment project" thesis in postmodern writings. See also Thomas Docherty, ed., *Postmodernism:*

A Reader (New York, 1993), p. 95; Peter Fitzpatrick, *The Mythology of Modern Law* (London, 1992), p. 44; and Hans Bertens, *The Idea of the Postmodern: A History* (New York, 1995), pp. 114, 118.

13. Docherty, *Postmodernism*, p. 445.

14. Joe Doherty, Espeth Graham, and Mo Malek, eds., *Postmodernism and the Social Sciences* (New York, 1992), pp. 2–3.

15. Terry Eagleton, "Nationalism, Irony, and Commitment" in Terry Eagleton, Fredric Jameson, and Edward W. Said, *Nationalism, Colonialism, and Literature* (Minneapolis, 1990), pp. 30–31. For a very similar view, see Chantal Mouffe, "Radical Democracy: Modern or Postmodern?" in Andrew Ross, ed., *Universal Abandon?: The Politics of Postmodernism* (Minneapolis, 1988), pp. 36, 38, 44. (My insertion of the term "Enlightenment" in Eagleton's quote is not an act of editorial discretion; the identification of the Enlightenment with "bourgeois ideology" is explicit.)

16. Joseph Goy, "Civil Code" in François Furet and Mona Ozouf, eds., *A Critical Dictionary of the French Revolution*, trans. Arthur Goldhammer (Cambridge, MA, 1989), p. 438.

17. Charles-Louis de Secondat, baron de Montesquieu, *Persian Letters*, trans. and ed. Christopher J. Betts (New York, 1973), p. 185.

18. For an additional perspective on Montesquieu as an enemy of the "abstract universalism of conventional natural law," see Donald R. Kelley, *The Human Measure: Social Thought in the Western Legal Tradition* (Cambridge, MA, 1990), pp. 219–222.

19. Max Weber, *Economy and Society: An Outline of Interpretive Sociology*, ed. Guenther Roth and Claus Wittich, trans. Ephraim Fischoff et al., 2 vols. (Berkeley, CA, 1978), 2: 854.

20. My analysis of the marriage of uniformity and local custom is indebted to James Whitman's discussion of the "mingling" of custom and reason in eighteenth-century legal thought. See James Q. Whitman, "Why Did the Revolutionary Lawyers Confuse Custom and Reason?" *The University of Chicago Law Review* 58 (1991): 1326–27, 1367–68.

21. Throughout this essay the term "creole" is invoked in its original eighteenth-century sense to refer to persons of any race born in the Caribbean colonies. Occasionally I will use the phrase in a looser sense—as in "creole culture" or "*créolité*—to refer to a movement of ideas organized around the principle of local custom, in which case the birthplace of the authors who express these ideas is less of an issue. Today the term is generally taken to mean any speaker of the various Creole languages.

22. For the notion of a "legal sensibility," see Clifford Geertz's essay "Local Knowledge: Fact and Law in Comparative Perspective" in his *Local Knowledge: Further Essays in Interpretive Anthropology* (New York, 1983), pp. 167–234.

23. Benedict R. Anderson, *Imagined Communities: Reflections on the Origin and Spread of Nationalism*, rev. ed. (New York, 1991), p. 60.

24. See William Doyle, *The Parlement of Bordeaux and the End of the Old Regime, 1771–1790* (London, 1974), pp. 23, 102, 210–214.

25. An excellent starting point is Charles Frostin, *Les Révoltes blanches à Saint-Domingue aux XVIIième et XVIIIième siècles* (Paris, 1975), pp. 342–379.

26. Robin Blackburn, *The Making of New World Slavery: From the Baroque to the Modern, 1492–1800* (New York, 1997), p. 300; and idem, *The Overthrow of Colonial Slavery, 1776–1848* (New York, 1988), p. 48.

27. There were some important exceptions to this generalization. Moreau de Saint-Méry, whom I will discuss below, seems never to have owned property in slaves throughout his many years in Saint-Domingue, though he grew up on a slave plantation in Martinique.

28. Charles-Louis de Secondat, baron de Montesquieu, *De l'esprit des lois* in *Oeuvres complètes*, ed. Roger Caillois, 2 vols. (Paris, 1951), 2: 229 [hereafter Montesquieu, *De l'esprit des lois*]. (Unless otherwise noted, all remaining translations in this essay are my own.)

29. The recent Cambridge translation of Montesquieu uses the term "mores," whereas the much older, contemporary translation by Thomas Nugent used "custom." The problem with "custom" is that it makes impossible any distinction between *coutume* and *moeurs*, but "mores" seems such a flat term in English that I will use the original French word in the rest of this essay.

30. "The empire of climate is the first of all empires." Montesquieu, *De l'esprit des lois*, p. 565.

31. Ibid., p. 566.

32. Ibid., p. 571.

33. Ibid., pp. 574–75.

34. Ibid., p. 565.

35. Ibid., pp. 495–96.

36. Kelley, *The Human Measure*, p. 195.

37. I borrow this term from the title of Patrick Chamoiseau, Jean Bernabé, and Raphael Confiant, *Éloge de la Créolité* (Paris, 1989).

38. For information on Petit, see the introduction by Arthur Girault to Emilien Petit, *Droit public, ou Gouvernement des colonies françaises*, Collection des économistes et des réformateurs sociaux de la France, (Paris, 1771; reprint, Paris, 1911), p. ix. Petit sat on one of the colony's two high courts (*Conseils Supérieurs*).

39. Ibid., p. 230.

40. Ibid., p. 232.

41. Emilien Petit, *Droit public, ou Gouvernement des colonies françaises*, 2 vols. (Paris, 1777), 1: 393. I have had to use two different editions of this work, but they are identical in everything except pagination. All further references to Petit's *Droit public* are from the two-volume, 1777 edition.

42. Frostin, *Les Révoltes blanches*, p. 21. See also the introduction by Lewis Leary to Michel René Hilliard-d'Auberteuil, *Miss McCrea: A Novel of the American Revolution*, trans. Eric LaGuardia (Gainesville, FL, 1958), pp. 6–11; and Gordon K. Lewis, *Main Currents in Caribbean Thought: The Historical Evolution of Caribbean Society in its Ideological Aspects, 1492–1900* (Baltimore, 1983), pp. 129–36.

43. Gabriel Debien, *Les Colons de Saint-Domingue et la Révolution: Essai sur le club Massiac* (Paris, 1953), p. 157.

44. Michel René Hilliard-d'Auberteuil, *Considérations sur l'état présent de la colonie française de Saint-Domingue*, 2 vols. (Paris, 1776–77), 1: 5.

45. Ibid., 2: 311, 316.

46. I mean this only partly in jest. Some sentences of the *Considérations* were literally copied word for word from *De l'esprit des lois*.

47. Hilliard-d'Auberteuil, *Considérations*, 1: 7.

48. Ibid., 2: 37.

49. Ibid., p. 38. Emphasis in the original.

50. For the argument that the *Essai* was compiled from passages of the *Histoire*, see the entry on Raynal in the *Biographie universelle, ancienne et moderne*, 52 vols. (Paris, 1811–28), 37: 182. For the (not incompatible) view that Malouet was the likely author, see Anatole Feugère, *Un précurseur de la Révolution: L'Abbé Raynal (1713–1796)* (Angoulême, 1922; reprinted Geneva, 1970), p. 364. Malouet and Raynal had been friends since well before the latter's return to France from exile in 1785.

51. The addition of these local details, read the preface, led "some persons" to doubt that Raynal was the bona fide author of the *Essai*.

52. Guillaume-Thomas Raynal, *Extrait d'un ouvrage intitulé: Essai sur l'administration de Saint-Domingue* (Port-au-Prince, Saint-Domingue, 1790), p. 30 [hereafter Raynal, *Extrait d'un ouvrage*].

53. Guillaume-Thomas Raynal, *Essai sur l'administration de Saint-Domingue* (Paris, 1785), p. xv [hereafter Raynal, *Essai*].

54. Ibid., pp. 6–7.

55. Ibid., p. ix.

56. See, for example, the parallel treatment of slavery in Hilliard-d'Auberteuil, *Considérations*, 1: 130–35.

57. "Arrêt du Conseil du Petit-Goave, qui ordonne l'exécution de la coutume de Paris, et des ordonnances de Sa Majesté, du 6 Mars 1687," in Médéric-Louis-Elie Moreau de Saint-Méry, *Loix et constitutions des colonies françaises de l'Amérique sous le Vent*, 6 vols. (Paris and Cap Français, Saint-Domingue, 1784–90), 1: 451.

58. Raynal, *Extrait d'un ouvrage*, pp. 26-27.

59. Hilliard-d'Auberteuil, *Considérations*, 2: 338-48; Petit, *Droit public*, 2: 167–84. It should be noted that Petit, in line with his royalist inclinations, was less polemical about the contradictions of colonial law.

60. The crux of this analysis was d'Auberteuil's discussion of the *coutume de Paris*. He measured the *coutume*'s articles against analogous provisions in Roman law and went on to point out areas of contradiction with the *Code Noir* of 1685. Hilliard-d'Auberteuil, *Considérations*, 2: 338-48. The rhetoric of this passage echoes François Hotman and the Renaissance humanist tradition.

61. See generally Emilien Petit, *Traité sur le gouvernement des esclaves*, 2 vols. (Paris, 1777).

62. Hilliard-d'Auberteuil, *Considérations.*, 2: 331–33. See also Raynal, *Essai*, pp. 173–75.

63. Hilliard-d'Auberteuil, *Considérations*, 2: 333. Raynal, *Extrait d'un ouvrage*, p. 27. For a much more detailed analysis of these issues than I have space to provide here, see Edith Géraud-Lloca, "La coutume de Paris outre-mer: l'habitation antillaise sous l'Ancien Regime," *Revue historique de droit français et étranger* (1982): 207–59. Colonial animosity toward absentee landlords is also illustrated in Raynal, *Essai*, p. 174.

64. Raynal, *Essai*, p. 176.

65. Hilliard-d'Auberteuil, *Considérations*, 2: 336. See also Raynal, *Extrait d'un ouvrage*, pp. 29.

66. Hilliard-d'Auberteuil, *Considérations*, 2: 365–66.

67. Petit gave voice to this strand of thought in a series of questions: "How will justiciable parties be informed of the system of their judges? How will they know the laws that an adjudicator is obliged to follow? Where is the compendium of laws that each court prescribes for itself? Above all, where is the law that grants this freedom and this power to the judges who claim it on their own behalf?" Petit, *Droit public*, 2: 181.

68. Quoted in C. L. R. James, *The Black Jacobins: Toussaint L'Ouverture and the San Domingo Revolution*, 2d ed., rev. (New York, 1963), p. 57.

69. Moreau de Saint-Méry, *Loix et constitutions*, 4: 440.

70. Emilien Petit, "Projet de *code civil* pour toutes les colonies," Anciens fonds français, Bibliothèque Nationale, Paris, ms. FR 12084; idem, "Projet d'ordonnance criminelle pour les colonies françaises de l'Amérique," Anciens fonds français, ms. FR 12085.

71. Petit, "Projet d'ordonnance criminelle." This manuscript is not paginated.

72. R. C. Van Caenegem, *Judges, Legislators, and Professors: Chapters in European Legal History* (Cambridge, 1987), p. 152.

73. In an autobiographical pamphlet published in 1790, Moreau noted that his family had been established in Martinique for more than 150 years. Médéric-Louis-Elie Moreau de Saint-Méry, *Mémoire justificatif* (Paris, 1790), p. 2. For biographical information on Moreau, see Anthony Louis Elicona, *Un colonial sous la Révolution en France et en Amérique: Moreau de Saint-Méry* (Paris, 1934); Augustin François, baron de Silvestre, *Notice biographique de M. Moreau de Saint-Méry . . . lue à la Société royale d'agriculture* (Paris, 1819); and the introduction to Médéric-Louis-Elie Moreau de Saint-Méry, *Description topographique, physique, civile, politique et historique de la partie*

française de l'isle Saint-Domingue, ed. Blanche Maurel and Étienne Taillemite, 2 vols. (Paris, 1958), 1: vii-xxxvi.

74. Moreau's mandate read in part as follows: "The king . . . wishing to fix the jurisprudence of the Colonies by more certain principles, has ordained that work be done . . . towards a general code of the Colonies." M. Merlin, ed., *Répertoire universel et raisonné de jurisprudence civil, criminelle, canonique, et bénéficiale,* 5th ed., 18 vols. (Paris, 1827–28), 3: 63.

75. Keith Michael Baker, *Inventing the French Revolution: Essays on French Political Culture in the Eighteenth Century* (Cambridge, 1990), p. 253.

76. Merlin, *Répertoire universel et raisonné,* 3: 63.

77. Moreau de Saint-Méry, *Loix et constitutions,* 1: vii–viii.

78. The reference to "false ideas" is from François de Neufchateau, *Les Etudes du magistrat; Discours prononcé à la rentrée du Conseil Supérieur du Cap, le Jeudi 5 Octobre 1786* (Cap Français, Saint-Domingue, 1786), p. 56. Neufchateau's pamphlet appears in Bibliothèque Moreau de Saint-Méry, Centre des Archives d'Outre-mer, Aix-en-Provence [hereafter Bibliothèque Moreau de Saint-Méry], 87 MiOM 4.

79. Moreau de Saint-Méry, *Loix et constitutions,* 1: viii.

80. Ibid., p. ix.

81. Ibid., p. x.

82. Ibid., p. xi.

83. Ibid., p. xii.

84. Ibid., p. xiii.

85. Ibid., p. xxi.

86. Ibid., p. xvi.

87. Ibid., p. xvii.

88. The philosophy behind Moreau's *code des colonies* would live on in such works as Coquille-Dugommier's *Projet d'une constitution générale-coloniale* (St. Pierre, Martinique, 1790), which is in the Bibliothèque Moreau de Saint-Méry, 87 MiOM 14.

89. For the details of this affair, see Elicona, pp. 26–76; and Moreau de Saint-Méry, *Mémoire justificatif.*

90. Weber, *Economy and Society,* 2: 848.

91. For a portrait of Montesquieu as the embodiment of a moderate, critical humanism, see Todorov, *Nous et les autres,* pp. 389–437. For the view that the Enlightenment catapulted individual autonomy to center-stage in the modern world, see Peter Gay, *The Enlightenment: An Interpretation,* vol. 1, *The Rise of Modern Paganism* (New York, 1977), p. 3.

92. Foucault, *The Foucault Reader,* p. 43.

93. Ibid. Foucault also argued that "we do not break free of [simplistic understandings] by introducing 'dialectical' nuances while seeking to determine what good and bad elements there may have been in the Enlightenment." Ibid. But there may be two separate issues at stake here, for it seems to me that discovering "nuances" within the Enlightenment—dialectical or otherwise—is an essential task. What must be avoided is the dogmatic mapping of these nuances onto polarized axes of good and evil, as Foucault correctly points out.

94. Ibid.

95. Alexis de Tocqueville, *The Old Regime and the Revolution, Volume 1: The Complete Text,* ed. François Furet and Françoise Mélonio, trans. Alan S. Kahan (Chicago, 1998), p. 280. I thank James Whitman for urging me to think more carefully about Tocqueville.

96. Neufchateau, *Les Etudes du magistrat,* p. 58.

MAN IN THE MIRROR

Language, the Enlightenment, and the Postmodern

ARTHUR GOLDHAMMER

Distaste for the Enlightenment is the pathognomonic sign of the post-modern. Language, once the centerpiece of the mouth-watering eight-eenth-century feast, has gone off, we are told, turned rotten. About language, they say, the old masters were always wrong: because their theories of language embody a dubious "metaphysics of presence,"[1] or overtly or covertly adopt one or another misleading "intentionalist" or "phenomenalist" doctrine of reference,[2] or peremptorily "impose a structure on the sign,"[3] or reduce language to representation, emphasizing the mimetic to the detriment of the poetic.[4] The "epistemology of conceptual language" is alleged to be "self-destructive" because it cannot "keep literal reference and figural connotation apart."[5]

This last quotation, from Paul de Man, is emblematic and worth pursuing. De Man would no doubt have rejected the label "postmodernist," but his interrogation of the Enlightenment conception of language is crucial for understanding the main point of contention. Indeed, Fredric Jameson, in a widely read work, remarks that "postmodernism may amount to not much more than theorizing its own condition of possibility."[6] Yet the chapter of that work entitled "Theory" itself amounts to "not much more" than a series of footnotes to de Man's reading of Rousseau. For Jameson, the pre-eminent American theorist of the postmodern, de Man is *the* crucial transitional thinker, a bridge from the postromantic to the postmodern. Hence, in order to explore what separates the postmodern from the Enlightenment on the central question of language, we would do well to recall de Man.

De Man's argument, reduced to essentials, is this: that for Rousseau, and for the Enlightenment in general, man is distinguished from the animals by his perfectibility; that this perfectibility is thought to rest on a specifically linguistic capacity, namely, the ability to ascribe names to general concepts; that the process of naming general concepts has "built into" it a "substitution of sameness for difference";[7] that "man" himself is a general denomination whose genesis involves the repression of a primal passion, fear of the other; and, therefore, that the concept of man, like all other supposed concrete universals, is incoherent at its root. Upon this claim about universal nominatives de Man builds a radical skepticism about the referential capacities of language itself. If "man" is in question, if the general concepts that are essential to his distinctive perfectibility are so many chimeras or repressive self-delusions, then what, indeed, is Enlightenment?

The centerpiece of de Man's case is his analysis of a brief passage in Rousseau's *Essai sur l'origine des langues.*[8] In this passage Rousseau describes the first encounter between a primitive man living in a state of nature and others of his species. His initial reaction, Rousseau asserts, is fear, and this fear makes "him see these men as larger and stronger than himself; he will give them the name *giants.*" But after many similar experiences, "he will discover that the supposed giants are neither larger nor stronger than himself" and "he will then invent another name common to them and him, such as, for example, *man,* and will retain the word *giant* for the false object that impressed him in his delusional state." De Man states that this passage is not about denomination as such but about "the linguistic process of conceptualization."[9] Moreover, "conceptualization . . . is an intralinguistic process, the invention of a figural metalanguage that shapes and articulates the infinitely fragmented and amorphous language of pure denomination." Up to this point he appears to be interpreting Rousseau. But now his argument takes one of those characteristic swerves that are at once the charm and the bane of his peculiar rhetoric: "To the extent that all language is conceptual, it always already speaks about language and not about things. . . . If all language is about language, then the paradigmatic linguistic model is that of an entity that confronts itself." Suddenly, out of nothing, a new concept, *language,* is born, staring at itself in a mirror.

But what sort of concept is *language,* which, we are told, "always already speaks" about itself? Like *man,* it is an assertion of sameness in the place of difference: just as "man" replaces the opposition between "self" and "giant," the general denomination "language" replaces the opposition between the "language of pure denomination" and the "figural metalanguage." And just as Rousseau creates the fiction of a primitive man frightened by the sight of the other, de Man gives us the fiction

of an uncorrupted "reader" of Rousseau plunged into civilized conster-
nation by the incoherence and self-contradiction he discovers in the very
texture of language: "as soon as a text knows what it states, it can only act
deceptively."[10] Here is the alleged rot, the source of the postmodern distaste. But this conclusion is drawn from an analysis, de Man concedes,
whose "intricacy . . . is obviously tied to the choice of the example."[11] For
Rousseau's commentator that choice is justified by the claim that language is "about language and not about things," a claim qualified by the
caveat that this is true only "*to the extent that all language is conceptual.*"[12]

To what extent is that?[13] To what extent can it be said that the
Enlightenment took all language to be conceptual language? In order
to begin to answer this question, let us set against the passage from
Rousseau that de Man so brilliantly analyzes a passage from another
roughly contemporary Enlightenment text, Diderot's celebrated discussion of the blind man of Le Puiseaux in the *Lettre sur les aveugles*. What,
Diderot asks, does this man, blind from birth, understand by the word
mirror? And his answer is that "a mirror is a machine which sets things
in relief at a distance from themselves if they happen to be suitably
placed in relation to it."

Diderot's choice of a case to study is as noteworthy as Rousseau's
choice of an example. In a sense, Diderot's blind man is the antithesis
of Rousseau's savage. The idea of putting sensualist metaphysics to the
test by studying the perception of the blind was of course a commonplace of the time. Concerning this point, William Molyneux had posed
a crucial question to John Locke,[14] and Pierre Coste's translation of
Locke's *Essay* had made Molyneux's question famous across the
Continent.[15] Any number of *philosophes* had pondered the matter. But
Diderot, as his editor notes, parted company with the others in at least
one important respect: where they saw "an abstract problem of justifying a philosophy, Diderot saw a human problem: the blind man lives in
a distinctive world, and if we are to make contact with him we must
bring to the task great patience, clever questions, and—something no
one else had thought of—an elite subject . . . a *blind philosopher.*"[16] Not
an inarticulate savage, then, lacking even the most basic concepts of
comparison, but a blind philosopher.

Diderot questions this philosopher in a way that suggests that he,
like de Man, believes that the moment singled out by Rousseau, of self-
confrontation mediated by confrontation with the other, is one worth
exploring in some detail. How does he go about this? He asks the blind
man what he understands by the word "mirror." Now, this is indeed a
"clever question," for what is a mirror? To the sighted, it is an instrument with the uncanny ability to make visible that which ordinarily one
cannot see: one's own face. To the other my face is my distinguishing

feature, the mark of my identity. In my face he reads who I am. In a world without mirrors a crucial aspect of my identity would thus remain forever beyond my ken, a part of the world that *is* but not of the world I *know*. The mirror fills in what would otherwise remain a gaping blank in my identity papers. It brings me face-to-face with myself *as* other. But only if I can see.

Now, when Diderot asks the blind philosopher what he understands by "mirror," the man responds that it is "a machine which sets things in relief at a distance from themselves." Diderot's interpretation of this response is an interesting foray into linguistic analysis. He wants to explain how the blind man can employ a term like "mirror" to which he can attach no perceptual image, or idea (as the eighteenth century used that word): "If he attaches no ideas to the terms he uses, he at least has the advantage over most people that he never misuses those terms."[17] According to Diderot, three things combine to make such pitch-perfect usage possible. First, the blind man brings his own distinctive experience to bear: he "knows objects only through the sense of touch." Furthermore, he knows from the reports of others that the sighted can identify objects at a distance, on sight. Yet they cannot, he has also been told, see their own faces except in a mirror. Combining these notions, part empirical, part hearsay, he deduces that the sighted use the word "mirror" to describe an instrument that allows them to employ the sense of sight, which for them is the primary means of apprehending the world, in order to apprehend what ordinarily they cannot, namely, the viewer's own face. But since the blind man understands "apprehending" only in tactile terms, this instrument must somehow "set objects in relief at a distance from themselves." Hence his answer to Diderot's question.[18]

Now, we may, since the hologram had not been invented at the time, assume that this relief-generating copy machine is a name without a referent. In this respect the blind philosopher's machine resembles Rousseau's "giant," for there were no literal giants in the primitive forest, only other hominids magnified into giants by fear. Both "giant" in the mouth of the fearful savage and "mirror" in the mouth of the blind *philosophe* are, to use de Man's term, "wild" metaphors, "to some degree aberrant."[19] What separates de Man's Rousseau from Diderot's philosopher is what happens next, or, rather, what has already happened that makes what happens next plausible, not to say inevitable. For according to de Man, "conceptualization is a double process."[20] Earlier he indicated that in the "encounter with other men, the first reaction of the primitive is said to be fear."[21] This fearful reaction "is certainly not obvious," the critic tells us. But half a page later we read that Rousseau's choice of fear of the other as his primary example in the genesis of conceptual terms "enriches the pattern to a considerable degree."[22] With this benediction paranoia is enshrined at the very heart of language. Conceptual thought is presented as a defense mechanism, a secondary elaboration erected upon a primal instinct, fear, in order to fix or, in de Man's word, "tame," energy that would otherwise remain "wild" and "aberrant."[23]

The blind philosopher's aberration is quite different in nature. For him, too, "conceptualization is a double process." For de Man, however, the conceptual term is the end product of this process, whereas for Diderot it is the beginning. For the blind philosopher, the word "mirror" *precedes* the explanatory discourse which produces, in response to a question, a justification of its use. Furthermore, that explanatory discourse is constructed out of reports elicited from sighted speakers about their usage of the term, together with inferences drawn from the blind speaker's own experience. Language, far from being "always already" about language, is "always already" embedded in *social forms*. Without sociability it would have no reason to exist. Meaning is use, and because he is a social being, capable of adjusting his behavior in light of the responses and expectations of others, the blind philosopher can use the word mirror appropriately without ever having seen a mirror. By combining experience with attentiveness to the reports of others, he has learned the rules, as Wittgenstein would say, of the language-game of the sighted community. Privately, however, he has contrived—in lieu, one might say, of a perceptual correlate, of an "idea" of the mirror—an explanation of those rules based upon his own quite different experience; this explanation, which takes palpation to be the pre-eminent mode of perception, is, we would say, aberrant. But it is also secondary. It survives because it is not incompatible with correct usage of the associated general term. It is not intrinsic to language but a mere epiphenomenon. Its associated aberrations are amenable to correction through sociable conversation. Diderot might have elicited further understanding of the blind man's linguistic universe by attempting to disabuse him of the notion that a mirror functions by setting objects in relief at a distance from themselves. Although he does not do this, he does explore the man's understanding of other optical instruments (telescopes, microscopes, etc.), and from this we see even more clearly how meaning is bound up with "forms of life."[24] We see this, for instance, in the blind philosopher's questions to Diderot about optical instruments whose function he understands but whose physical form cannot be deduced from that function. Is the microscope, which makes small things large, smaller than the telescope, which makes large things small? In the blind man's life world, the sense of touch is primary, hence the heft of material things is a matter of keen interest to him. He therefore puts first questions that would not occur to a person who had learned the use of the word telescope by *seeing* a telescope in use.[25] For him, it is plausible to think that the attribute "enlarges" might bear a causal relation to the thing possessing that attribute: the microscope's power to enlarge might in some way be related to its size. Language thus has a generative power: questions grow out of the nature of words by parthenogenesis, as it were, without the impregnation of perception.

Thus the blind man can use the noun "mirror" as a "name" for a "concept," but the act of naming does not exhaust the meaning of the term, does not, as Foucault would have it, "name its being."[26] His engagement in society, his use of language not as a simple mirror of reality but as a compass with which to orient himself and find his way among his fellow men, exemplifies a power of *poiesis* that postmodernism wrongly asserts the Enlightenment suppressed in favor of more disciplined and circumspect *mimesis*.

Here, then, we have two models of the operation of language and, more specifically, of conceptual terms within language. For de Man, language functions as a repressive institution: it is a means by which an individual subject imposes sameness ("man" as universal) in order to repress the memory of an aberrant passion (fear of the other as putatively different). For Diderot, on the other hand, language is a social institution: it is a means by which two or more individuals whose experience differs (the blind and the sighted, say) can communicate about matters of mutual interest, correct misperceptions and misinterpretations, and develop an intuitive grasp of the implicit rules that permit them to coexist in harmony.

Each of these models leaves something out, however. What is left out of de Man's account of Rousseau's thinking is an explanation of how a conceptual term generated by an intrasubjective psychological process becomes intelligible to other individuals: how, in other words, does the universal term "man" become part of a public and not simply a private language? And what is left out of Diderot's account is how a general term like "mirror," which the sighted community shares with the blind, comes into being in the first place. De Man's account of language is thus genetic but lacks a social component, whereas Diderot's is descriptive and functional but lacks a genetic component.

It might be objected that de Man implicitly offers a psychoanalytic in lieu of a social component. It is as if language for de Man, like civilization for Freud, were an edifice built out of a multitude of repressions, with concomitant discontents. We can converse because the speaking self in each of us stands where the inarticulate id used to be. Whatever plausibility such an argument for bridging the gap between individual and collective experience may have in psychoanalysis, however, it seems less applicable to language, whose primary processes are more varied than those of psychic development. Unless, as de Man seems at times to suggest, fear is the universal experience. Why else single out an episode of fear as the essence of Rousseau's philosophy of language, when that philosophy is, as we shall see, considerably more eclectic than de Man's version would have us believe (that is why I refer to de Man's version as de Man's, rather than Rousseau's). Perhaps fear seemed to de Man, who lived in an age distinguished by darkness rather than Enlightenment, *the* universal experience.

If the Enlightenment can be said to have had a universal experience, surely it was one of astonishment at the breaking down of barriers. Indeed, a central metaphor seized upon by Daniel Roche to describe France in the Enlightenment is that of *désenclavement*.[27] Social barriers fell as men and women of different estates and conditions mingled in salons and academies. Geographic barriers were overcome by improvements in roads, waterways, and means of conveyance. And linguistic barriers were reduced if not eliminated by translators such as Pierre Coste[28] and Denis Diderot, to whom I shall return in a moment. But first consider the psychic consequences of such *désenclavement*. When barriers fell, man confronted his other, just as he had in the primal forest of Rousseau's imagination. Was his first reaction one of fear, as Rousseau would have it in the *Essai*, or one of triumph, curiosity, wonder, admiration, interest, and sometimes envy?

On Rousseau's own account it could be both. In the Turin dinner scene described in Book 3 of *Les Confessions* and admirably analyzed by Jean Starobinski,[29] Jean-Jacques goes from "a state of separation and anxiety" caused by "the pain of distance (whether social or amorous)" to a "jubilant moment of triumph" after he successfully explains the meaning of an obscure word in the motto of an aristocratic family. But "he is then plunged back into separation and aridity," though "not without the bittersweet pleasures of memory and hope."[30] Here, Rousseau has transposed the encounter with the savage into an eighteenth-century salon. At the first sight of the Other, magnified to gigantic proportions by social superiority, Jean-Jacques suffers "anxiety" and the "pain of distance." Then, however, his linguistic mastery smashes the social barrier, winning a brief but jubilant triumph. Only then does the quintessential Other, Mademoiselle de Breil, the object of Rousseau's desire, become sufficiently his Like to make plausible the transmogrification of desire into love. Language becomes an instrument of conquest, and pre-eminently of sexual conquest. Indeed, the obscure word that Jean-Jacques explains to his amazed betters is *fiert*, which they, to whom French is a foreign tongue, mistake for a corrupt spelling of *fier*, proud, but which he contends is a corruption of the old French *ferit*, "he strikes, he wounds," so that the family motto, on his reading, becomes "some strike and do not kill." For Rousseau, this scene is a paradigm of linguistic conquest: language is *par excellence* the instrument by which the man of hidden genius strikes the world, leaves his mark upon it, and thereby stakes his claim to the otherwise inaccessible Woman. Language, which for Rousseau is a private treasure, a psychic hoard, is momentarily exchanged for the social currency that establishes the speaker's rightful place in the world.

Diderot is at once more worldly and less miserly. For him, the linguistic gift is what common sense was for Descartes, the thing most widely shared in the world. He displays an unrivaled capacity for amazement at the genius of others. Thus he says of the blind man of Le Puiseaux that his explanation of the phenomena of sight is no less clear and therefore all the more wonderful than that of Descartes' *Dioptrique*. And just as he is keen to explore the meaning of sight by engaging a blind man in conversation, he is eager to explore the meaning of society by conversing with an outsider, Rameau's bohemian nephew. Not as eager as some, who make of bohemians like the nephew "their familiar acquaintances, even their friends," but still eager enough because the outsider is the "grain of leavening . . . that restores a portion of each person's natural individuality . . . brings the truth, reveals the good people, unmasks the scoundrels. And so the man of good sense listens, and unravels his world." Conversation with the outsider has this power because Rameau's nephew is the socialized man's other, who has thrown off "the tedious uniformity that our education, our social conventions, and our customary proprieties have introduced."[31]

"Tedious uniformity": if Rousseau's savage evolved the concept "man" to fix and stabilize the gnawing anxieties stemming from his fear of *the other*, Diderot's *moi* engages in conversation with Rameau's bohemian nephew because he fears *the same*. *Désenclavement* introduced a disorienting uniformity into the world: "It is almost impossible to distinguish people by their exterior. The shopkeeper dresses like a gentleman. . . . *Adieu la différence*."[32] Equality has its discontents. While it may procure relief from terror of the other's greater power or strength or wealth or talent, the social rapprochement that equality permits frustrates the expression of the individual's enabling sense of difference: "One is vain, scornful, and consequently unjust whenever one can be so with impunity," writes Helvétius. "Who does not believe himself to be the best person of his society, and who does not catch himself now and then pretending that he is the foremost person in the world? . . . Who does not desire public confirmation of the high opinion he has of himself?"[33] Baffled in this quest for difference, the self may feel trapped, caught in a fatal web of determinations: "Can I not be me?" asks Jacques le Fataliste. "And, being me, can I do other than I do?" Nothing less than liberty is at stake. The language that can speak only equality, the language that lacks the style to accommodate, express, or conjure with difference, is, for Rousseau, the language of animals, the grunt of natural need: "The animals that speak [these "natural" languages] have them from birth . . . and everywhere [they are] the same; they do not change, they make no progress whatsoever."[34] Human language, the language of change, hence of liberty and progress, must therefore not only express difference, it must create it; it must be not just conceptual language "constative" of difference but a "performative" instrument, a carillon of the self.[35] "Style," Buffon said contemporaneously, "is the very man." And that creature of style, Rameau's nephew, offers an apt metaphor for the relation between self and language when he speaks of the relation between melody and words in opera: "The words must be thought of as one line and the melody as another which snakes around it."[36]

What is distinctively human about language, then, is not just the capacity to ascribe universal denominations to concepts but the ability to project the movement, the passions, the velleities of the self that each speaker's unique utterances enfold. Language is not always conceptual language, which substitutes sameness for difference. Language—*parole* as opposed to *langue*—is also voice, style, the art of variegating sameness.

How is such an art learned? Again we have divergent answers, depending on whether one would shun society or seek it. For Helvétius, the art of language is not so much learned as imbibed in "silence and solitude. If the muses, as the poets tell us, are fond of woods, meadows, and fountains, it is because one savors there a tranquillity that shuns the city, and when a person, detached from the petty interests of society, there reflects upon himself, he will reflect upon man in general, and his thoughts will belong to, and please, all mankind." Sociability, in other words, is the enemy of universality. For sociability depends on reciprocal esteem, and the thinker who seeks the esteem of any *société particulière* is obscurely aware that such esteem would prove only "the similarity of his ideas" to those of others. Universality is the reward of the thinker prepared to subject himself to the rigors of isolation, just as "the pride of giving orders to kings compensated the Romans for the harshness of their military discipline."[37]

Diderot, however, offers another answer: imitate—not nature but others who possess qualities of style that one envies and would like to emulate. Culture is not, or at any rate not only, the work of isolated culture heroes; it is (also) a commerce in which comparative advantages are sometimes to be found in one place or another. Rameau's nephew recommends that the French pay heed to the Italians so as to experience "with what facility, suppleness, and suavity the harmony, prosody, and ellipses of the Italian tongue lend themselves to the art, movement, expression, and turns of melody and the measured value of sound."[38] Of course they would even then "continue to ignore how stiff, dull, clumsy, cumbersome, pedantic, and monotonous" their own language is, for such is human nature, but eventually "my trinity . . . the true, the good, and the beautiful" will prevail, for art, the play of difference, offers relief from the "tedious uniformity" of philosophy. Now, this rhetorical gesture of the nephew's is in one sense merely a nationalization of the quarrel of the ancients and the moderns: for just as it had been possible in the sixteenth century to wonder whether the French or the Italian language lacked the resources for great poetry so manifestly abundant in Latin and Greek, so, too, was it possible, *mutatis mutandis,* to extol the one modern tongue over the other by adducing the same alleged qualities of vigor, vivacity, and sinew.[39] This was the natural rhetoric, the intrinsic symptomatology, of the anxiety of influence.

If nations felt that anxiety, so, too, and no less acutely, did individuals. It was the inevitable counterpart of *désenclavement.* The fallen barriers had been landmarks as well as walls. One response was withdrawal to the "woods, meadows, and fountains" of which Helvétius speaks: "se cacher pour mieux se montrer," as Rousseau put it. Another was to venture forth in borrowed robes. Diderot, still a youth unsure of his voice, chose this course when he translated Shaftesbury's *Essay.* Of course "translation" is not a strictly accurate description of Diderot's appropriation of Shaftesbury's text. He interpolated passages of his own. Daniel Gordon has pointed to one of these in particular, which interests the historian of sociability because of the analogy it draws between social feeling and worshipful reverence: "Avoir les affections sociales entières . . . c'est imiter, c'est représenter l'Etre suprême sous une forme humaine."[40] There is an admirable force to the paratactic structure of this passage (a parataxis not present, incidentally, in Shaftesbury): *c'est . . . , c'est. . . .* (one is reminded of Montaigne's *parce que c'était lui, parce que c'était moi,* the classic expression of the ineffability of "social affections"). To feel unalloyed affection for one's not unalloyed fellow man, for man, that is, not in the abstract but in the concrete otherness of his social existence, may well require nothing less than *imitatio dei,* or emulation of divine forbearance. Or, taking the other clause of the parataxis, to feel unalloyed social affection is "to represent the Supreme Being in human form," that is, to exhibit in a mode accessible to human understanding an invisible, inaccessible form of affection, divine love (Diderot was, at the time he made this translation, still a theist). So much for the metaphoric reading of the passage; but there is also a metonymic reading: Diderot as translator is both *imitating* Shaftesbury (his voice, his aristocratic ease, which Diderot the bourgeois writer eagerly coveted) and *representing* him (as an emissary carrying his ideas about social affection across the chasm separating

Protestant, commercial, constitutional Britain from Catholic, mercantilist, absolutist France). If civilization was a source of anxiety, perhaps it was because it had to be smuggled across borders as contraband. Translators were smugglers of the new. If language in one of its modes was for the Enlightenment an instrument for variegating sameness, so was translation at its highest pitch. The eighteenth century anticipated Walter Benjamin's advice that the translator must allow "his language to be powerfully affected by the foreign language."[41]

It would be a mistake, however, to think that all variety came from abroad. The eighteenth century was a time of exuberant technical progress, and Diderot was among the first to recognize what an impoverishment of language would result if working men were banished from the *beaux quartiers*: "What diversity is introduced into language every day by the arts, machines, and manual skills (*manoeuvres*)."[42] The *Encyclopédie* was conceived in part as a compendium of these specialized tongues, a compendium that would be not just a passive record of the jargons of the trades but an artful selection designed with a political goal in mind, namely, to further progress by initiating a conversation—for it is "through the inveterate habit of conversing among themselves that working men understand one another, and far more by repeatedly facing the same situations (*par le retour des conjonctures*) than by relying on any fixed terminology"[43]—and thus making the trades mutually intelligible, thereby "eliminating the traditional barriers between guilds."[44]

Traditionally in France the institutions of the monarchy had made language a matter of distinction. The best French was that spoken by the *sanior pars* of French society, the court. Eloquence was a matter of *police*, meaning at once polish and discipline. The Académie served, its historian reminds us, both to civilize and to enforce.[45] It was a sort of hothouse of the tongue, and as with all hothouse plants there was a danger of etiolation in unnatural and isolated profusion: "Words have multiplied endlessly, and knowledge of things has fallen behind."[46] The language had been drained of its substance, in other words, and Diderot aimed to reinvigorate it by embracing rather than shunning those who remained in contact with things, whose knowledge of the world, like the blind man's, was tactile and direct. Yet even an ecumenical undertaking like the *Encyclopedia*—ecumenical in the root sense, meaning about the "world which we inhabit"—could not be so utopian as to dispense altogether with *police*: there are too many words in the world, too many specialized words intelligible only within particular milieus—so that an editor must be careful not so much "to introduce new terms as to banish [superfluous] synonyms."[47] Again, a balance is to be struck between fearful exclusion of the other and the "tedious sameness" of indiscriminate reduction to equality.

Diderot leaves no doubt about where disruption of the necessary balance between sameness and difference, equality and distinction, may lead. "People will spit on a petty thief," he has the nephew say, "but they cannot withhold a kind of respect from a great criminal."[48] He has, moreover, a precise notion of the kind of crime to which the avidity of distinction bred by tedious sameness will give rise: the "renegade of Avignon" is a man capable of befriending a Jew and then denouncing him to authorities committed to the extirpation of difference in the name of purity of the faith. The Jew, rendered different from his fellow man by a slanderous speech act, dies in the holocaust of the Inquisition, and the renegade seizes his fortune. The criminal's depravity of character has already revealed itself in the mirror of language, however: "Can a vicious person speak in an even tone?" the nephew asks. Language keeps no secrets.

It will be clear by now that to describe the language of Enlightenment as "a substitution of sameness for difference" is to create a self-describing artifact, a text which, as de Man alleged, "acts deceptively" because it "knows what it states." Yet it cannot be denied that this deception has enjoyed a considerable measure of success. That success requires explanation. It is a fact verified daily in college literature courses that rhetorical modes lose their effectiveness. Words that once stirred the soul or brought tears to the eyes elicit only snickers: Rousseau's *Julie* is a case in point. Rousseau would have been surprised, for he believed that the qualities of language were essential rather than historical and contingent: "There are languages favorable to freedom," he wrote in the *Essai*. "They are sonorous, rhythmic, harmonious . . . Ours are made for the buzz of the couch."[49] In order to change the quality of the language one spoke, it was necessary to change the person one was, to accept that harsh Roman discipline to which Helvétius alluded. This Rousseau saw himself as having accomplished, and it would have astonished him to discover that the virile language of liberty he believed he had forged had become fit only for the buzz not of the couch but of the seminar room.

What might have helped him to explain the fate of his style was what he of course could not know, his place, as it were, in history. His savage among giants was like Hobbes's man among wolves, the taming of whose aberrant energies required an absolute monarch whose fate it was to be beheaded by Rousseau's "man." Rousseau could not have known this because his understanding of the sovereignty of the general will was like the blind philosopher's understanding of the mirror, synthetic *a priori*, perfect for articulating a political discourse in conformity with the rules governing the language-game of an age that had never yet seen a republic of free and equal citizens.

This particular mirror we can now perceive with the clarity of hindsight, and the image it reflects fills us with the usual ambivalence of self-recognition. The blind philosopher's description disturbs us because it reminds us of how beautiful we thought we might be before belated sobriety dimmed our bright fancies. Yet if we can now see the mirror, we still see ourselves only as we were, never as we are. To the present we remain blind. Perhaps the point of Diderot's parable is that we should not expect, ever, to see ourselves as we are: those who think they *can* see should listen to the blind and converse with those who work with their hands in order to find out what they are missing. Clairvoyance is not ours. What we do have, all we have, is the ability to discuss what a mirror would have to be like in order to reflect an image of such creatures as we take ourselves to be. Man in the mirror of language is thus what Jameson calls a simulacrum, "a copy for which no original has ever existed."[50] If a fascination with simulacra is the hallmark of the postmodern, then the postmodern begins with Diderot.

NOTES

1. Jacques Derrida, *De la grammatologie* (Paris, 1967), p. 444.
2. Richard Rorty, *Philosophy and the Mirror of Nature* (Princeton, 1979), pp. 288ff.
3. Jean Baudrillard, *Pour une critique de l'économie politique du signe* (Paris, 1972), pp. 173ff.
4. Michel Foucault, *Les Mots et les choses* (Paris, 1966), p. 136: "The fundamental task of classical 'discourse' was to *attribute a name to things,* and *in that name to name their being.* . . . When it named the being of all representation in general, it was philosophy: theory of knowledge and analysis of ideas."
5. Paul de Man, *Allegories of Reading* (New Haven, 1979), p. 158.
6. Fredric Jameson, *Postmodernism, or The Cultural Logic of Late Capitalism* (Durham, 1991), p. ix.
7. De Man, *Allegories,* p. 148.
8. Jean-Jacques Rousseau, *Essai sur l'origine des langues* (Paris, 1990), pp. 67–68.
9. De Man, *Allegories,* p. 152.
10. Ibid., p. 270.
11. Ibid., p. 152.
12. Ibid.
13. The rhetorical structure of de Man's sentence, with the all-important qualification placed in apposition to the bald central assertion that "language is always already about language," has the effect of suppressing the qualification, and indeed de Man argues in the remainder of his text as though language in general were indeed "always already" about language. By a trick of the pen the world is erased.
14. Molyneux's question concerned a man blind from birth and taught by touch to distinguish a cube from a sphere. If he regained his sight, could he, when presented with a cube and a sphere, identify them by sight alone? For Locke's discussion, see John Locke, *An Essay Concerning Human Understanding,* Book II, Chap. IX, Section 8.
15. Condillac, for instance, takes up Molyneux's question in the *Essai sur l'origine des connaissances humaines;* see Diderot, *Oeuvres philosophiques* (Paris, 1964), p. 76.
16. Paul Vernière, introduction to "Lettre sur les aveugles" in Diderot, *Oeuvres philosophiques,* p. 76.
17. Diderot, "Lettre sur les aveugles" in *Oeuvres philosophiques,* p. 84.

18. Ibid., pp. 85.
19. De Man, *Allegories*, p. 153.
20. Ibid.
21. Ibid., p. 149.
22. Ibid., p. 150.
23. Once again, the effect of de Man's rhetorical strategy is to ensure that an argument predicated on analysis of a special case (a case in which a primal passion, fear, is repressed by the introduction of an objective general denomination, "man") is read as a universal explanation of the operation of language in general.
24. Curiously for a literary theorist as keen to engage with philosophy as de Man, he has nothing to say about Wittgenstein, whose terminology I mimic here.
25. Diderot, "Lettre sur les aveugles," p. 85.
26. Cf. n. 4.
27. Daniel Roche, *La France des Lumières* (Paris, 1993).
28. On Coste, see Margaret Rumbold, *Traducteur huguenot: Pierre Coste* (New York, 1991).
29. Jean-Jacques Rousseau, *Confessions*, Book 3; Jean Starobinski, *The Living Eye*, trans. Arthur Goldhammer (Cambridge, MA, 1989), pp. 181ff.
30. Starobinski, *The Living Eye*, p. 186.
31. Diderot, "Le Neveu de Rameau" in *Oeuvres Romanesques* (Paris, 1959), p. 397.
32. Antoine de Montchrétien, quoted in Daniel Gordon, *Citizens Without Sovereignty: Equality and Sociability in French Thought, 1670–1789* (Princeton, 1994), pp. 37–38.
33. Helvétius, *De l'esprit* (Paris, 1973), pp. 98, 103.
34. Rousseau, *Essai*, p. 65.
35. One sees this Austinian distinction applied to the nominative "man" in Shakespeare's *Macbeth*, when Macduff, adjured to "dispute like a man" the murder of his wife and children, replies, "I shall do so, but I must also feel it as a man." In so enunciating the difference between action and pathos, his pain becomes as real for others as it already is for himself. Here the distinguishing passion, though subsumed as in Rousseau's example within the universal substantive, is not effaced: Macduff is both a man who avenges a wrong (and he who does not avenge a wrong is not a man), but he is also a man capable of making the pain of that wrong visible to others: both justice and eloquence speak in his behalf.
36. Diderot, "Neveu," p. 464.
37. Helvétius, *De l'esprit*, p. 102.
38. Diderot, "Neveu," p. 466
39. Marc Fumaroli, "Le génie de la langue française" in Pierre Nora, ed., *Lieux de mémoire*, vol. 3: *Les France*, part 3 (Paris, 1992), pp. 921–76.
40. Gordon, *Citizens*, p. 83.
41. Walter Benjamin, "The Task of the Translator." Benjamin is quoting Rudolf Pannwitz.
42. Quoted in Jacques Proust, *Diderot et L'Encyclopédie* (Paris, 1962), p. 212.
43. Diderot, quoted in ibid., p. 213.
44. As Jacques Proust remarks, ibid., p. 220.
45. Marc Fumaroli, "La Coupole" in Pierre Nora, ed., *Lieux de mémoire*, vol. 2: *La Nation*, part 3 (Paris, 1986), pp. 321–89.
46. Diderot, *Pensées*, p. 59.
47. Diderot, quoted in Proust, *Diderot*, p. 214.
48. Diderot, *Le Neveu*, p. 458.
49. Rousseau, *Essai*, p. 144.
50. Jameson, *Postmodernism*, p. 20.

AN EIGHTEENTH-CENTURY TIME MACHINE

The *Encyclopedia* of Denis Diderot

DANIEL ROSENBERG

In 1755 the French philosopher Denis Diderot published his article "Encyclopedia" in the fifth volume of a work he was then editing with the mathematician Jean le Rond d'Alembert. The importance of this work, the *Encyclopedia, or a Rational Dictionary of the Sciences, Arts, and Trades* (1750–72), to the Enlightenment is difficult to overestimate. Robert Darnton, for example, refers to it as the "supreme work" of the period.[1] It remains so familiar today that it is most often simply referred to as the *Encyclopedia*. The article "Encyclopedia" served Diderot as an opportunity to reflect on the nature of the enterprise.

Diderot's article is preoccupied with two problems, the relationship between the encyclopedia and *language* and the status of the encyclopedia in *time*. Of these two concerns, scholars know much more about the first. Indeed, it has become quite common for intellectual and cultural historians, philosophers and literary scholars to study the Enlightenment through the lens of its ideas about language.[2] Language served the Enlightenment as an essential model for the structure of thought and knowledge, and during that period the study of language and the study of reason frequently converged.[3] As the philosopher Etienne Bonnot de Condillac put it, "Every language is an analytic method, and every analytic method, a language."[4] Condillac's own work bears this out in many domains. For example, his textbook on algebra and geometry takes the form of a discourse on what he calls the "language" of calculation. And he means this literally. He treats mathematical operations as a kind of syntax, and the algebraic sign as a kind of purified linguistic marker. Diderot's *Encyclopedia* has often, and not incorrectly, been seen in a similar light. Among other things, it is a philosophical lexicon, a "rational dictionary," a sourcebook and repertoire to accompany the rational syntax of a philosopher like Condillac. Diderot discusses this at some length in the article "Encyclopedia."

The other preoccupation of Diderot's article "Encyclopedia," the problem of the relationship between knowledge and time, has been less well explored. This is in part because it is so often taken for granted that the linguistic turn of the eighteenth century was a turn away from considerations of history and time and toward a purely universalizing perspective on the domain of knowledge. There are elements of truth in this judgment. But, as the philosophically important eighteenth-century projects on etymology, neology, and language origins all suggest, the tension between the project of seeing philosophy through the lens of language and of accounting for history, contingency, act, and change occurs during this period as just that, a tension, and many Enlightenment writers address it from one perspective or another. As Diderot's article makes plain, the question of the status of knowledge in time should be central to the project of any encyclopedia. Moreover, the importance of addressing it only intensifies given Diderot's view, and the view of many contemporaries, that the process of change in the many domains of knowledge seems to be accelerating manyfold. For Diderot, the question of how to construct an encyclopedia is crucially a question of how to construct an encyclopedia in (historical) time.

In fact, this is a question in many ways novel in the Age of Enlightenment, and it echoes questions heard throughout philosophy and natural philosophy at the time. One of the distinctive aspects of this historical moment in contrast to the centuries that precede it, is a sense of vertiginous opening in the horizons of past and future. In the 1760s, for example, the natural scientist Buffon raised eyebrows among scientists and hackles among theologians by arguing that the earth might be as much as 75,000 years old. But even as he published these figures, Buffon was entertaining the possibility that the earth might be millions, not tens of thousands, of years old.[5] Buffon's perspective (and his change in perspective) was far from unique. Historians of science refer to this moment in biology, geology, astronomy, and other areas as that of the "discovery of deep time." While this development has roots that extend earlier, its importance only became clear in the eighteenth century. To the philosophers of the Enlightenment, it appeared that much had changed very quickly. Indeed for writers such as Diderot and Buffon, it seemed that *everything* had changed in the short period since the beginning of the century, in the short period since even Isaac Newton himself had engaged in a serious attempt to reconcile astronomical chronology with the literal chronology of the Bible.[6]

It is interesting to note that Buffon recognized very clearly how great a cognitive leap would be required in order to give up the notion that the earth was really 6,000 years old, as the Church had long taught. Clearly, Buffon's hesitations in publishing his speculations about the long geological history of the earth were in part motivated by his concerns about the censorship of his ideas and the problems they posed for scriptural interpretation; but as Paolo Rossi has shown, part of his tentativeness had to do with his acknowledging the difficulty of contemplating what he called the "dark abyss" of geological and biological time. Indeed, when first presenting his new time scales, he intentionally collapsed them by tenfold or more. "This abbreviated version," he wrote, "was necessary . . . to preserve the order and the clarity of the ideas. . . . Although it is quite true that the more we stretch time, the closer we get to the truth . . . still, we must shorten it as much as possible in order to conform to the limited power of our intelligence."[7] Over time, Buffon grew bolder, but he was always conscious of the cognitive and cultural strangeness of thinking of time in new ways.

As the dimension of the past began to burst open during the eighteenth century, a parallel development began within the dimension of the future. With the unsettling of the traditional 6,000-year history of the earth, the meaning of the future changed immensely. As J. B. Bury and Reinhart Koselleck have shown in different ways, during the Enlightenment, the meaning of the future became arguable in a way quite unfamiliar to Europeans only a generation removed.[8] Koselleck explains that this new territory of the future, freed from the straightjacket of eschatology, "is characterized by two main features: first, the increasing speed with which [the future] approaches . . . , and second, its unknown quality. 'Unknown' because this accelerated time . . . abbreviated the space of experiences, robbed them of their constancy, and continually brought into play new, unknown factors."[9] With the end no longer in plain sight, Koselleck argues, imaginative demands on the future intensify sharply.

This is a period of flowering for the *uchronian* imagination, for the shift of *utopian* themes into narratives of the future. In the twentieth century it is so common to locate our *utopian* visions somewhere in the chronological future (whether in the tomorrowlands of Disney World or Star Trek), that it is difficult to remember that this convention is actually very young. Indeed, it can be dated fairly precisely to the decade of the 1770s in which, seemingly out of nowhere, a spate of novels on the great year 7603, or 1850, or 2440 all of a sudden begin to appear.[10] The German critic Lessing identified a new species of writer emerging in this period, one who, "cannot wait for the future," who "wants this future to come more quickly, and . . . wants to accelerate it [himself]."[11] These cultural and intellectual developments can be formulated, as they are in J. B. Bury's classic study, as elements of the invention of *the idea of progress*. But during the Enlightenment, progress *itself* was only one element in a large and contested field of ideas, perceptions, figurations, and constructions of the future and past. In contrast to the idea of progress, the more basic development in this period, recognizable as much in works of historiography, natural philosophy, philology and other fields as in explicitly progressive or futurological works, was a problem and a problematization of time.

Diderot's *Encyclopedia* makes an interesting and important study in this regard first because it figures so centrally in the conception of the Enlightenment put forward by the *philosophes*, and second because it may not be immediately evident how questions of time might influence the formulation of an encyclopedia, a work aimed, as Diderot puts it, "to collect all the knowledge that now lies scattered over the face of the earth."[12] It may be interesting all the more since, for Michel Foucault and the many historians and scholars influenced by him, the *Encyclopedia* figures so centrally as an artifact of an epistemological disposition to classify and tabulate, which either suppresses or ignores the dimension of time.[13] In this version of the Enlightenment, language and knowledge meet in the form of the encyclopedia itself, as a great synchronic taxonomy of the world which transcends and contains any possible temporality. As Foucault puts it, characterizing the *épistémè* of the eighteenth century:

> In so far as language can represent all representations it is with good reason the element of the universal. There must exist within it at least the possibility of a language that will gather into itself, between its words, the totality of the world, and, inversely, the world, as the totality of what is representable, must be able to become, in its totality, an Encyclopaedia.[14]

In the course of this paper I want to cast a somewhat different light on the eighteenth-century *Encyclopedia*, a work that has come to seem very familiar, perhaps too familiar to us. It seems to me that the *Encyclopedia* serves so often as a symbol of the order, stability, and universalism of the Enlightenment imagination, that it is sometimes difficult to remember or recognize how much this document speaks from and to a sense of time and the times. I want to argue that even if we recognize the *Encyclopedia* frequently expresses a longing for the synoptic, we should not lose sight of the fact that in Diderot's work this is always paired with an acute sense of time's presence and evanescence.

That the *Encyclopedia* heralded and interrogated a new kind of time is nothing one would have needed to tell an eighteenth-century observer. Contemporary readers of the *Encyclopedia* experienced it as a volatile and epoch-making text. From historians such as Robert Darnton, John Lough, and Jacques Proust, we know that the *Encyclopedia* stirred lively controversy, and that a complicated drama of underground commerce and circulation began after the French censor withdrew permission for a work that appeared increasingly irreligious and materialist.[15] We also know from contemporary sources that the *Encyclopedia* registered as much as *event* as it did as text. An eighteenth-century commentator named Jean-Baptiste Suard summed up his own reaction to the work as follows:

> What a moment! and of what an era [the *Encyclopedia*] gave promise! . . . [I]t was . . . as though [its] wishes for the human race showed an almost divine force. . . . [N]early drunk with so much hope for the progress of reason, [the *Encyclopedia*] prophesied a Jerusalem of philosophy that would last more than 1000 years.[16]

Diderot himself never adopts quite this millennial tone; indeed he tells us that he is uncertain about the stability of intellectual progress in the epoch that the *Encyclopedia* seems about to usher in, but as much as Suard, he understands the *Encyclopedia* as both the sign and the mechanism of a new kind of intellectual time.

One of the basic aims of the *Encyclopedia* is empiricist. Diderot and his original collaborator, d'Alembert, make much of the fact that in contrast to older works, the *Encyclopedia* would in important ways constitute a *primary* study of its objects. The contributors to the *Encyclopedia* would all be in some way familiar with the fields for which they were to take responsibility. The *Encyclopedia*, as they put it, would be the work of a *société de gens de lettres* and not just the scribbled summary appreciations of one or two closeted editors or the dusty accumulations of a royal academy. As the "Preliminary Discourse" to the *Encyclopedia* makes clear, the plan for the work involved legions of writers including philosophers of the most general talents such as Voltaire (who wrote the entry on "history" among others) and Rousseau (who contributed many articles on music), to writers with more specialized knowledge including scientists, teachers and men from all walks of professional life.

Diderot frames the work as a tool for a world in which "[one dares] to raise doubts about the infallibility of Aristotle and Plato," and in which "works that still enjoy the highest reputation . . . begin to lose some of their great prestige"—and may even be "forgotten entirely."[17] The *Encyclopedia* is a manifesto for an explosion of the arrogance of canonical texts and for an active engagement in the material world. This aspect of the work is beautifully attested to by many rich and historically useful articles, and even more vividly by the work's broad and precise collection of plates illustrating the sciences, arts, and trades of the day, plates which in the words of Roland Barthes practice a kind of autonomous "philosophy of the object."[18]

But the problems that motivate the *Encyclopedia* and the strategies it deploys are more complex than its empiricist aspect suggests. The problem of the *Encyclopedia* is not just returning to the things themselves, but constructing a literary and intellectual mechanism capable of accounting for them in a way that will not be subject to immediate obsolescence or irrelevance. Diderot feels this problem acutely. To all appearances, in the eighteenth century the half-life of books is diminishing at an unaccountable rate. Works intended to serve generations outlive their usefulness in only ten or twenty years. Diderot writes, "[I]n every work destined for the general instruction of men, one must . . . resolve to work only for the generations to come because our moment passes and hardly will a great enterprise be completed before our generation exists no longer."[19] Moreover, a work that takes too many years to appear invariably suffers a literary stillbirth, becoming an artifact for the historian.

The fortunes of Pierre Bayle's very important *Historical and Critical Dictionary* (1697) make a case in point. In only decades a work as substantial and as important to the *philosophes* as this had acquired the air of old age. "[I]f such has been the fate of Bayle, how much worse would have been the fate of an *Encyclopedia* executed during his time?" Diderot asks.[20] In the view of Diderot and d'Alembert, Bayle's generation was still too much obliged to the memory of old ideas. A monument of criticism, Bayle's *Historical Dictionary* nonetheless remained torn between the act of criticism and the conventional texts that it critiqued. Its very form brought quick obsolescence. Although its outward appearance was that of a dictionary much like Diderot's own "dictionnaire raisonné," Bayle's work could not shake free of the old conventions of commentary. The *Encyclopedia* alphabetized a diverse list of objects, concepts, and names in a system that placed equal value in all of these potential objects of knowledge. Bayle's *Dictionary* was a repertoire of old names. The very organization of the page in the work marks the hold of tradition. According to d'Alembert, the important parts of Bayle's book are invariably found not in its body, but in the apparatus in the margins. D'Alembert writes, "Bayle's dictionary is only improperly referred to as a historical dictionary; it is a philosophical and critical dictionary in which the text is only the pretext for the notes."[21] By contrast, the *Encyclopedia* would abandon the convention of notes, favoring the *renvois* or cross-reference where additional commentary on a particular issue was required. In this way, the *Encyclopedia* would elevate the work of criticism to the same epistemological status as the positive work of description and synthesis. This is part of its claim to modernity.

Diderot and his coeditor d'Alembert register the shock of the new in different ways. D'Alembert responds mainly to the blinding speed with which books become obsolete. Diderot responds to the same development but also to the phenomenon of language change which appears to outstrip conventional means of accounting for it.[22] The very mechanisms of knowing with which the *Encyclopedia* responds to its objects are themselves changing. Indeed, it is this reflexive aspect which most distinguishes this encyclopedia from its predecessors: Diderot's *Encyclopedia* recognizes itself both as a symptom and an instrument of change.[23]

Thus, while Diderot and d'Alembert argue that an encyclopedia such as their own had never been possible before the 1750s, by the time it had become possible, it could not be delayed another instant.[24] "An Encyclopedia," writes Diderot, "should be begun, carried through, and finished within a certain interval."[25] In the "Age of Louis XIV," major philosophical, scientific, and linguistic works had taken decades to appear. The time of the Sun King expanded itself without limit. With vested interest in the extension of the time of its self-representation, absolutist bureaucracy had extended the moment of knowledge into an irrecoverable pause. The very delay instituted by academic bureaucracy had become a corruption of knowledge. "A sordid self-interest always asserts itself to prolong any work that a king has commissioned."[26] What better monument to the interminableness of the academic institution than the 1694 *Dictionary of the Académie Française*? "[O]ur French academicians," Diderot writes, "had toiled sixty years on their dictionary before having published its first edition!"[27] By the time it had been published as a whole, in the formerly antineological bastion of the Académie Française, a neological supplement had now to be prepared. Diderot writes,

> If one should devote to a universal and systematic dictionary all
> the long years that the vast scope of its subject matter seems to
> require, it would come about, thanks to the revolutionary changes
> which are scarcely less rapid in the arts and sciences than in lan-
> guage, that this dictionary would be that of a century past, just as a
> dictionary of language composed slowly could only end up a list of
> words from an age already passed.[28]

In all of these passages language appears as the very element of change. Revolutions in the sciences and in the arts follow after revolutions in language. Genius itself becomes possible only when the genius of language permits.[29]

Diderot and d'Alembert imagine the *Encyclopedia* as a kind of time machine, a mechanism to release learning from the periodicity of the academies, the endless cycle of séances without progress. "Literary projects which great noblemen conceive," Diderot writes, "are like the leaves that appear in the spring, grow dry in the autumn, and fall in a heap in the depths of the forest where the sustenance they give to a few sterile plants is all the effect that they can be seen to produce."[30] The opening pages of the article "Encyclopedia" are consumed by almost mechanical repetition of this argument against repetition and wasted time.[31] Diderot conceives of the *société de gens de lettres* responsible for the *Encyclopedia* as a kind of counteracademy. In earlier times great works of synthesis were written by individuals and the production of works by groups tended to contribute to their tardiness and insipidness. Bayle wrote his *Dictionary* alone. The *Dictionary of the Académie Française* was written by committee. But as speed became more of an issue, the economies of time possible with a large group of collaborators became more important. The more workers, the faster the work.[32]

According to Diderot, the institutional problem of timeliness multiplies almost beyond control in an age when sciences change so fast that the time between a scholarly work's composition and publication might bring discoveries which would make it out of date. Diderot writes,

> Opinions grow old and fade away just as do words; our interest in particular discoveries grows weaker day by day and then extinguishes itself. If the work is drawn out over time, we will get stuck on problems of the moment which have ceased to be at issue, and we will have said nothing about others whose time has come and gone.[33]

This problem is not one that the *Encyclopedia* is entirely capable of avoiding. Diderot continues, "We ourselves have given evidence of this difficulty, as a quite significant period of time has passed between the date of this work and the moment of my writing."[34] For Diderot, the delay necessitated by editing and publishing books is itself a matter of great concern. Even the act of writing implies the threat of receding time.[35]

The technical issue of how to produce quickly a good encyclopedia is crucial to Diderot not only because he values intellectual progress in general, but also because he understands the *Encyclopedia* to be a document and an artifact of a "siècle philosophe."[36] He confronts the problem of imagining a universal book in a moment, of defining his encyclopedia as a dynamic act, of telling the story in which it plays a role even by coming into existence. We live in a time, Diderot explains, when "the least common ideas of the century passed . . . become more and more common every day."[37] Not two-thirds of the words in use in the past century, he speculates, remain in use now.[38] The vortex of change enters language itself. What were once the languages of experts, the most difficult and abstruse of words, are today common coin. He continues,

> There is not a woman who has received some education who does not employ with discernment the whole range of expressions con-

secrated to painting, to sculpture, to architecture, and to belles lettres. How many children are there . . . who have learned to draw,
who know geometry, who are musicians, to whom the language of
the home is no more familiar than that of the arts. . . . The language, even the popular language, will come to change.[39]

Diderot's characterization of women's speech is another indication that
perceptions of language are changing. Molière's caricatures of *les pré-
cieuses* are only the best known examples of the very common seventeenth-
century association of women and neologism. As the passage above
attests, by the time of the *Encyclopedia*, men of science, art, and industry
came to imagine themselves as the primary sources of new expressions,
and the project of neology (as opposed to neologism which became the
derogatory term) took on new philosophical and political importance.
As an account of language, the encyclopedia was an account of change,
and as an account of change, of language.

For Diderot a contemporary encyclopedia must be time-bound,
both in the sense that its production is subject to the constraints of time
and that (regardless of universal intentions) it necessarily becomes a
document of its own time. But that very fact forces us to write as much as
possible into the future. Again, Diderot: "[I]n every work destined for
the general instruction of men, one must . . . resolve to work only for the
generations to come because our moment passes and hardly will a great
enterprise be completed before our generation exists no longer."[40]

For Diderot, the principal difficulty associated with older encyclopedias has less to do with the truth of their content than with their formal inability to register and make navigable the rapids of time. In other
words, the difficulty with older encyclopedias is that in the intellectual
conditions of Enlightenment, they simply age too quickly:

> Think of the progress that has been made . . . in the sciences and
> the arts! Think of the many truths that are unveiled today which
> were not dreamed of [a century ago]! True philosophy was in its
> cradle; the geometry of infinity was not yet in existence; experi-
> mental physics had scarcely appeared; dialectics did not exist; laws
> of sound criticism were entirely unknown.[41]

Certainly, in 1755, encyclopedias had existed for many years. Indeed,
Diderot was aware of the great tradition of Renaissance encyclopedias.
But today, Diderot asks, "What would these encyclopedias be for us?"[42]
The temporal condition of Enlightenment demands not only a new
encyclopedia, but an encyclopedia of a new kind.

Diderot portrays his *Encyclopedia* as a transitional work relative to
these orders of knowledge and progress. He originally proposed the

work in 1745 as a translation of a twenty-year-old encyclopedia by the Englishman Ephraim Chambers, called simply *Cyclopedia*. But by the time that Diderot's *Encyclopedia* had begun to appear, it had metamorphosed almost beyond recognition.[43] The arena of the *Cyclopedia*, Diderot writes, "expands under our feet."[44] According to Diderot the problem was not that Chambers's book was wrong, but that increasingly no book traditionally conceived could claim to be sufficient to the task of an encyclopedia. In a sense, it is the very bookness of the book that constitutes the problem, the fact that the book seals itself off against the world, explaining it, illustrating it, attempting to mirror it in structure, but finally reconstituting it as a dead object bound between two covers.[45]

Understood in a certain way, we might think of this problem as an aspect of the condition of intellectual progress known as the Enlightenment. This is the condition that Diderot points to when he catalogs an explosion of novelties in philosophy, science and art, when he characterizes philosophy as having emerged from its "cradle." But Diderot's discussion of progress here is only one aspect of what he understands to be a broader phenonemon of accelerated intellectual production and change. This is Diderot, from the article "Encyclopedia," discussing the future of the book:

> As long as the centuries continue to unfold, the number of books will grow continually, and one can predict that a time will come when it will be almost as difficult to learn anything from books as from the direct study of the whole universe. It will be almost as convenient to search for some bit of truth concealed in nature as it will be to find it hidden away in an immense multitude of bound volumes.[46]

This vision of a kind of Borgesian Library of Babel occurs in the context of a discussion of what an encyclopedia is and does and why the present intellectual moment in particular demands such a work. The passage is somewhat surprising. On the one hand, Diderot is trumpeting some of the important intellectual advances of the day. On the other hand, he is diagnosing a condition of accelerated and accelerating intellectual production *which is anything but progressive*. He perceives the possibility of intellectual production accelerating beyond intelligibility.

In a somewhat dystopian mode, Diderot locates the *Encyclopedia* at a turning point in the history of textual production and culture. He identifies the Enlightenment with the maturity and perhaps the exhaustion of the print age. In the old scriptural economy, Diderot explains, there were few writers and many copyists. But, "if you look ahead to a future age," he continues, "and consider the state of literature after the printing press, which never rests [and which] has filled huge buildings with books, you will find again a twofold division of labor." And some men

> will . . . devote themselves to investigations which will be new, or
> which they will *believe* to be new. . . . The others, . . . incapable of
> producing anything of their own, will be busy night and day leaf-
> ing through these books, taking out of them the fragments they
> consider worthy of being collected and preserved.[47]

For Diderot, the distinctiveness of the *problem* of knowledge in the
Enlightenment lies in its reflexive character. Diderot shifts the focus of
epistemology to the concealment of truth within the realm of knowledge itself. As he bluntly puts it, "If we are even now ignorant of a part
of what is contained in so many volumes . . . , [in the future, one] will
know still less of what is contained in those same books, augmented as
they will be by a hundred—a thousand—times as many more."[48]

Thus, when Diderot writes that "an attempt at an encyclopedia could
only belong to a philosophical age," he is up to something more complicated than promoting his own work or praising the philosophical
advances of his day.[49] He is arguing that an encyclopedia of the sort that
he proposes is both a symptom and necessary response to a condition of
intellecutal hyperactivity. The modern encyclopedia is not only incon-
ceivable prior to the mid-eighteenth century, by the mid-eighteenth century a world without an encyclopedia has become unthinkable.

From a statistical point of view it has been well documented that in
the mid-eighteenth century there were more books, more journals,
more places to read, and more readers than ever before.[50] But the numbers do not capture the contemporary sense of vertigo. Practices and
technologies of writing, print, and reading were associated with novelty,
immediacy and change in a way that, from the point of view of our own
"information age," must seem both very strange and very familiar. In
Roger Chartier's account, the eighteenth-century bookshop appears the
very picture of activity and anticipation. New forms of commerce and
circulation appear including commercial lending libraries. The time of
reading seems to accelerate, breaking the book into smaller pieces and
redistributing it across assignments of time. In these days, comments
one of Diderot's contemporaries, "There are works that excite such a
ferment that the bookseller is obliged to cut the volume into parts in
order to be able to satisfy the pressing demands of many readers; in this
case you pay not by the day but by the hour."[51]

The *Encyclopedia* is fundamentally an artifact of this moment. It
addresses this sense of accelerated time not only by providing the kind
of digest mentioned earlier, but by posing the question, how can an
account of knowledge comprehend and represent a process of intellectual becoming? How can an account of knowledge itself take on tempo-

ral form? Diderot's anxiety about the quickening of time is matched by his ambition for the *Encyclopedia*. A self-proclaimed manifesto of a "siècle philosophique," the *Encyclopedia* is in a special sense "historical." By virtue of its ability to make new, it creates a formal dilemma, how to remain in the present while accelerating the very process of becoming-past.

But why an encyclopedia? How does that form address the kind of temporal acceleration that Diderot perceives? Why an encyclopedia now? According to Diderot, an *Encyclopedia* is at once something more and something less than a book. More precisely, the *Encyclopedia* is what comes after books. Traditionally, an encyclopedia was understood to be a compendium. As Diderot notes, the etymology of the word, en-cyclo-pedia, suggests a compass or an encompassing of knowledge.[52] But as we already know, Diderot understood the arena of the encyclopedia to be expanding under his feet. Diderot's encyclopedia was in this sense to be more than a book. Its ambitions were enormous, and over the course of a quarter of a century and 28 or more volumes (depending on how you count), the *Encyclopedia* described, explained, cataloged, narrated, analyzed, and depicted a breathtaking panorama of objects, ideas, and events.

At the same time Diderot's *Encyclopedia* was to be something less than a book, or less than a traditional encyclopedia. The *Encyclopedia* followed the form of another sort of work, the alphabetic dictionary: hence, the full title, *Enyclopedia, or a Rational Dictionary of the Sciences, Arts, and Trades*. The *Encyclopedia* constructed by Diderot and his collaborators disposes of the notion of a single and eternal order of knowledge, the very ordering that the term "encyclopedia" traditionally implied. It also dispenses with context and linearity. In the past, encyclopedias were usually organized in a thematic fashion, what Diderot called an "encyclopedic order," so their structure might mirror the fundamental categories of the universe of knowledge.[53]

In order to loosen the hold of traditional categories, Diderot structured his encyclopedia as a *dictionary*, organizing the work by following the arbitrary order of the alphabet. This is not to say that in choosing "dictionary order" Diderot dispensed with the ambition to organize the universe of knowledge. It is rather to say that he insisted that such acts of ordering were just that, acts, products of a structuring imagination, and furthermore that there ought to be many ways of organizing this universe. This, he considered not only an intellectual principle but a compositional imperative in the accelerated condition of Enlightenment. The eighteenth-century linguistic turn appears to have more than just a taxonomic dimension.

The *Encyclopedia* is an *interface*. Diderot planned four basic interactive mechanisms to operate in the work. First, it could be accessed alphabetically, as an intellectual lexicon. Second, its articles could be traversed from one to another by means of embedded cross-references or *links*. Third, the reader could begin by following either the genealogical or the rational divisions of the domains of knowledge offered in appendices to the work. Or, finally, one could begin with the plates which were themselves complexly cross-referenced with the text. Without abdicating the responsibility of conceptualizing relationships among the subjects treated, the *Encyclopedia* attempts to leave room for the active participation of its readers. D'Alembert's famous analogy between the *Encyclopedia* and a world map, which is sometimes taken to suggest the univocal and totalizing character of the work, is, in fact, intended to convey the arbitrariness of any given perspective on it. As d'Alembert puts it, "one can create as many different systems of human knowledge as there are world maps having different projections, and each one of these systems might even have some particular advantage possessed by none of the others."[54] The multiply-indexed structure of the *Encyclopedia* emphasizes the "projective" role of the reader and the readerliness of the encyclopedic text.[55]

Alphabetical order, Diderot admits, is a kind of disorder. But according to Diderot (slyly evoking again an empiricist rhetoric), the disorder of the *Encyclopedia* is not so unlike the disorder one finds and sometimes appreciates in the world. He writes,

> Often, alphabetical order produce[s] burlesque contrasts; an article on theology [is] relegated to the page across from the mechanical arts. . . . I insist on the liberty and the variety of this distribution.

He goes on,

> In this respect, the construction of an Encyclopedia is much like the foundation of a city. One must not build all of the houses on exactly the same model even if one has found a general model, handsome in itself and suitable for any location. The uniformity of the buildings, bringing with it a uniformity in public passages would give to the whole city a sad and tiring appearance.[56]

For Diderot, the qualities of "dictionary order" extend right up to chance, juxtaposition, and burlesque. The *dis-order* of the *Encyclopedia* demands an active intellectual engagement. It demands that reading be thought of as a constructive intellectual enterprise.

Thus Diderot defends the encyclopedic dictionary against the objections of traditionalists (which must seem familiar to us today) who claimed that making information accessible completely apart from context, completely apart from the necessity of reading long abstruse analytic or narrative works would "contribute to extinguishing the taste for work and study."[57] In addition to giving the work a dynamic self-renewing quality, from even a formal perspective, the *Encyclopedia* would encourage an enlightened kind of reading. As Wilda Anderson has suggested in her excellent book on eighteenth-century scientific dictionaries, for the *philosophes* part of the critical effectiveness of a dictionary stems from the choice allowed the reader and the constant formal suggestion that every order of knowledge is in some way instrumental.[58] Structuring the *Encyclopedia* in this fashion not only provides it with the flexibility to survive changing ideas about the order and use of knowledge, it also gives it (in Diderot's famous words), "the character . . . of a good dictionary . . . which is to change the general way of thinking."[59]

While it may be possible to regard the organizational apparatus of the *Encyclopedia* as static—formal, systematic and mechanical—it seems to me that such an approach drains from the work much of its interest and urgency. It is true that Diderot considered the *Encyclopedia* to be a kind of machine, but it seems to me that as historians we should be especially careful not to erase either the motivation for the invention nor the role of the mechanic in operating it. Diderot's mechanism demands an operator.

From the outset the *Encyclopedia* admits the *provisional* character of its structure. As we have seen, the work claims its authority on the basis of its ability to be new and to renew in the face of accelerating time. The progress of the reader through the work is envisioned as the motor of that renewal, a process that produces its own logic of progress. This logic interacts with but is not determined by a grand historical narrative of progress. This comes through most clearly perhaps in Diderot's and d'Alembert's presentation of the problem of progress itself. Consistent with the widely shared Enlightenment practice of "conjectural history," d'Alembert juxtaposes what he calls a "genealogical tableau" of the progress of the human mind with both an "encyclopedic tableau" and historical accounts in general. He notes that the organization of each is different, and their critical and positive values differ as well.

The genealogical tableau represents a grand narrative of progress; it is history *as it should have happened.* This is in contrast with any possible narrative of history that actually occurred. According to Diderot and d'Alembert, the interest of *either* narrative derives from its relation to the other. For the editors as for many of their contemporaries, the example of the Middle Ages serves as a constant reminder that progress of human understanding must be ever renewed and is without guarantee. The abstraction of conjectural history provides a critical key for understanding the actual history of the human mind, but never predicts or accounts for it directly. Histories constantly frustrate the story of linear progress that Reason would write for itself.[60] Thus, the *Encyclopedia* alternately narrates itself in histories with different purposes, and provides the materials for still more writings and readings. Progress, for Diderot and d'Alembert, is necessarily an act. It is a constant process of re-narration, a process located at what Bronislaw Baczko has referred to as the *fringe* of utopia, a space of utopian aspiration without a utopian script.[61]

During the eighteenth century in Europe, certainties about the meaning and pace of time to a significant extent unraveled, and in turn, as Koselleck argues, imaginative demands on the future intensified. In my view, the case of the *Encyclopedia* bears this out. But it does so in perhaps unexpected ways. Koselleck and others such as Fredric Jameson have emphasized the formal and cultural difficulty of maintaining narratives without ends. But in some respects this is precisely what Diderot and d'Alembert set out to do. In place of the figural and proleptic imagination of Christian prophesy (in the end, this will have had meaning, the proleptic statement par excellence), Diderot and d'Alembert substitute an open and activist vision of the future of human knowledge (this will have had meaning once you have read it).

It is worth emphasizing that the *Encyclopedia* cannot be reduced to only this aspect. As a collective project, the *Encyclopedia* was one of the most complex works of its day, and the many issues that it raises deserve careful and individual attention. But it is equally worth emphasizing that to leave out of our account this element of the *Encyclopedia*, to treat the *Encyclopedia* as a totality rather than as a project, would be to miss a major element of the constructive and pedagogical dimensions of the work; it would also be to miss an important episode in the eighteenth-century struggle to reconceptualize past and future.

Looking backward, the success of Diderot's *Encyclopedia* is in so many ways remarkable. Centuries later the *Encyclopedia* still serves as a model for philosophical works of all sorts. It is still itself widely used in a modern edition. Students today are all familiar with the faces of the creators of the *Encyclopedia*. And schoolchildren even learn their ABC's from the names of these great men . . . Alembert, Blondel, Cahusac, Diderot, and so on.

This is what we learn from the narrator of a time-travel story written by Louis-Sébastien Mercier in 1771.[62] In this novel, entitled *The Year 2440*, an eighteenth-century Frenchman, a contemporary of Diderot, falls asleep and is awakened miraculously some seven hundred years later. In the story the time traveler makes the acquaintance of a twenty-fifth-century philosopher who guides him on a tour through the astonishing cityscape of future-Paris. The time traveler marvels at a world in which streets are clean, government is accountable to the governed, and the uncomfortable hats of the eighteenth century have finally been replaced.

But not every artifact or memory of eighteenth-century France has been eliminated. When the subject of education arises, the guide tells the traveler, "As soon as [our children] have reached the age of reason, we put in their hands your famous *Encyclopedia.*" To which the traveler responds, "You surprise me! The *Encyclopedia* as a primer! Oh, what a leap you have taken toward the advanced sciences, and how ardently I desire to take instruction with you! Open your treasure chests to me, so that I may, at one fell swoop, enjoy the accumulated works of six centuries of glory!"[63]

This is nothing less than an encyclopedist's dream, transport into the future (six centuries of intellectual glory at one fell swoop): mastery of time, that slipperiest and most troublesome of eighteenth-century problems.[64] With only the minor innovation of time travel, Mercier solves not only one of the most difficult of epistemological problems but, for the Enlightenment, one of the most timely. For better or for worse, in the *Encyclopedia* Diderot was not blessed with the kind of fictional possibilities possessed by Mercier's narrator, and was forced to confront the same sense of an expanding future with the tools at hand: text, image, and print. His solution to the these problems was to create a mechanism that resembled a book but also represented an attempt to move beyond it. Today, at a moment when posthistories of all sorts have been declared, when, to many, the book seems to have exhausted itself, and when novelties of various sorts are supposed the only constants, it may be interesting to think about the ways in which such formulations can be understood as historically particular, and perhaps also the extent to which, since the Enlightenment or the year 2440, they may not be new at all.

NOTES

1. Robert Darnton, *The Business of Enlightenment: A Publishing History of the* Encyclopédie, *1775–1800* (Cambridge, MA, 1979), p. 4.

2. Outside intellectual history, this association has probably been most influential upon the subject of the French Revolution. See, for example, François Furet, *Interpreting the French Revolution*, trans. by Elborg Forster (Cambridge, MA, 1977); Lynn Hunt, *Politics, Culture and Class in the French Revolution* (Berkeley, 1984); Keith Michael Baker, *Inventing the French Revolution* (Cambridge, 1990). More directed studies include Michel de Certeau, Dominique Julia, and Jacques Revel, *Une Politique de la langue: La Révolution française et les patois* (Paris, 1975); Jacques Guilhaumou, *La Langue politique et la Révolution française: De l'évenement à la raison linguistique* (Paris, 1989); and Sophia Rosenfeld, "A Revolution in Language: Words, Gestures, and the Politics of Signs in France, 1745–1804" (Ph.D. diss, Harvard University, 1996). Recent historiography of the American Revolution has taken a similar turn. See Michael Warner, *The Letters of the Republic: Publication and the Public Sphere in Eighteenth-Century America* (Cambridge, 1990); Jay Fliegelman, *Declaring Independence: Jefferson, Natural Language, & the Culture of Performance* (Stanford, 1993); Christopher Looby, *Voicing America: Language, Literary Form, and the Origins of the United States* (Chicago, 1996).

3. The most widely influential work in this regard is Michel Foucault's *The Order of Things: An Archaeology of the Human Sciences* (New York, 1973 [1966]); a great num-

ber of recent works on the Enlightenment and the French Revolution rely in one way or another on Foucault's arguments. Other essential works on the relationship between language and the philosophy of the Enlightenment include Noam Chomsky, *Cartesian Linguistics: A Chapter in the History of Rationalist Thought* (New York, 1966); Sylvain Auroux, *La Sémiotique des Encyclopédistes: Essai d'épistemologie historique des sciences du langage* (Paris, 1979); Daniel Droixhe, *La Linguistique et l'appel de l'histoire (1600–1800): Rationalisme et révolutions positivistes* (Geneva, 1978); and Hans Aarsleff, *From Locke to Saussure: Essays on the Study of Language and Intellectual History* (Minneapolis, 1982).

4. Etienne Bonnot de Condillac, *La Langue des calculs* in *Oeuvres de Condillac*, v. 23 (Paris, 1798), p. 1. On Condillac and the question of time, see Daniel Rosenberg, "Making Time: Language, History, and Origin in Enlightenment France and Britain," (Ph.D. diss., University of California, Berkeley, 1996), ch. 2. See also, Hans Aarsleff, *From Locke to Saussure*; Suzanne Gearhart, *The Open Boundary of History and Fiction: A Critical Approach to the French Enlightenment* (Princeton, 1984); and Jacques Derrida, *The Archeology of the Frivolous: Reading Condillac*, trans. John P. Leavey, Jr. (Lincoln, NB, 1980 [1973]).

5. Paolo Rossi, *The Dark Abyss of Time: The History of the Earth and the History of Nations From Hooke to Vico*, trans. Lydia C. Cochrane (Chicago, 1984), pp. 108–10. In the same chapter Rossi discusses Diderot's own claim to have "inserted" the idea of succession into the definition of nature. On the problem of time in various scientific fields during this period, see also, Stephen Toulmin and June Goodfield, *The Discovery of Time* (New York, 1965); Arthur O. Lovejoy, *The Great Chain of Being: A Study of the History of an Idea* (Cambridge, MA, 1936); François Jacob, *La Logique du vivant: Une histoire de l'hérédité* (Paris,1970); Charles Coulston Gillispie, *Genesis and Geology: A Study in the Relations of Scientific Thought, Natural Theology, and Social Opinion in Great Britain, 1790–1850* (Cambridge, MA, 1951); Stephen Jay Gould, *Time's Arrow, Time's Cycle: Myth and Metaphor in the Discovery of Geological Time* (Cambridge, MA, 1987).

6. See Frank Manuel, *Isaac Newton, Historian* (Cambridge, MA, 1963).

7. Rossi, *Dark Abyss of Time*, p. 108.

8. J. B. Bury, *The Idea of Progress* (New York, 1932); Reinhart Koselleck, *Futures Past: On the Semantics of Historical Time*, trans. Keith Tribe (Cambridge, MA, 1985).

9. Koselleck, *Futures Past*, pp. 17–18.

10. See I. F. Clarke, *The Pattern of Expectation, 1644–2001* (London, 1979); Brian Aldiss, *Billion Year Spree: The History of Science Fiction* (London, 1973); and Bronislaw Baczko, *Utopian Lights: The Evolution of the Idea of Social Progress*, trans. Judith L. Greenberg (New York, [1978]). On the relationship between the idea of progress and the science fiction novel, see Fredric Jameson, "Progress versus Utopia; or, Can We Imagine the Future?" in Brian Wallis, ed., *Art after Modernism: Rethinking Representation. New York: New Museum of Contemporary Art* (New York, 1984); and Fred Pfeil, "These Disintegrations I'm Looking Forward To: Science Fiction from New Wave to New Age" in *Another Tale to Tell: Politics and Narrative in Postmodern Culture* (London, 1990). On the development of the time-travel story in the nineteenth and twentieth centuries, see Darko Suvin, *Metamorphoses of Science Fiction: On the Poetics and History of a Literary Genre* (New Haven, 1979); and Mark Rose, *Alien Encounters: Anatomy of Science Fiction* (Cambridge, MA, 1981).

11. Gotthold Ephraim Lessing from *Education of the Human Race* (1780), quoted in Koselleck, *Futures Past*, pp. 17–18. Koselleck writes, "The bearer of the modern philosophy of historical process was the citizen emancipated from absolutist subjection and the tutelage of the Church: the *prophète philosophe*, as he was once strikingly characterized in the eighteenth century. Present at the baptism of this prophetic philosopher in the role of godfather was a combination of political calculation and

speculation on a future liberated from Christian religion."

12. Denis Diderot, "Encyclopédie" [1755] in Denis Diderot and Jean le Rond d'Alembert, eds., *L'Encyclopédie ou dictionnaire raisonnée des sciences, des arts et des métiers* (Paris, 1780; reprint as compact edition, New York, 1969), v. 1, p. 635. I have referred to the following edition for guidance in translation: Denis Diderot, *Rameau's Nephew and Other Works*, trans. by Jacques Barzun and Ralph H. Bowen (New York, 1956).

13. See Michel Foucault, *The Order of Things* and, equally, *The Birth of the Clinic: An Archaeology of Medical Perception*, trans. A. M. Sheridan Smith (New York, 1975 [1963]). Many readers have emphasized this aspect of Foucault's argument more than Foucault himself, particularly in service of a contrast between eighteenth- and nineteenth-century epistemologies. See, for example, Jonathan Crary, *Techniques of the Observer: On Vision and Modernity in the Nineteenth Century* (Cambridge, MA, 1990), p. 56.

14. Foucault, *The Order of Things*, pp. 85–86.

15. Both Darnton and Proust give good orientations in this literature. See Darnton, *Business of Enlightenment*; Jacques Proust, *Diderot et l'Encyclopédie* (Paris, 1967); John Lough, *The Encyclopédie* (New York, 1971).

16. P.-J. Garat, *Mémoires historiques sur la vie de M. Suard* (1820), quoted in Bronislaw Baczko, *Utopian Lights*, p. 31. On Suard, see Daniel Gordon, *Citizens without Sovereignty: Equality and Sociability in French Thought, 1670–1789* (Princeton, 1994), ch. 4.

17. Diderot, "Encyclopédie," p. 636a.

18. Roland Barthes, "The Plates of the *Encyclopedia*" in *New Critical Essays*, trans. Richard Howard (Berkeley, 1990 [1972]), p. 23.

19. Diderot, "Encyclopédie," p. 637.

20. Ibid., p. 636a.

21. Jean le Rond d'Alembert, "Dictionnaire" [1755] in Denis Diderot and Jean le Rond d'Alembert, eds., *L'Encyclopédie*, v. 1, p. 967.

22. Concerns about language change had been voiced more and more often since the linguistic fashions of the late seventeenth century, and many neological dictionaries had appeared. In one of the best known, *La Dictionnaire néologique*, the notorious abbé Desfontaines had claimed that the language at court changed so quickly that it was necessary to write a primer for those in the provinces in order that they might understand and be understood at court. Molière had parodied the *préciosité* of neologism (by reflexively or unreflexively inventing the term *préciosité*). While the concerns of many of these works had more to do with fashion than science, the problem of language change was understood as pervasive. On the history of neology in eighteenth-century France, see Daniel Rosenberg, "Making Time," ch. 6.

23. In his most apocalyptic tone, Diderot argues that the moment of revolution is the privileged moment of the encyclopedia: "The most glorious moment for a work of this sort would be that which might come immediately in the wake of some catastrophe so great as to suspend the progress of science, interrupt the labors of craftsmen, and plunge a portion of our hemisphere into darkness once again. What gratitude would not be lavished by the generation that came after this time of troubles upon those men who had discerned the approach of disaster from afar, who had taken measures to ward off its worst ravages by collecting in a safe place the knowledge of past ages!" (author's translation). Diderot, "Encyclopédie," p. 637.

24. D'Alembert, "Dictionnaire," p. 967.

25. Diderot, "Encyclopédie," p. 636.

26. Ibid.

27. As much as the crown claimed to have an interest in fixing the standards of the

language, volumes of the *Dictionary* of the Académie Française appeared at a snail's pace. In fact, at least one "immortal," Furetière, had created a scandal by rebelling against the dictionary project and in short order issuing his own dictionary. See, especially, Ferdinand Brunot, *Histoire de la langue française des origines à 1900* (Paris, 1905–53), tome IV: La langue classique (1660–1715).

28. Diderot, "Encyclopédie," p. 636.
29. This claim echoes Condillac's theory that genius only becomes possible at moments of linguistic exhaustion, and that it necessarily manifests itself as a way of speaking newly. Diderot makes a related point in the following passage when he describes temporalities of fashion and genius. Ibid., p. 644a.
30. Ibid., p. 636.
31. Ibid.
32. "[I]f you wish to have your work remain fresh and useful for a long time to come— by virtue of its being far in advance of the national spirit, which marches ceaselessly on—you must shorten your labors by multiplying the number of your collaborators" (author's translation). Ibid., p. 637. For the reason of promptness, Diderot recognizes that an encyclopedia can no longer be the work of one person. He writes, "When one comes to reflect upon the vast subject matter of an encyclopedia, the one thing that can be perceived distinctly is that it cannot be the work of a single man. For how could one man, in the short space of his lifetime, hope to know and describe the universal system of nature and of art, seeing that the numerous and erudite society of academicians of *La Crusca* has taken forty years to compose its dictionary, and that the members of our French Academy worked sixty years on their *Dictionary* before publishing its first edition!" (author's translation). Again and again, Diderot and d'Alembert entwine themes of mortality and knowledge. Ibid., p. 635. An interesting parallel can be drawn with Samuel Johnson's *Dictionary* (1755). As Alvin Kernan has shown, while Johnson liked to portray himself as a solitary author, he in fact employed a great number of assistants, and the organization of the enterprise was in great measure conditioned by the logic of capitalist economies of scale. No such mythology haunted Diderot's *Encyclopedia* which was explicitly meant to be a collaborative project. The composition of both works was governed by a perceived imperative of speed. See Alvin Kernan, *Printing Technology, Letters & Samuel Johnson* (Princeton, 1987). On the literary textures of time in Johnson and other seventeenth- and eighteenth-century British writers, see Stuart Sherman's suggestive *Telling Time: Clocks, Diaries, and English Diurnal Form, 1660–1785*.
33. Diderot, "Encyclopédie," p. 636a.
34. Ibid.
35. The perceived relationship between writing and deferral is not new to Diderot's works. Jacques Derrida has traced the formula to Plato and has examined its implications across Western philosophy and literature. And in this respect Diderot could certainly be written into a Derridean frame. But we do this at the peril of losing perspective on the specific historical sense of this relationship for Diderot. Without objecting to the Derridean analysis from a philosophical point of view, we may from a historical point of view nonetheless observe that in Diderot's view there is something novel about the problem of the relationship between writing and deferral. And for Diderot, recognizing the problem is precisely what makes one modern. An interesting parallel may be drawn in this respect with the sense of post-ness attributed to Derrida's own position. See *Of Grammatology*, trans. Gayatri Chakravorty Spivak (Baltimore, 1976 [1967]). On the "mode of temporality" of writing and publishing in the eighteenth century, see Carla Hesse, "Books in Time" in Geoff Nunberg, ed., *The Future of the Book* (Berkeley, 1996).
36. Diderot, "Encyclopédie," p. 644a. On the idea of the century during the eighteenth

century, see Daniel Milo, ". . . Et la Révolution 'créa' le siècle" in *Trahir le temps (histoire)* (Paris, 1991) and Bronislaw Baczko, *Utopian Lights*, pp. 80–81.

37. Diderot, "Encyclopédie," p. 636a.
38. Ibid., p. 637.
39. Ibid., p. 636a.
40. Ibid., p. 637.
41. D'Alembert and Diderot, *Discours préliminaire* in idem., *Encyclopédie*, p. xxxiv. Translations modified from *Preliminary Discourse to the Encyclopedia of Diderot*, trans. Richard N. Schwab and Walter E. Rex (Indianapolis, 1963).
42. Ibid.
43. Ibid., pp. xxxiv–xlv (esp. pp. xxxiv–xxxv). The usual account of this is drawn from Rousseau's *Confessions*.
44. Ibid., p. xl.
45. On the question of the end of the book, see esp. Geoffrey Nunberg, *Future of the Book*; Carla Hesse and Randolph Starn, eds., "Future Libraries," (special issue) *Representations* 42 (spring 1993); George Landow, *Hypertext 2.0: The Convergence of Contemporary Critical Theory and Technology* (Baltimore, 1997); and Mark Poster, *The Second Media Age* (Oxford, 1995).
46. Diderot, "Encyclopédie," p. 644a.
47. Ibid.
48. Ibid. It is not unimportant in this regard that this is also the period of the birth of the modern review essay. Such reviews may be found, not least of all, in the *Journal Encyclopédique*. For this observation, I am grateful to Sophia Rosenfeld.
49. Diderot, "Encyclopédie," p. 644a.
50. Among the many important works in this field, see esp. Lucien Febvre and Henri-Jean Martin, *L'Apparition du livre* (Paris, 1958); Gerald Graff, *The Legacies of Literacy: Continuities and Contradictions in Western Culture and Society* (Bloomington, IN, 1987); and Roger Chartier, *The Cultural Uses of Print in Early Modern France*, trans. Lydia G. Cochrane (Princeton, 1987).
51. Louis-Sébastien Mercier from *Tableau de Paris* (1782–83), quoted in Roger Chartier, *The Cultural Origins of the French Revolution*, trans. Lydia G. Cochrane (Durham, NC, 1991), p. 70.
52. Diderot, "Encyclopédie," p. 636.
53. This often meant the *trivium* and *quadrivium*. See, for example, Peter Sharatt, ed., *French Renaissance Studies, 1540–70: Humanism and the Encyclopedia,* (Edinburgh, 1976).
54. D'Alembert and Diderot, *Discours préliminaire*, p. xv.
55. On the literary character of these formal structures, see Roland Barthes, "Plates of the *Encyclopedia*"; James Creech, "'Chasing after Advances': Diderot's Article 'Encyclopedia'." *Yale French Studies* 63 (1982): 183-97; Daniel Brewer, *The Discourse of Enlightenment in Eighteenth-Century France: Diderot and the Art of Philosophizing* (Cambridge, 1993); Jean Starobinski "Remarques sur l'encyclopédie," *Revue de métaphysique et de morale* 75 (1970): 284–91.
56. Diderot, "Encyclopédie," p. 642.
57. D'Alembert and Diderot, *Discours préliminaire*, p. xxxiv. See also, d'Alembert, "Dictionnaire," p. 968. The editors point out that this approach would clear up obscurities created by the increasing specialization of knowledges. By breaking up hierarchical arrangements of subjects into generic entries that might be drawn upon by readers in many different fields, the *Encyclopedia* would work to counteract the compartmentalization of knowledge. Thus, a single entry on "analysis" referring likewise to grammar and chemistry makes a point that would more likely be lost if embedded in separate accounts of separate fields. It is interesting that Diderot also argues that if an encyclopedic arrangement had been chosen, it might

have been difficult to convince scholars to work cooperatively on the project, as each would essentially have been writing an integral treatise and would see no particular reason not to publish it as such. Diderot's insight may be borne out by the number of spinoff works that the later *Encyclopédie méthodique* produced. On the other hand, unlike the *Encyclopédie*, the *Encyclopédie méthodique* was capable of swallowing books whole as was the case for Charles de Brosses's *Du Culte des dieux fétiches* (1760), for example. The criticism of encyclopedias to which Diderot responds here is similar to criticisms made of new technologies and forms of information access from writing to CD-ROM. On Plato's critique of writing, see Jacques Derrida's "Plato's Pharmacy" in *Dissemination,* trans. Barbara Johnson (Chicago, 1981 [1972]).

58. Wilda Anderson argues that the dictionary "presents at least two systems of judgment . . . the institutionalized or accepted way of viewing the world is presented explicitly in each dissertation, but the totality is fragmented by the arbitrary structure of the alphabetical ordering. . . . The system of cross-references provides at least one other implicit judgment on the explicit world-view: the network of connections and oppositions brings into contact ideas which would never before have been considered in terms of each other." Wilda Anderson, *Between the Library and the Laboratory: The Language of Chemistry in Eighteenth-Century France* (Baltimore, 1984), p. 36.

59. Diderot, "Encyclopédie," p. 642a. Ernst Cassirer contextualizes this statement in his discussion of the role of agency in the philosophy of the Enlightenment. See chapter one of his *The Philosophy of the Enlightenment,* trans. Fritz C. A. Koelln and James P. Pettegrove (Princeton, 1951 [1932]). On the theory of the *renvois,* Diderot continues: "Cross references to things clarify the subject; they indicate its close connections with other subjects that touch it directly as well as its more remote connections with still other matters that might otherwise be thought irrelevant; and they suggest common elements and analogous principles. They also put added stress on elements of internal consistency within groups of facts, they elaborate upon the connections that each special branch of knowledge has with its parent tree, and they give to the whole *Encyclopedia* that unity so favorable to the establishment of truth and to its propagation" (author's translation). Diderot, "Encyclopédie," pp. 642a. Diderot develops d'Alembert's contrast among kinds of encyclopedic arrangement into a kind of tropology of the reference. Cross-references do more than create an economy of definition and a fabric of shared concepts. They confirm and refute inferences that may be drawn from articles, they allow for implication, and even satire. Diderot writes, "Finally, there is a kind of cross reference—it can refer either to words or to things—which I should like to call satirical or epigrammatic. Such, for example, is the one to be found in one of our articles where, at the end of a pompous eulogy, one reads: *see* CAPUCHON. The comic word, *capuchon* [monk's hood], together with what the reader will find under the heading CAPUCHON, can easily lead him to suspect that the pompous eulogy was meant ironically, and that it is wise the read the article with the utmost precaution and with attention to the careful weighing of every word." (author's translation). Ibid., p. 643.

60. D'Alembert and Diderot, *Discours préliminaire,* p. xx. For the editors of the *Encyclopedia* the specter of the decline of civilization and the loss of learning is always present. No *stage* of history, including a dark age, recedes to an unrepeatable past. And the *Encyclopédie,* envisioned as a document and a mechanism of historical progress, is imagined and justified under the sign of historical loss. Diderot writes, "May the Encyclopedia become a sanctuary, where the knowledge of man is protected from time and from revolutions. . . . Therefore, let us do for centuries to come what we regret that past centuries did not do for ours. We daresay that if the

ancients had carried through [an] encyclopedia, as they carried through so many other great things, and if that manuscript alone had escaped from the famous Library of Alexandria, it would have been capable of consoling us for the loss of the other." (author's translation). Ibid., pp. xxxviii–xxxix.

61. Baczko emphasizes that in addition to the "utopia in its classic paradigmatic forms," the Enlightenment gave rise to an increase "on the fringes of utopia" of alternative imaginations. Baczko, *Utopian Lights*, p. 20. Thanks to Omar Metawally for his insights about Baczko.

62. Louis-Sébastien Mercier, *L'An deux mille quatre cent quarante, rêve s'il en fut jamais* (1771), translated in excerpt in Robert Darnton, *Forbidden Bestsellers of Pre-Revolutionary France* (New York, 1995), pp. 300–36.

63. Ibid., p. 315.

64. Indeed, Mercier flags this with his subtitle, "A Dream If Ever There Was One."

VIRTUOUS ECONOMIES

Modernity and Noble Expenditure from
Montesquieu to Caillois

ELENA RUSSO

Paradoxically, the aspect of Montesquieu's social thought most indicative of its age is a critique of modernity that would have great resonance
in the romantic and modernist critique of bourgeois economy in the
nineteenth and twentieth centuries. I am thinking of the importance
Montesquieu gives to the role of the nobility as a bulwark against
encroachments of absolutist power, and his praise of aristocratic morality and honor. This position has been interpreted mostly as a symptom
of Montesquieu's attachment to the interests of his class. I intend to
show that its source is quite different. Montesquieu's praise of aristocratic moral economies and the role he assigns the nobilities of the
sword and the robe must be seen as an effect of his interest in the ethics
of ancient republics and in republican civic virtue. This allows us to recognize his profound ambivalence toward the emergence of commercial
society. For Montesquieu, remnants of ancient political virtue can still
be found in the moral economy that distinguishes the nobility, and that
alone can save the French state from the moral decline caused by the
absolutist marketplace. His fascination for the ancients anticipates—
and indeed inspires—Rousseau's critique of the commercial spirit and
Rousseau's archaic utopianism. Montesquieu's case, however, is far
more interesting: unlike Rousseau, he does not believe that the ancient
moral economy can be resurrected within modern society; his fondness
for the virtue of the past runs as an undercurrent through his work, but
is never adopted as a system, nor does it assume a programmatic value.
Precisely because he cannot integrate it into his vision of the modern

age, ancient virtue keeps resurfacing; as a result, Montesquieu, much more than Rousseau, produced the most complex and disturbing description of an ethos that was to play such a crucial role in the revolutionary script and in the postrevolutionary reflection on social ethics.

The originality of Montesquieu's critique of the moral economy of his time appears more forcefully when we highlight its debt to traditional themes of aristocratic discontent. In the *Lettres persanes* he manifests ambivalence toward the emergence of a society he sees as too individualistic and fragmented; the density and complexity of individual private lives are a result of the civic and political disaffection of those who have surrendered their civic responsibilities to the centralized monarchy. The result is a society in which the individual is both self-absorbed and insignificant, where efforts to distinguish oneself lead individuals to fall prey to the fashions that radiate from the court. He detects social anomie and a loss of values issuing from the monarch's despotic whim; every activity may be exchanged for another because all activities have become empty symbols of prestige without intrinsic value. He criticizes the power of money, that great equalizer able to buy the symbolic capital of prestige and exchangeable for honor.

Most of these themes were part of a critique that Montesquieu did not formulate alone; they can be found, in various forms, in the writings of La Rochefoucauld, Fénelon, and Boileau, to mention a few.[1] All consider the market the product of a self-interested and dishonest mode of exchange ultimately expressed in social relations at large: namely, giving as little as possible in order to gain as much as possible. This is roughly the position of La Rochefoucauld in his *Maximes*, in which amour-propre plays the role of the dishonest merchant.[2]

Economic affairs are inevitably conceived in terms of morality because the marketplace is seen as a product of individual passions and desires. Montesquieu criticizes the market by devoting much attention to archaic modes of exchange—generally described under the broad concept of "virtue"—a term covering practices as diverse as self-sacrifice, generosity, frugality, construction of communal sentiment, and love for the "patrie."

Montesquieu's critique reflects aristocratic and feudal resentment against the modern, commercial society that emerged with monarchical centralization. This led to the marginalization of an aristocracy increasingly alienated from its traditional callings and thus forced to seek social promotion through bourgeois economic activity or dependency on the vagaries of court politics. A persistent sense of frustration found expression through a nostalgia for more heroic times, in which merit was rewarded, social relations were open and transparent, and society was organized in an organic fashion. Most of the critique directed against absolutism carried the imprint of aristocratic dissatisfaction. Paul Bénichou correctly notes that the Roman and republican scenario that ruled the revolutionary act had its origin in the frustration of those who, like Montesquieu, fancied themselves heirs of Roman senators, harbingers of liberty, crushed under the weight of Augustus's tyranny.[3] But even if Montesquieu's critique owes much to the aristocratic tradition (the analysis of which is yet to be written), the impact of his representation of modernity resonates far beyond its origin, into the postrevolutionary era of romanticism.

Montesquieu illustrates the coming to consciousness of modernity as a condition of loss and displacement, of *inquiétude* and disunion. Modernity begins to conceive itself in terms of guilt by inventing a past that includes humanity's fall from a state of harmony and grace. Even before Montesquieu, Montaigne and Lahontan had inaugurated that move with the figure of the good savage.[4] The theme of the *inquiétude* of the soul, a traditional Christian motif, resonated in moralist discourse throughout the seventeenth century, as demonstrated most notably by Pascal, Nicole, Malebranche, and Bossuet. But the moralists tended to think ahistorically, conceiving the fall as a sacred event outside historical time, and they viewed history as the repetitive enactment of a battle between the love of God and the love of man. Rousseau will recapture the moralists' inherent ahistoricity in his description of a conflict between the state of nature and the fall into the social state.[5] Montesquieu, on the contrary, is too aware of the complex structuring of any given period, of the multiplicity of factors that contribute to create the moral blueprint of an epoch, its *esprit général*, to dream of resurrecting the morality of times past.[6] His own history is not mythical; it is a form of resistance to the mythifying tendencies strong in the culture of his time. The world of the ancients and, more particularly, that of republican Rome, which he inherits from the pedagogical tradition of Oratorian and Jesuit colleges, is indeed a mythical one, and Montesquieu's efforts are to demystify it.

Yet, regardless of such debunking, Montesquieu never abandons some measure of admiration for what he is busy demolishing: he never completely ceases to treat the world of the ancients as a moral exemplum for his own time. The power of his work lies precisely in this unreconcilable movement between history and myth, faith and disenchantment, critical analysis and belief. On the one hand, Montesquieu uses the model of the ancient world as a foil to the vices of modern monarchy and modern individuals; on the other, he finds himself compelled to examine this model on its own specific historical terms. Montesquieu may well declare himself a citizen of the ancient world, but in the end he runs the risk of finding himself (as a punishment, his editor Caillois would say, for his "perverse" disguise in the *Lettres persanes*) without a home.

Montesquieu's opposition between a world of tradition, of unreflective and unwritten *moeurs*, of a noble economy of the gift, when private and public life merge, and the modern world of written law, rationalized commercial exchange and separated private and public lives would prove fruitful throughout the nineteenth century. From Rousseau to Constant, Hegel and Nietzsche, down through the tradition of romantic anthropology running from Emile Durkheim to Marcel Mauss, Georges Bataille, and Roger Caillois and their joint venture in the *Collège de Sociologie*, these oppositions define the moral identity of modernity by confronting it with a past of mythical loss and normative ideal.

My intent in this essay is twofold. The first is to extract from Montesquieu's writings on virtue the elements of a theory of aristocratic exchange, and to highlight the political relevance for his own time of ancient virtue to the relationship between the state and civil society. This will show that Montesquieu uses literary material from his classical education in the Oratorian college much as an ethnologist in the Maussian tradition: to understand and compare, take distance from himself, recapture in the other the shadow of his own past, and draw some wisdom for the future.

Second, I will close with an examination of some pertinent themes in contemporary accounts of archaic, aristocratic economies, as they appear in the ethnographic work of Mauss, Bataille, and Caillois. The latter is especially relevant given his position as editor of Montesquieu's complete works for the Gallimard "Pléiade" edition published in 1949. Caillois was a student of Mauss and Georges Dumézil at the Ecole Pratique des Hautes Etudes, where he majored in sociology in the early 1930s, and he founded, with Bataille and Michel Leiris, the short-lived but ambitious *Collège de Sociologie*. This organization, devoted to the study of closed communities and modern manifestations of the sacred, nurtured the ambition of concretely implementing its own theories. An earlier experience with surrealism, as well as the influence of Nietzsche and Baudelairian and Balzacian dandyism, led Caillois to inject into his ethnographic studies a confused fascination for extreme manifestations of social communion; these included secret, elective societies, heretical sects, and monastic, military and terrorist organizations all supposedly animated by an ethos of heroism, the free expenditure of energy, sacrifice and violence. For Caillois, these extreme social expressions represent the antithesis of a modern ethos of social indifference and fragmentation, the product of "an extremely dissipated society in which no mediation remains between the passions of the individual and the

State apparatus."⁷ Caillois favors manifestations of social excess and vitalistic expression, such as the orgiastic exaltation of the ritual *fête*, the free expenditure of the potlatch, the experience of the sacred—"a dangerous and incomprehensible energy" of "a sacred of dissolution" that regenerates society by transgressing rules and violating boundaries.⁸ He seeks experiences of irrational communion that would overcome feelings of weakness and the anxiety of belonging to a declining society, one in which he feels like a helpless creature of the twilight (thus echoing Nietzsche's words about the weakness of "human beings of late cultures and refracted lights"). A few years later, disenchanted and exiled in Argentina to escape the war, he thus evokes his mood in those years: "We did not belong to the dawn. We feel the cold and fly clumsily, we are quick to hide in holes in the walls; we lie in wait only for small prey. We are the sinister and cautious bat of twilight, the bird of experience and wisdom, who comes out after the rumblings of day, even fearing the shadows that day heralds. We should call ourselves twilight creatures."⁹

It would be neither possible nor enlightening to make a sustained and extensive comparison of Montesquieu's description of ancient societies and Caillois's and Bataille's use of Mauss's ethnographic reflections on primitive peoples. Caillois acknowledges Montesquieu as a precursor, the first sociologist "who accomplished for himself the sociological revolution," and recognizes in him something akin to his own "Luciferian spirit."¹⁰ Yet we would be hard-pressed to demonstrate a direct influence. My purpose is to examine the crucial role played in their respective works by the construction of a myth of a lost state of wholeness and social organicity, one in which the economic sphere is not yet emancipated from the moral universe, but subordinated to it. Montesquieu, Mauss, and Caillois make moral, exemplary use of their study of an "other" that has strange affinities with their own fellow citizens, of times past that have some resonance with their own times. For them, ethnographic studies help define the contours and identity of their own society: the lesson delivered by the ancients, as well as by "primitive" peoples, is that an early experience of organicity and cohesion has been replaced by one of fragmentation, uncertainty, isolation and moral indifference. For them, the study of archaic social structures holds the hope of regeneration. In that respect, Montesquieu inaugurates the fundamental move of modernity's questioning of its own values through an imagined and idealized past, while Caillois and Bataille illustrate one of the dangers of that move: a flight into irrationality.

Daniel Gordon has pointed out that several scholars (such as Polanyi, Dumont, and Arendt) have mistaken the moralization of self-interest that took place in the second half of the eighteenth century for an outright endorsement of the hegemony of market economy over civil society; he notes Arendt's argument in *The Human Condition* that the rise of society in the Enlightenment "indicates a stark contrast between the Greek conception of the public sphere as a locus of communication and virtue, and the Enlightenment conception of civil society as a network of 'laborers and jobholders.'"[11] In reality, the insistence on virtue, generosity, and noninstrumental giving in social, religious, and political spaces is yet another manifestation of an opposition to the dominance of a discourse of the market economy in the moral and civic domain that characterizes Enlightenment thought well before the Revolution. What is more, Arendt's and Dumont's own turning toward the Greek city-state as a model of civic virtue and participation, and as an alternative to the modern marketplace, is a move made possible by the Enlightenment's introduction of that theme.

Following the same line of reasoning, we can draw a parallel between the Enlightenment's fascination with archaic economies and contemporary interest in "primitive" theories of exchange, prestige consumption, and "dépense" (in particular Mauss's work on the potlatch and Bataille's notion of pure expenditure). Vincent Pecora has convincingly argued that this interest is part of a tendency within modernism to nurture a nostalgia for archaic, aristocratic forms of status-oriented economies of sacrifice, extravagant expenditure, and ritual—a nostalgia that fuels modernism's rejection of capitalist, rationalized exchange for profit. Pecora detects in the ethnological dream of an economy of symbolic exchange and esthetic, nonprofit-driven ways of life (which, he argues, is yet another version of the Aristotelian notion of magnanimity and the noble *oikos*),[12] the inspiration of the postmodernist critique of representation illustrated by Lévi-Strauss, Derrida, Baudrillard, and Goux. The latter all imply "the 'deconstructive' possibility of a circulation of signifiers, rather than gifts, without the rational good of the intended signified, without the promise of any intellectual (or linguistic) profit from production and exchange."[13] Postmodernism has inherited Romanticism's nostalgia and idealization of an allegedly organic, prerational past. It appears that twentieth-century ethnological visions of noncapitalist societies with economies embedded harmoniously in social relations (Mauss's notion of "phénomènes sociaux totaux" or "prestations totales") are indebted to an obsession with noble forms of expenditure that have preoccupied social thought since the Enlightenment—that is, since the dawn of capitalism and the decline of feudal economies. It is therefore somewhat ironic that the work of Mauss and anthropologists informed by his theory of the potlatch should come full circle. Maussian conceptions of noble expenditure in traditional Melanesian, Polynesian, Australian, and North American societies are in fact being invoked as explanatory tools by scholars working on modes of aristocratic interaction in early modern Europe. Norbert

Elias's notion of a "court-aristocratic figuration" relying upon "prestige consumption" in which resources are squandered for the sake of prestige, is indebted to Mauss's idea of the potlatch, which Elias quotes as proof of the endurance and depth of antibourgeois feelings.[14] More recently, Elizabeth Goldsmith, who has used the ethnographic work of Marshall Sahlins (also indebted to Mauss's description of the gift) to account for "generalized reciprocity" among individual members of Madeleine de Scudéry's conversational group, has gone to the heart of the matter with her bemused remark that "curiously, this radically civilized version of sociable interaction seems more analogous to the social structures characterizing primitive cultures than to those of contemporary society."[15] Such analogies seem curious indeed.

That these convergences among European cultures and so-called primitive societies appear so convincing should incite us to be cautious. We are, after all, uniquely equipped to appreciate the moral beauty of a society that squanders and destroys what we accumulate and preserve. We do have venerable models of archaic forms of aristocratic exchange that are exclusively homegrown and European, from Aristotle's notion of magnanimity and *oikos* in the *Nicomachean Ethics*, to Seneca's description of the gift in *De Beneficiis*, Cicero's *De Officiis*, and the highly moralized vision of republican Rome disseminated in seventeenth- and eighteenth-century French colleges. Therefore, the structure of the potlatch might have more to do with our own indigenous preoccupations with, as Pecora puts it, "a pleasantly romantic vision of 'primitive' life before the advent of capitalism . . . a pastoral alternative to the European marketplace," than with the traditions of Polynesian and North American peoples.[16] In seventeenth- and eighteenth-century France, insistence on archaic reciprocity was part of a nostalgia-driven reaction against the laws of economic exchange then being implemented. Has the reaction now come full circle, carried down to us by ethnological discourse—itself a form of nostalgia?

Montesquieu devoted much attention to the discussion of virtue as normative value and a principle of government (that is, as the human passion that rules republican government): to describe adequately its various facets and implications in such a limited space is impossible. I shall focus therefore on the one aspect that concerns us here, namely virtue as selfless action and sacrifice. Virtue for Montesquieu is above all a system of exchange in which the moral and economic order coincide. Virtue means a willingness to act without expecting immediate reward. It is not unmotivated, gratuitous, or irrational action, as in Bataille's *dépense*; it is action determined not by calculating self-interest, but unmediated love for (or identification with) something that transcends the self, such as duty toward the *patrie* and a sense of one's obligations toward society. It is a "passion générale" as opposed to a "passion parti-culière."[17] It is dominant in communities where individuality is not yet fully deployed and people are unenlightened: "souvent [le peuple] a tiré de la médiocrité de ses lumières un attachement plus fort pour ce qui est établi" (5,2). Even though virtue involves a "renoncement à soi-même" and a "sacrifice de ses plus chers intérêts" (3,5)—"un sacrifice continuel de soi-même et de ses répugnances" to the state (5,19), "une préférence continuelle de l'intérêt public au sien propre" (4,5)—it does not suppress or humiliate the self. Self-sacrifice is compatible with pride and ambition when the self identifies so strongly with the State that no blunt distinction is made between personal interests and those of the community. This is how early republican Romans discharged greedy and violent impulses onto external enemies of the *patrie*, and thus put their destructive and rapacious forces at the service of com-munal good.[18] One wonders whether it remains possible to speak of sac-rifice in that context: Benjamin Constant will pick up Montesquieu's argument and push it forward, arguing that a sacrifice of "passions par-ticulières" to the State is relatively natural and easy in societies where private life is entirely subsumed under the public, and where those pas-sions are quite rudimentary. Constant's point, of course, is that modern societies cannot expect such sacrifices.[19] Montesquieu, however, does not discuss this matter explicitly and leaves the issue unclear.

The argument about the extent and nature of such sacrifice could also be made in respect to the category of virtue found in religious and mystical discourse current in Montesquieu's time. Montesquieu is care-ful to note that he means political, not Christian virtue, yet his view of civic virtue is clearly indebted to Christian thought.[20] It makes histori-cally little sense to separate Christian from pagan and political virtue, when one considers that first exposure to the Roman world was usually experienced in Jesuit and Oratorian colleges (Montesquieu studied with the Oratorians of Juilly), which enforced moral rules with gram-matical ones.[21] The Roman world, represented in the seventeenth and eighteenth centuries, is to a great extent Christianized. Civic virtue is structurally a secularized version of Augustinian *charité* and of Salesian and Fénelonian *pur amour*, two notions central to the Christian concept of the psyche at a time when discourse about human motivation was dominated by the Church (albeit not always by the official Church: in fact, both Jansenism and Fénelonian quietism found little favor with the authorities). Both in civic virtue and its Christian correlatives the degree of self-concern and rational calculation of profit is crucial in measuring the moral worth of an action. Selfless action is always privileged, and Fénelon establishes various degrees of selflessness which escalate toward moral perfection as we love God for his own sake and not for the interest of our personal salvation. When Montesquieu writes that "pour être homme de bien, il faut . . . aimer l'Etat moins pour soi que pour lui-même" (3,6), he is really treading in the same steps as Fénelon, who wrote "this love [of charity] seeks God for His sake and prefers Him to everything else, with no exception."[22] Fénelon had praised the condition of *pur amour*, in which the self is obliterated and lost in the love of God, and used political language in order to describe this blessed loss of individuality, highlighting the affinities between the Christian love of God and the devotion ancient republican citizens felt for the community: "this idea of pure disinterestedness dominates the political theories of all ancient legislators."[23] Such disinterestedness involves merging the self with the transcendent body—the latter may be called God or *Patrie*—which, rather than diminishing, widens the boundaries of the self, allowing it to share the glory of the mystical body it has joined.

For Montesquieu, the relevant source of civic virtue, the one from which all the other virtues flow, is this merging of the self into a larger communal body, which he opposes to the narrow self-interest of modern individuals: "Les politiques grecs, qui vivaient dans le gouvernement populaire, ne reconnaissaient d'autre force qui pût les soutenir que celle de la vertu. Ceux d'aujourd'hui ne nous parlent que de manufactures, de commerce, de finances, de richesses et de luxe même. Lorsque cette vertu cesse, l'ambition entre dans tous les coeurs qui peuvent la recevoir, et l'avarice entre dans tous. . . . La république est une dépouille; et sa force n'est plus que le pouvoir de quelques citoyens et la licence de tous" (3,3). That virtue is a moral economy (that is, an individual morality involving a general economy) is demonstrated by the fact that virtue is always played against the economy of the marketplace as Montesquieu knows it: commerce, industry, a complex financial system, money, and luxury. Montesquieu views economy as coextensive with morality because individual passions shape social and political situations. Both the system of virtue and that of the marketplace are determined by, and determine in their own turn, a specific ethics: "dans les bonnes républiques, on dit: Nous, et dans les bonnes monarchies, on dit: Moi."[24] When love for the *patrie* wanes, communal feelings disappear, replaced by love of the self. The marketplace is the consequence of that love. Montesquieu's praise of virtue is thus indistinguishable from his critical evaluation of the economy and the ethics of his time: both are strictly correlated and must therefore be discussed together.[25]

The passage above deserves closer scrutiny because it is ambiguous. In fact, it mixes two different temporalities and suggests a comparison between two incongruous time frames: that of the republic and that of the modern monarchy ("les politiciens grecs . . . ceux d'aujourd'hui"), which should have no direct historical connection with each other. In this chapter, devoted to the "principe de la démocratie" (that is, to virtue), Montesquieu purports to describe a process of political corruption within the ancient republic, and the examples given concern the strength and weakness of Athens at two different historical moments and the corruption of Carthage at the time of its fall to the Romans. And yet, right in the middle of his argument, he inserts an unexpected reference to modern times: "Ceux d'aujourd'hui ne nous parlent que de manufactures, de commerce, de finances, de richesses et de luxe même." The consequence is to introduce ambiguity in the referent of his discourse on political corruption: when he describes the disappearance of virtue, the breakdown of law and the destruction caused by "avarice," is he talking about the decline of the ancient republic or about the French monarchy? The question is significant, because it reveals not only that Montesquieu has his own society in mind when describing the past, but also that he feels deeply ambivalent about the moral economy of contemporary France. However, the picture he usually draws of the French monarchy, critical as it may be, is never as starkly negative as the evocation of social collapse, corruption and rapacious anarchy that comes through in this passage, which deals ostensibly with a decaying republic.

Indeed, Montesquieu's position toward the morality of the modern age is difficult to pin down. Unlike Rousseau, he is not an unequivocal enemy of modernity. His position is subtle and nuanced, and he is careful to situate commerce within its political and social context; the role of commerce is always evaluated in relation to the general conditions of the country (for instance, his distinction between the positive, civilizing effects of commerce upon the "moeurs barbares" and its corrupting effect upon the "moeurs pures" is well known).[26] Montesquieu is not one to discard the positive effects of economic development for the material conditions of the population in the name of some ideal in moral perfection: he is too convinced that a society functions best not when its members are morally irreproachable, but when different forces within it, including potentially destructive but natural instincts such as *inquiétude* and ambition, are carefully balanced against each other. However, in spite of his Mandevillian praise of the civilizing role of the *petit-maître* and the social utility of negative passions such as vanity,[27] Montesquieu is not moved by considerations of utility alone. He is more concerned with the symbolic structure of society than its material well-being: with rank, not with the material control of the means of production; he conceives wealth mainly as a sumptuary source of prestige, as symbolic capital, and not as accumulation and multiplication of commodities. For him wealth is (or ought to be) regulated by tradition and custom; it is ritualistic and not at all ruled by individual *jouissance*, unlike the ridiculous expenditure of the parvenus. "La fortune est un état, et non pas un bien. Elle n'est bonne qu'en ce qu'elle nous expose aux regards et nous peut rendre plus attentifs; elle nous oblige à rendre un compte d'elle-même" (*Mes pensées*, 72). Following Artistotle's description of noble magnanimity, Montesquieu praises the Roman custom of sacrificing personal wealth to the state, making religious offerings and contributing to the construction of public buildings.[28]

As Pierre Rétat has pointed out, Montesquieu experiences to the fullest the contradictions of the nobility of his time, and the impossibility of reconciling aristocratic values such as honor and glory with economic interest and general profit: hence his flight toward the ideal of republican frugality and virtue. In fact, Montesquieu is able to transcend customary grievances of the nobility; his critique attacks the very roots of the private and public divide that characterizes modern life in a bureaucratic state. Significantly, the message of virtue as an ideal is not fully endorsed in his published work, but comes through much more forcefully in his unpublished notebooks, of which he disclaimed full responsibility.[29] Not only does he allow himself more critical expression, but most of the direct comparisons between the economy of virtue and that of contemporary monarchical commerce appear in the notebooks: in his major works they are often marginal and almost involuntary, a recurrent but repressed motif.

"C'est l'amour de la patrie qui a donné aux histoires grecques et romaines cette *noblesse* que les nôtres n'ont pas. Elle y est le ressort continuel de toutes les actions, et on sent du plaisir à la trouver partout, cette vertu chère à tous ceux qui ont un coeur. Quand on pense à la petitesse de nos motifs, à la *bassesse* de nos moyens, à l'avarice avec laquelle nous cherchons de *viles récompenses*, à cette ambition si différente de l'amour de la gloire, on est étonné de la différence des spectacles, et il semble que, depuis que ces deux grands peuples ne sont plus, les hommes se sont raccourcis d'une coudée."[30] This passage contains a regressive tendency to assimilate civic virtue with the customary ideals of the feudal, military nobility: "noblesse" involves glory, moral grandeur, beauty of action, courage, and a complementary tendency to see commercial pursuit as "low," "vile," and "small." Loss of the noble ideal of virtue has led to a sort of moral degeneration, a scaling down of the individual. Montesquieu is usually less pessimistic about the commercial ethos and willing to recognize that the spirit of commerce may involve the exercise of certain lesser virtues: "L'esprit de commerce entraîne avec soi celui de frugalité, d'economie, de modération, de travail, de sagesse, de tranquillité, d'ordre et de règle." (5,6). Those virtues, however, are limited in scope and reducible to a minimal "justice exacte" which is by no means sufficient to create a communal feeling or a livable society: "Mais, si l'esprit de commerce unit les nations, il n'unit pas de même les particuliers. Nous voyons que dans les pays où l'on n'est affecté que de l'esprit de commerce, on trafique de toutes les actions humaines, et de toutes les vertus morales: les plus petites choses, celles que l'humanité demande, s'y font ou s'y donnent pour de l'argent. L'esprit de commerce produit dans les hommes un certain sens de *justice exacte*, opposé d'un coté au brigandage, et de l'autre à ces vertus morales qui font qu'on ne discute pas toujours ses intérêts avec rigidité, et qu'on peut les négliger pour ceux des autres" (20,2 emphasis added).

Montesquieu is targeting here the Dutch, for whom he has very harsh words in his travel notes: "Le coeur des habitants des pays qui vivent de commerce est entièrement corrompu: ils ne vous rendront pas le moindre service, parce qu'ils espèrent qu'on le leur achètera. . . . Tout paye; tout demande; à chaque pas que vous faites, vous trouvez un impôt."[31] Everything is for sale with the Dutch: hardened to any human sympathy, they ignore the generosity and exchange of "services" that form the basis of sociable living and ground the aristocratic exchange of favors that constitutes the patronage system. Paradoxically, the commercial spirit, a product of our heightened awareness of others ("on a plus de désirs, plus de besoins, plus de fantaisies quand on est ensemble," 7,2), becomes a source of isolation, constraining the self within limited horizons. Dutch society is neither unjust nor immoral in a strict sense: but it is ugly and unlovable. In the "noble" way of life, such as the one illustrated by the ancient republics, "les actions humaines" are not negotiable in monetary terms, they cannot be exchanged for money, but only for other actions of the same nature, which reinforce the feeling of communal unity. Monetary compensation breaks the circle of the exchange of "services" and thus creates isolation and indifference, because it allows people to meet too easily their reciprocal social debts.[32] Virtue, on the contrary, creates an uninterrupted network of debtors and creditors, who never cease to depend upon each other and are ever willing to give and receive more services and favors: "L'amour de l'égalité dans une démocratie, borne l'ambition au seul désir, au seul bonheur de rendre à sa patrie de plus grands services que les autres citoyens. . . . En naissant on contracte envers elle *une dette immense* dont on ne peut jamais s'acquitter" (5,3, emphasis added). Significantly, the ancients held toward the *patrie* the same sense of indebtedness that Christians hold toward God: "inquiets sur les anciennes dettes, jamais quittes envers le Seigneur, nous devons craindre d'en contracter de nouvelles." (24,13). Both the Christian and the ancient citizen feel that no effort or sacrifice can extinguish the debt owed to the transcendent body of which they are members.

The question of the "récompense" of our actions is therefore crucial to a discussion of virtue and recurs in various contexts throughout

Montesquieu's work.[33] While the moderns seek "de viles récompenses," the ancients were satisfied with symbolic rewards: "A Rome, à Athènes, à Lacédémone, l'honneur payait seul les services les plus signalés. Une couronne de chêne ou de laurier, une statue, un éloge, était une récompense immense pour une bataille gagnée ou une ville prise. Là, un homme qui avait fait une belle action se trouvait suffisamment récompensé par cette action même. Il ne pouvait voir un de ses compatriotes qu'il ne ressentît le plaisir d'être son bienfaiteur";[34] "et n'est-ce pas beaucoup d'obliger les hommes à faire toutes les actions difficiles, et qui demandent de la force, sans autre récompense que le bruit de ces actions?" (3,7). Since the debt cannot be repaid, the reward for good action can only be a "témoignage," a symbolic object whose only significance is a renewed demand for more good actions. A good reputation ("le bruit de ces actions") is nothing but the expectation that one will continue to act in the same way. If the demand for services is inexhaustible, so is the offer. The ancient citizen is noble because he is boundless and bountiful; he has an infinite supply of energies at the service of the *patrie*. Indeed, he is almost divine: "c'est ressembler aux dieux que de contribuer au bonheur d'une société entière."[35]

In the modern world, in contrast, moral resources are limited and avarice narrows expectations. The king may well provide "gratifications" to those he favors, but those rewards are degrading: "Il ne croit pas que la grandeur souveraine doive être dans la distribution des grâces, et, sans examiner si celui qu'il comble de biens est homme de mérite, il croit que son choix va le rendre tel."[36] The king is a despot because he wants his idiosyncratic will to play a foundational role as value-giver: one is compelled to honor not what is publicly taken to be honorable, but what the king, arbitrarily, recognizes as such. In a monarchy when such a disjunction between power and justice, reality and symbols, "honneur" and "les honneurs" (the outward marks of esteem) exists, truly deserving people go unrecognized. Who are those people? Those who serve the state, (we have to observe that Montesquieu did much to destroy the sacredness of the king and transfer it to the State, which has become the sacralized embodiment of duty and service). In modern times a few people remain who are willing to forgo the commercial ethos, who do not seek profit, but are ready to devote their energies without demanding material, or even visible, satisfaction. The true heirs of the virtuous citizens of antiquity are those who are willing to serve the state obscurely and secretly, without any tangible reward except "le témoignage de leur conscience": the magistrates and the sword nobility.

Montesquieu has a sacrificial view of the role of the military nobility which, by a self-immolating gesture, wastes its wealth and consumes its energies to serve the state. He praises "cette noblesse toute guerrière qui pense . . . qu'il est honteux d'augmenter son bien, si on ne commence par le dissiper; cette partie de la nation qui sert toujours avec le capital de son bien; qui, quand elle est ruinée, donne sa place à une autre qui servira avec son capital encore . . . qui, quand elle ne peut espérer les richesses, espère les honneurs, et lorsqu'elle ne les obtient pas, se console parce qu'elle a acquis de l'honneur." (20,22). Elsewhere he mentions "cette noblesse qui depuis onze siècles est couverte de poussière, de sang et de sueur" (31,8). In this context noble honor is, like virtue, a willingness to spend and waste oneself, to serve the state at the price of self-destruction, only to be replaced by yet another sacrificial family; the state owes its existence to this long succession of self-immolating noble families who surrender their fortunes and lives on the battlefields. Montesquieu is tempted by this representation of morality as wasteful expenditure: "dissipation" is honorable per se. Wasting is a sign of power; only those with an infinite supply of resources can waste, but it is even more heroic to waste the necessary, to give beyond the impossible, unto death.[37]

His praise of the noblesse de robe is equally inspired: "En France, cet état de la robe qui se trouve entre la grande noblesse et le peuple . . . cet état qui laisse les particuliers dans la médiocrité tandis que le corps dépositaire des lois est dans la gloire; cet état encore dans lequel on n'a de moyen de se distinguer que par la suffisance et par la vertu; profession honorable . . . toutes ces choses ont nécessairement contribué à la grandeur de ce royaume" (20,22). "Le respect et la considération sont pour ces ministres et ces magistrats qui, ne trouvant que le travail après le travail, veillent nuit et jour pour le bonheur de l'empire" (13,20). Montesquieu's occasional admiration for the heroic exploits of the battlefield is offset by his vision of a "heroic" class of state bureaucrats. The true heroes of modern times are the magistrates who toil away in obscurity, who work day and night so that the institution to which they belong, "le corps dépositaire des lois," the true heart of the state and the protector of its fundamental laws, can shine in glory. Unlike Rousseau, Montesquieu does not idealize virtue as sheer energy and excess; he finds nothing to admire in bodily strength and military exercise: for all their virtue, he sees the Spartans as barbaric and brutish. There is nothing of the Cornelian admiration for heroic pride in his consideration of virtue: "Pour qu'un seul homme s'élève au-dessus de l'humanité, il en coûte trop cher à tous les autres," says Eucrate, in the remarkable *Dialogue de Sylla et d'Eucrate*. The dictator Sylla, the murderous hero, is willing to sacrifice all the citizens of Rome to preserve the freedom of its institutions, but he considers the obscure and patient work of the governmental administrator beneath himself: "J'ai cru avoir rempli ma destinée, dès que je n'ai plus eu à faire de grandes choses. Je n'étais pas fait pour gouverner tranquillement un peuple esclave. J'aime à remporter des victoires, à fonder ou détruire des Etats, à faire des ligues, à punir un usurpateur; mais pour ces minces détails de gouvernement où les génies médiocres ont tant d'avantages, cette lente exécution des lois, cette discipline d'une milice tranquille, mon âme ne sauroit s'en occuper."[38]

Montesquieu puts at the pinnacle unheroic, ordinary bourgeois virtues such as patience, slowness, perseverance, tranquility and discipline because they are moderating forces that preserve society from destructive excess. All the haughty moral claims of Sylla come to nothing, because they are rooted in contempt for others and an unlimited will to power ("délice à dominer les autres"). Virtue is dangerous when employed as a force, as an unbounded energy that ignores limits: "C'est une expérience éternelle que tout homme qui a du pouvoir est porté à en abuser; il va jusqu'à ce qu'il trouve des limites. Qui le dirait! la vertu même a besoin de limites" (11,4); "Par un malheur attaché à la condition humaine, les grands hommes modérés sont rares; et comme il est toujours plus aisé de suivre sa force que de l'arrêter, peut-être dans la classe des gens supérieurs, est-il plus facile de trouver des gens extrêmement vertueux que des hommes extrêmement sages" (28,41). In spite of his marked distaste for the mere pursuit of wealth, Montesquieu gives a noble hue to the bourgeois qualities that enter into the construction of commercial wealth, such as ambition and patient work. This accounts for his favorable attitude toward the venality of offices: successful commercial families should be rewarded with access to state service and the ennoblement it brings. It is noble to serve, and those who serve are noble, or deserve to become so. Nobility may appear as a tradition embodied by a caste, but it is primarily a moral attitude; in that respect Montesquieu fully shares Marivaux's and Mme de Lambert's own moralization of the concept of nobility, which is for them a normative ideal of behavior rather than a closed group.[39] His praise of nobility comes from a conviction that society needs symbols and values not founded on utility alone. Nobles are for him those able to see their activity in reference to the social bond and to look beyond considerations of strict utility; he believes that what ultimately motivates them is pure love of the social, invested with transcendent value, as their constant search for reputation and honor demonstrates. That he makes awareness of the importance of symbolic values the specific attribute of the nobility to which he belonged indicates his historical limitation; one that is perhaps more understandable than the facile, all-inclusive, "democratized" notion of nobility propounded in more recent times by Bataille.[40]

Yet, virtue transcends the quest for recognition that motivates honor and glory: virtue is the conquest of sovereign autonomy, as Caillois has noted in his introduction to Montesquieu's works: "virtue does not feel it is entitled to any advantages. It finds its reward in itself and in the inalienable happiness it enjoys. Merit only can conquer it, and no accident can deprive a person of it, so that it is protected from the vagaries of chance."[41] In a passage praising the Stoics, Montesquieu celebrates not only the religion of the social, the need to create an organic unity in which the happiness of others becomes one's own happiness, but also an ethics in which the generous, sacrificing self achieves sovereignty over his passions and self. This accomplishment recalls that of Descartes's *généreux*, a modern version of Aristotle's magnanimous, noble individual, who is precisely "a character that suffices to itself":[42] "elle seule [la secte stoïcienne] savait faire les citoyens; elle seule faisait les grands hommes; elle seule faisait les grands empereurs . . . Nés pour la société, ils croyaient tous que leur destin était de travailler pour elle: d'autant moins à charge, que leurs récompenses étaient toutes dans eux-mêmes; qu'heureux par leur philosophie seule, il semblait que le seul bonheur des autres pût augmenter le leur" (24,10). Virtue yields autonomy and sovereignty, the attributes of nobility in the traditional Aristotelian sense. There is in Montesquieu a yearning (not an actual nostalgia, because he is very little the utopian) for a society in which such attributes would be achieved effortlessly and unselfconsciously; an organic and harmonious community with no division of functions and labor, in which *moeurs* and customs would have the efficacy of laws, the political order would reflect the ethical order of personal conduct, and the duties of public life would merge harmoniously with those of the private sphere.

The social thought that the philosophes (most notably Montesquieu, Rousseau, and Diderot) develop under the general concept of "virtue," and which emerges from an idealization and Christianization of the world of antiquity, recurs in various forms throughout Romanticism in the nineteenth and the early twentieth centuries (particularly in the works of Constant, Hegel, Nietzsche, Durkheim, and Mauss). Paradoxically, the discourse of virtue, a product of the Enlightenment's self-critique, gives rise to an archaic utopianism that is the negation of the Enlightenment. It does so by glorifying nondiscursive, nonrational values, such as sacrifice, that reintroduce the sacred in the secular domain. The Enlightenment's questioning of the moral foundations of civil society and their relation to the economic sphere generates an interest, as well as a confused nostalgia, for "primitive" or "traditional" gift economies based on friendship and human solidarity rather than utilitarian notions of production, consumption and material efficiency.[43] Paradoxically, however, a philosophy that originally aspired to give moral grounding to society, which was looking for a morality more noble than the bourgeois rational negotiation of interests, ends up rejecting reason and the social altogether, taking refuge in an irrationalist estheticism that celebrates nonproductive expenditure, violence, excess, the archaic, the enchanted, the sacred, the "interpenetration of reason and bestial unreason,"[44] and, finally, in postmodern theories of language, the nonrepresentable.

The period between the two world wars experienced a blossoming interest in forms of generous exchange in French ethnological literature (indeed, more literary than ethnological). In Mauss, Caillois, and Bataille, ethnology became a tool to critique modern bourgeois morality and capitalism; for Caillois and Bataille, it merged with a sort of revolutionary estheticism. Caillois's interest in a modern moral aristocracy during his early days with the Collège de Sociologie betrayed his debt to Baudelairian dandyism (which he called "the privileged form of modern heroism"), as well as a fascination with Cornelian heroism (he produced an annotated edition of *Le Cid*). In one of his conferences at the college he translated the Nietzschean opposition between master and slave into a more "contemporary" opposition between producer and consumer that glorified the artist pitted against the rest of society: "these words simultaneously evoke the economic substratum and translate a vital attitude that, without being completely determined by this substratum, in the simplest cases is often only its direct consequence. One would successfully characterize as consumers those who are turned toward pleasure (*jouissance*); who, unproductive on their own, as parasites of others only assimilate; who do not reach, in their judgment, the principle of the agreeable. Consumers are incapable of generosity, and, even more, of that gift that the producers' very nature obliges them to make of what they create, which, because the taste for producing is so tenacious that they even scorn pleasure and reward, is not for their own use."[45]

The longing for an aristocratic ideal of magnanimity is translated in a general rejection of bourgeois ethics and economy, and in the search for modern forms of heroism; but such rejection is based less on a rational argument than a cluster of metaphors and confused aspirations. In his search for a communal bond that would protect the isolated individual from direct confrontation with the anonymous body of the state ("an extremely dissipated society"), Caillois turns to the idea of a secret, elective society of superior beings mystically united in a fashion that both exalts and transcends individualism; however, he ends up rehashing a bookish version of Baudelairian and Balzacian dandyism. Hollier notes the role that such conspiratorial, aristocratic revolutionism was to play in fascism and the French Communist Party.[46] Caillois is less interested in exchange and reciprocity than the suprarational notion of expenditure, in those phenomena of subversion and transgression that for him express the sacred and allow a society to "regenerate" itself through ritual explosions of energy: "*Economy, accumulation,* and *moderation* define the rhythm of profane life; *prodigality* and *excess* define that of the festival, the periodic and exhilarating interlude of sacred life that cuts in and restores youth and health."[47] Caillois's fascination for the *fête* in primitive societies leads him to write a lyrical evocation of war (published with glaring insensitivity after the Second World War) as a modern analogue of the unleashing of festive energies in traditional societies and the effect of a traditional desire for ritual violence "proclaiming the sacred triumph of death."[48] Both Bataille and Caillois use ethnology to ground their philosophy, which consists of a romantic rejection of economy, utility, and rationality. The social is exalted only insofar as it represents some form of excess such as the fête, violence and sacrifice. The social bond is envisioned only as communion, as mystical, ecstatic fusion, not as balance nor as democracy (that is, discursive exchange and compromise in view of a rational purpose).

More radical than Caillois, Bataille deems any teleology "servile." Bataille is fascinated by aspects of human experience not reducible to processes of production and conservation—sexual pleasure, excrements, dirt, animality—and by what he calls "unproductive expenditure: luxury, mourning, war, cults, the construction of sumptuary monuments, games, spectacles, arts, perverse sexual activity (i.e., deflected from genital finality). All these represent activities which, at least in primitive circumstances, have no end beyond themselves."[49] They are characterized by a willingness to endure the greatest loss. Only by activating an indefinite loss can we free ourselves from the slavery of bourgeois life and material necessity. Hence, for Bataille, generosity is based on an irrational willingness to endure loss for no reason other than the enjoyment of an affirmation of life in the present moment. Bataille's search for an ideal of generosity induces him to favor a progressively disembodied and irrational form of generosity, as if all generosity had to be predicated on irrationality. Irrational expenditure has a value of subverting the social as rational, purpose-oriented construction. He praises the "sovereign dignity of the gift-giver,"[50] who showers the receiver with presents so as to establish his own superiority, a mirror image of Aristotelian magnanimity ("and he is the sort of man to confer benefits, but he is ashamed of receiving them; for the one is the mark of a superior, the other of an inferior").[51] Yet nothing seems to satisfy his excessively purist notion of sovereignty and truly generous expenditure. "What distinguishes sovereignty is the consumption of wealth, as against labor and servitude, which produce wealth without consuming it. . . . Life beyond utility is the domain of sovereignty."[52]

The Aristotelian language of magnanimity does not lose its moral and political connotations, but it does assume a wider, metaphorical significance. It indicates a metaphysical rejection of necessity, utility, subordination to time and rationality; it becomes the search for some plenitude of the moment lived in the consciousness of its impossibility. "It is *servile* to consider duration first, to employ the *present time* for the sake of the *future*, which is what we do when we work. . . . We don't see the sovereign moment arrive, when nothing counts but the moment itself. What is sovereign in fact is to enjoy the present time without having anything else in view but this present time."[53] Religious sacrifice, eroticism, violence, and death are all instances of denying duration and rationality, which, Bataille says (with a curiously perverse Kantianism) forces the world of things and human beings to become means to an end (which is precisely servility). In that perspective he praises the senseless violence of combat: "glory . . . expresses a movement of senseless frenzy, of measureless expenditure of energy, which the fervor of combat presupposes. Combat is glorious in that it is always beyond calculation at some moment . . . ," but he condemns all combat that has a purpose other than its pure immanence in view, for instance the acquisition of social rank.[54] The sacralization of the esthetic jouissance of the moment lived beyond all utility induces Bataille to label the practice of the potlatch, described by Mauss, as servile, because it is subordinated to a logic determined by utility and prestige: "In a sense the presents are repaid with interest. Thus the gift is the opposite of what it seemed to be: To give is obviously to lose, but the loss apparently brings a profit to the one who sustains it"; "acquisition is nonetheless its ultimate purpose"; "Actually, as I have said, the ideal would be that a potlatch could not be repaid."[55] The threshold of generosity is placed so unreasonably high that for Bataille nothing but the most extreme form of self-destruction can approach it.

Generosity takes an entirely different meaning in the work of Mauss, who greatly inspired Caillois and Bataille, but who, unlike them, was not a revolutionary estheticist but an active socialist in the tradition of Jean Jaurès. Mauss debated moral questions that originated with the Enlightenment and the Revolution; his anthropological work complements his political militancy. Like his uncle Durkheim, Mauss attempted to detect, within the modern, industrial world, the recurrence of traditional forms of social regroupings and associations that set as their purpose the transmission and maintenance of moral activity; he tried to integrate the concepts of exchange, generosity, and the gift into a corporatist view of society.[56] For Durkheim, the source of all moral activity was the readiness to subordinate particular interests to the general interest, an attitude involving a disposition to "sacrifice and abnegation."[57] For Mauss, it was important to re-create among nations and social classes the exchange of services, moral obligations, and solidarities that characterized primitive societies (hence, for instance, his endorsement of the internationalism of the League of Nations, his advocacy of the improvement of public education and the development of workers unions).[58] Mauss's account of the potlatch is familiar; I will therefore focus on the lesser known social and political contextualization of his idea of the gift within the modern industrial world. Like Montesquieu, Mauss is concerned with recovering social and moral forms that for being archaic are no less symptomatic of universal, atemporal patterns. At the closure of his *Essai sur le don*, he writes: "One can see how this concrete study can lead not only to a science of customs [moeurs], to a partial social science but even to moral conclusions, or rather, to adopt once more the old word, to 'civility,' or 'civics' as it is called nowadays."[59] Mauss argues against the hegemony of utilitarian views; he believes that economic exchange should fulfill basic needs of social cohesion that obey a moral imperative rather than considerations of utility. "We possess more than a tradesman morality"; "In ancient systems of morality of the most epicurean kind it is the good and pleasurable that is sought after, and not material utility. . . . It is our Western societies who have recently made man an 'economic animal'. But we are not yet all creatures of this genus. Among the masses and the elites in our society pure and irrational expenditure is commonly practised. It is still characteristic of a few of the fossilized remnants of our aristocracy."[60] The archaic gift exchange represents both a survival of an ancient, universal mode of exchange now superseded by other forms, and something which must be preserved as a normative ideal and antidote to modern social problems; it still survives, to our days, in the form of elective societies, labor unions, charity associations, corporative solidarity, and other manifestations of cooperation. Like Montesquieu, Mauss admires the publicly oriented expenditure of the Romans in the civic realm: "We return, as return we must, to habits of 'aristocratic expenditure'": in modern societies, "the rich must come back to considering themselves—freely and also by obligation—as the financial guardians of their fellow citizens."[61]

The numerous convergences joining Montesquieu's and Mauss's conception of wealth and honor betray their common debt to the Aristotelian tradition of magnanimity and to models inherited from Roman and Greek antiquity in general. Both have a ritualistic, sumptuary conception of wealth, in which its material dimension is only the support of its symbolic value within a general network of symbolic relations that unite the members of society.[62] Mauss explicitely compares the "noble" commerce of the *kula* among the peoples of the Trobriand Islands (which he gets secondhand from Malinowski), in which an agonistic and sumptuary exchange of gifts establishes the prestige of the clan and its chief ("such trade is noble, replete with etiquette and generosity") to the Aristotelian notions of magnificence and *elefteria,* or liberality.[63]

Mauss's notion of exchange, both commercial and sumptuary, is decidedly holistic; no rational separation exists between the giver and the object given. The exchanged objects assume a symbolic and even magical dimension whereby they serve to strenghten ties between individuals and clans: "The goal is above all a moral one. . . . In short, this represents an intermingling. Souls are mixed with things; things with souls. Lives are mingled together, and this is how, among persons and things so intermingled, each emerges from its own sphere and mixes together. This is precisely what contract and exchange are."[64] Likewise, society is an organism in which the members are united not only by mutual obligations and debts, but also by an incapacity to sense themselves as separate individuals: "In these societies neither the clan nor the family is able to isolate itself or dissociate its actions. . . . The chief is merged with his clan, and the clan with him. Individuals feel themselves acting in a unified way. . . . In reality this symbol of social life—the permanence of influence over the things exchanged—serves merely to reflect directly the manner in which the subgroups in these segmented societies, archaic in type and constantly enmeshed with one another, feel that they are everything to one another."[65] Mauss's romantic vision of an organic, supraindividual body composed of members united by a perpetual offering of gifts and services reproduces an aspiration that emerged from the Enlightenment's own self-critique: the longing for a mystical body social, the utopian aspiration to a reconciliation of conflicts and the end of all divisions—not through political negotiation among powers, not by argumentative and discursive reason, but through the re-enactment of a world of unreflective traditions and collective identification that most likely existed only as a reverse image of its own.

NOTES

1. For an analysis of the critique launched against the urbanization and feminization of aristocratic mores, see Carolyn Lougee's classic *Le Paradis des Femmes: Women, Salons and Social Stratification in Seventeenth-Century France* (Princeton, 1976), and Fénelon's *De l'éducation des filles* and *Télémaque*. Boileau's *Satire V*, an attack against the new alliance of capital and curialized nobility, gives a very concise expression to those views. Céline Spector provides a sensitive analysis of Montesquieu's social critique and his conception of the role of the passions in *Montesquieu, les "Lettres persanes": De l'anthropologie à la politique* (Paris, 1997).
2. Of course, others will argue that the market relies upon such qualities as trust and honor, virtues wrongly seen as the exclusive attributes of a noncommercial ethic. A whole literature argues for an ethical reconsideration of commerce. Among the many titles: *Le Commerce honorable* (Nantes, 1646), *Le Négociant patriote* (Amsterdam, 1748), *L'Apologie du commerce, essai philosophique et politique* (Geneva, 1777). What appears in La Rochefoucauld as a critique of the market economy is in fact an indictment of the failure of traditional noble ethics, and the dissolution of the bond between morality and social utility. The critique of an economy based on self-

interested exchange is thus a vehicle for the expression of an aristocratic self-critique. See Henry C. Clark's "La Rochefoucauld and the Social Bases of Aristocratic Ethics," *History of European Ideas* 8 (1987) 1: 61–76, and "Passions, Interests, and Moderate Virtues: La Rochefoucauld and the Origins of Enlightenment Liberalism," *Annals of Scholarship* 7 (1990) 1: 33–50, as well as Bradley Rubidge's *The Code of Reciprocation in Corneille's Heroic Drama*, forthcoming. Montesquieu himself does not condemn commerce, which he praises for its civilizing role. The object of his criticism is less commerce than the supposed interference of a commercial spirit in social relations, particularly in connection with the decline of the aristocratic ethos of generosity.

3. But he was wrong in suggesting that Montesquieu's admiration for Roman liberty went no further than an idealized Cornelian heroism and stopped short of realizing the political implications of the Roman ideal of the state. See *Man and Ethics; Studies in French Classicism*, trans. Elizabeth Hughes (Garden City, NY, 1971), pp. 71–74.

4. There are much earlier traces of this attitude in classical antiquity, especially in Seneca, who was, of course, one of the major sources of inspiration for the reappearance of these motifs in the Renaissance, from Montaigne onward. See Arthur O. Lovejoy and George Boas, *Primitivism and Related Ideas in the Antiquity* [1935] (Baltimore, 1997).

5. See *Second Discours*: "Let us begin, therefore, by laying aside the facts, for they do not affect the question. The researches in which we may engage on this occasion are not to be taken for historical truths, but merely as hypothetical and conditional reasonings." *The Social Contract and the Discourse on the Origin of Inequality*, ed. Lester G. Crocker (New York, 1967), p. 177. The state of nature is not a historically observable fact, but a normative notion that allows Rousseau to formulate a moral evaluation of human progress.

6. Among the various formulations of the *esprit général*, see the early essay "De la politique" (1725) in *Oeuvres complètes*, ed. Roger Caillois (Paris, 1949) vol.1, pp. 114–15.

7. Quoted in Denis Hollier, ed., trans. Betsy Wing, *The College of Sociology* (Minneapolis, 1988), p. 302.

8. *L'Homme et le sacré* [1948] (2nd ed. Paris, 1950), p. 21.

9. Text composed in 1940 for the journal *Sur*, which he founded in Argentina, and republished in French in 1946 in *Le Rocher de Sisyphe*. Quoted in *The College of Sociology*, p. 378. See also Bataille: "These young writers, more or less clearly, felt that society had lost the secret of its cohesiveness and that that was exactly where the vague, uneasy and sterile efforts of a poetic fever were aiming." "Le sens moral de la sociologie," *Critique* 1 (1946), quoted in *The College of Sociology*, pp. 383–84.

10. In his preface to Montesquieu's *Oeuvres complètes*, p. xiv. For the meaning of "Luciferian spirit," see *The College of Sociology*, pp. 400–401, n. 5.

11. Quoted in *Citizens Without Sovereignty: Equality and Sociability in French Thought, 1670–1789* (Princeton 1994), p. 71.

12. *Households of the Soul* (Baltimore, 1997), pp. 175–76. For an assessment of the relevance of Aristotle's *oikos* in contemporary anthropology, with conclusions very similar to Pecora's, see Lucette Valensi, "Anthropologie économique et histoire: L'oeuvre de Karl Polanyi" in *Pour une histoire anthropologique: La notion de réciprocité*, *Annales* 29 (1974): 1311–17.

13. *Households of the Soul*, p. 50.

14. Norbert Elias, *The Court Society*, trans. Edmund Jephcott (Oxford, 1983), pp. 67–68.

15. She quotes Sahlins's description of primitive exchange: they "give freely . . . no payment is demanded in return, and in fact all mention of a counter-obligation is scrupulously avoided. This does not mean that there is none, but it is crucial to the success of the interaction that no reckoning is overtly made. There must be a sus-

tained pretense that the resources being offered are abundant, even unlimited.";
Goldsmith notes that for Sahlins the "idea of generalized reciprocity . . . combines
the aristocratic ideal of sociability with the principle of the potlatch," *Exclusive
Conversations* (Philadelphia, 1988), pp. 11–12.

16. *Households of the Soul,* p. 294.

17. *De l'esprit des lois,* book 5, chapter 2, ed. Robert Derathé, 2 vols. (Paris, 1973). All
    my references to this work will be to this edition and will include only the number
    of the book followed by that of the chapter.

18. See especially his *Considérations sur les causes de la grandeur des Romains et de leur déca-
    dence* (1734).

19. See *De l'usurpation,* chapter 6 in *De l'esprit de conquête et de l'usurpation* (1814). I dis-
    cuss this issue further in "The Youth of Moral Life: The Virtue of the Ancients
    from Montesquieu to Nietzsche," *Studies on Voltaire and the Eighteenth Century,* forth-
    coming.

20. Robert Shackleton believes, with Emile Faguet, that we should attribute to the
    word *virtue* its "full sense" since "in spite of all that has been written to the con-
    trary, by Montesquieu as well as by his commentators, virtue for Montesquieu
    means moral goodness," *Montesquieu* (Oxford, 1961), p. 273.

21. Orest Ranum writes in *Paris in the Age of Absolutism* (New York, 1968), pp. 188–89:
    "Behind the unbelievable number of grammatical rules which they memorized lay
    hidden a rigid moral code. The rules themselves were precepts, usually drawn from
    Cicero and selected to illustrate some point of grammar, but also to convey a moral
    principle. . . . Since classical works were rarely assigned in their entirety in the early
    years, and because the precepts were selected by the religious to present an edify-
    ing ethic, there was no possibility for students in the collège to find any disagreement
    between Christian doctrine and classical letters. The Roman world was for 17th-
    century students a world of heroes, of generals, emperors and great statesmen. . . .
    Idealized and heroic, the Roman world, as presented in the collège, became a
    coherent ethical and psychological system which offered an alternative to the cor-
    porate mentality." See also Marc Fumaroli, "L'héroïsme cornélien et l'idéal de la
    magnanimité" in *Héroïsme et création littéraire sous les règnes d'Henri IV et de Louis XIII,*
    Actes du Colloque de Strasbourg published by Noémi Hepp et Georges Livet
    (Paris, 1974), pp. 53–76; and Jean Ehrard "Rome enfin que je hais?" in *Storia et
    ragione,* ed. Alberto Postigliola (Napoli, 1984), pp. 23–32.

22. *Explication des maximes des Saints, Oeuvres,* ed. Jacques Le Brun, vol. 1 (Paris, 1983),
    p. 1009.

23. Quoted in Nannerl Keohane, *Philosophy and the State in France* (Princeton, 1980), p.
    342. Keohane points out similarities between political and mystical language,
    between the Fénelonian utopia of a perfect community in *Télémaque* and his vision
    of spiritual salvation: "The essential similarity is the radical denial of the self in
    favor of something greater than the self . . . in both cases the starting point is the
    loss of individuality in something greater, purer, finer—participation in a worthy
    whole," p. 342. Montesquieu was acquainted with Fénelon's work through the lat-
    ter's influence on Mme de Lambert and her salon; Montesquieu respected her and
    acknowledged her influence.

24. *Mes pensées,* p. 233.

25. Even though I will focus mainly on the two poles of civic virtue and the self-interest
    of the commercial world, it must be acknowledged that Montesquieu does consider
    a range of middle virtues that fill the gap between the two: those virtues are
    described under the concept of honor, and they function as a substitute for real
    virtue in modern monarchical society. The idea of honor is one and requires a
    detailed analysis of its own. From a utilitarian point of view, honor is an adequate
    substitute for virtue, it functions "as if" it belongs to the realm of the "utile," as

opposed to that of the "honnête," but from a moral standpoint, honor is an inferior virtue rooted in amour-propre and not selfless love: "cet honneur faux est aussi utile au public que le vrai le serait aux particuliers" (3,7): "false" honor is useful because it sets in motion the commercial machine and contributes to the greatness of the State, but it does not contribute to the moral perfectioning of the individual. The political order is thus cut off from the moral order: one can very well be a "bon citoyen" without being an "homme de bien" (3,6; see also *Mes pensées*, 628). In that respect Montesquieu is in line with the Augustinian tradition illustrated by Pascal: his opposition virtue/honor is a replica of the opposition charity/concupiscence: "We have used concupiscence as best we can to make it serve the common good, but this is mere sham and a false image of charity, for essentially it is just hate," *Pensées* (Lafuma 210), trans. A. J. Krailsheimer (Harmondsworth, 1966), p. 97–98.

26. See 20,1. Pierre Rétat's insightful article is an essential reference on that topic: "De Mandeville à Montesquieu: honneur, luxe et dépense noble dans *l'Esprit des lois*" *Studi Francesi* 50 (1973): 238–49. See also Daniel Gordon's brief but useful remarks, *Citizens Without Sovereignty*, pp. 130–33.

27. See in particular *Lettres persanes*, letter 106, and *De l'esprit des lois* 19,9.

28. "Magnificence is an attribute of expenditure of the kind which we call honorable, e.g., those connected with the gods—votive offerings, buildings and sacrifices—and similarly with any form of religious worship, and all those are the proper objects of public-spirited ambition," *Nicomachean Ethics*, (1122b19–33). See *De l'esprit des lois*, 5,3.

29. See "Avertissement," *Mes pensées*, 3, *Oeuvres complètes*, vol. 1. The collection of notes which Montesquieu carefully classified, numbered, and annotated, and which was published for the first time in 1899–91, is an ample reservoir of material woven into Montesquieu's work, sometimes in the same form. I refer to that work by the number of the pensée.

30. *Mes pensées*, 598, emphasis added.

31. *Voyages*, *Oeuvres complètes*, vol. 1, p. 864.

32. Montesquieu makes a strict distinction between "richesse" and "honneur:" "Tout est perdu lorsque la profession lucrative des traitants parvient encore par ses richesses à être une profession honorée . . . l'honneur y perd toute sa considération, les moyens lents et naturels de se distinguer ne touchent plus, et le gouvernement est frappé dans son principe" (13,20). However, he is also aware of the fact that "richesse" may, in its turn, be translated into "honneur," because money itself may be turned into symbolic capital of prestige: people crave wealth not only for the material advantages it brings, but also because they hope it will acquire them honor together with "honneurs" and the admiration of others: the financiers "sont méprisés comme de la boue pendant qu'ils sont pauvres; quand ils sont riches, on les estime assez: aussi ne négligent-ils rien pour acquérir de l'estime," he writes ironically in *Lettres persanes*, letter 98 (ed. Paul Vernière, Paris, 1975), p. 204. In France the "noble" desire to gain distinction and the esteem of others is universal and cuts across all ranks of society; but the ways of achieving it are vastly different, and range from actions motivated by a love for justice (which may or may not be rewarded with public distinction) to actions motivated by mere vanity. However, even vanity is preferable to pure greed (cet intérêt bas qui n'est proprement que l'instinct animal de tous les hommes," *Mes pensées*, 604) because it is an implicit recognition of the respect for public opinion that binds us to each other. Montesquieu considers the Dutch utterly immune to any notion of honor, hence unsociable: for him, a society without institutionalized nobility has diminished access to the realm of symbolic, "noble" values (that is, the constellation of glory, ambition, vanity, the desire for reputation and esteem) upon which rests the consciousness of the social bond.

33. The question of the motivation of virtuous actions is crucial to the totality of moral philosophy during the seventeenth and eighteenth centuries. For an excellent overview of the matter, see Arthur O. Lovejoy, *Reflections on Human Nature* (Baltimore, 1961), especially lecture 5.

34. *Lettres persanes*, letter 89.

35. *Lettres persanes*, letter 89.

36. *Lettres persanes*, letter 37.

37. See also his paean to the dead soldiers of the Invalides and the secular cult of the victims of the *patrie* in *Lettres persanes*, letter 84: "Quel spectacle de voir rassemblées dans le même lieu toutes ces victimes de la Patrie, qui ne respirent que pour la défendre, et qui, se sentant le même coeur, et non pas la même force, ne se plaignent que de l'impuissance où elles sont de se sacrifier encore pour elle!"

38. *Oeuvres complètes*, p. 501.

39. See in particular Marivaux's *La Vie de Marianne* (1731–42) and Mme de Lambert's moral essays recently republished in *Oeuvres*, ed. Robert Granderoute (Paris, 1990).

40. "In the past, sovereignty belonged to those who, bearing the names of chieftain, pharaoh, king, king of kings, played a leading role in the formation of that being with which we identify ourselves, the human being of today. . . . But further, it belongs essentially to all men who possess and have never entirely lost the value that is attributed to gods and 'dignitaries.' . . . For I shall always be concerned, however it may seem, with the apparently lost sovereignty to which the beggar can sometimes be as close as the great nobleman, and from which, as a rule, the bourgeois is voluntarily the most far removed," *La Souveraineté*, 1976; trans. *Sovereignty* (New York, 1991), p. 197.

41. *Oeuvres complètes*, p. xxvii.

42. *Nicomachean Ethics*, 1125a14

43. "A certain strain of romantic anthropology in the nineteenth and twentieth centuries would also look to savage or primitive societies in an attempt to recover the virtues of noble mastery no longer supportable at home. On the whole and quite in spite of the racist superiority that remained a part of its heritage, this modern anthropology rediscovered Aristotle's mastery and noble oikos not in terms of Europe's own dominant position but rather as an element of "primitive," "archaic," or "traditional" society itself. Aristotle's proud, magnanimous man—whose honor rests on his power to give, his distance from the market, his freedom from need or servile labor, his attachment to an esthetic (symbolic) rather than utilitarian mode of activity, his capacity for great expenditure, in short, his position in a network of noble, rather than necessary, exchanges—is recovered by a variety of anthropological and sociological discourses as the basis of primitive or archaic modes of exchange . . . It is in Mauss, one might say, that the noble ethics of Aristotle's master is most fully recovered for use as a putatively egalitarian critique of, and remedy for, modern, bourgeois, capitalist society"; Vincent Pecora, op. cit., pp. 175–76.

44. The expression is of Allan Stoekl in his introduction to Georges Bataille, *Visions of Excess, Selected Writings, 1927–1939* (Minneapolis, 1985), p. xii.

45. *The College of Sociology*, p. 39.

46. See his remarks regarding the "Letter from Marcel Mauss to Elie Halévy," and the letter itself, in *The College of Sociology*, pp. 347–50.

47. *The College of Sociology*, p. 298.

48. *L'Homme et le sacré*, p. 244.

49. "The Notion of Expenditure" in *Visions of Excess*, op. cit., p. 118.

50. *Sovereignty*, p. 347.

51. *Nicomachean Ethics*, 1124b6.

52. *Sovereignty*, p. 198.

53. *Sovereignty*, pp. 198–99, emphasis in the text.

54. *La Part maudite*, 1967, trans. *The Accursed Share* (New York, 1988), p. 71.

55. *The Accursed Share*, op. cit., pp. 70, 72.

56. We should note that Durkheim wrote his doctoral dissertation on Montesquieu and Rousseau as "precursors of sociology" (*Montesquieu et Rousseau, précurseurs de la sociologie*, Bordeaux, 1892). He saw in the notion of "esprit général" a prefiguration of his collectivist sociology and a confirmation of his organicist and biological view of society as a living body (although Montesquieu's model of a society is more mechanical than organic). See Luc Fraisse, "De l'imitation à l'organicisme: Montesquieu à la lumière des sociologues en 1880," *Revue d'histoire littéraire de la France* (1989): 195–219.

57. See pp. xv–xvii, Introduction to the 2nd edition of *De la division du travail social*, Paris [1930] (10th ed. Paris, 1978).

58. See Pierre Birnbaum, "Du socialisme au don," *L'Arc* 48 (1982): 42–46.

59. Originally published in *Année sociologique* 2 (1923–24) and reprinted in *Sociologie et anthropologie* (Paris, 1950), trans. W. D. Halls, *The Gift. The Form and Reason for Exchange in Archaic Societies* (London, 1990), p. 83.

60. Ibid., pp. 65, 76.

61. Ibid., pp. 68–69.

62. "There would be a place for studying the notion of wealth itself. From our point of view, the rich man is one who has *mana* in Polynesia, *auctoritas* in Rome, and who, in these American tribes, is 'open-handed', *walas*. But strictly speaking we need only point out the relationship between the notion of wealth, that of authority, and the right of commanding those who receive presents, and the potlatch: it is a very clear relationship" p. 115, n. 148; "Riches are from every viewpoint as much a means of retaining prestige as something useful. Yet are we sure that it is any different in our own society, and that even with us riches are not above all a means of lording it over our fellow men?" p. 75. Bataille, too, is drawn to the sacrifice Romans were willing to make of their fortune in unproductive social expenditures such as festivals, spectacles, and games. See "The Notion of Expenditure," *Visions of Excess*, p. 123.

63. Ibid., pp. 37, 100, n. 28.

64. Ibid., pp. 19–20.

65. Ibid., pp. 32–33.

RATIONALIZING THE ENLIGHTENMENT

Postmodernism and Theories
of Anti-Semitism[1]

RONALD SCHECHTER

The Jews of France did not wait for postmodernism before criticizing the Enlightenment. In response to an anti-Jewish libelist who in 1786 accused the Jews of being "superstitious," Isaiah Berr Bing of Metz defended himself and his coreligionists in a published letter:

> I do not know what you call superstitious; is it to show the most inviolable attachment to a religion in which you do not dare ignore the mark of divinity? Is it to observe very scrupulously all that it prescribes? If it is in that that we appear superstitious to you, I shall willingly admit that we are, that I hope quite sincerely that we shall always be; in spite of the progress of fashionable philosophy, in spite of its aversion for the ceremonial, and for everything that it cannot, as it were, touch with its finger.[2]

Yet it would be mistaken to characterize Bing as somehow against the Enlightenment. Indeed, in his pamphlet he drew liberally from the *philosophes*, postulated the natural equality of men and urged religious toleration. His philippic against the tendency of "fashionable philosophy" to encourage what Max Horkheimer and Theodor Adorno would later call the "disenchantment of the world" was a rhetorical ploy designed to make his opponents appear overly abstract and cerebral. This was a prudent strategy, since Bing knew that his audience valued the piety and sincerity of the naïve believer over the intellectual dexterity of the hair-splitting rationalist. (If this statement seems doubtful, I hope to convince the reader of its veracity by the end of this essay.) Moreover, he knew that

Christians tended to attribute precisely the traits he ascribed to his adversaries—a mentality of calculation and excess of reason over feeling—to the Jews themselves. Thus his apparent defiance of a dominant trend was really the expression of a widely held set of values.

Yet historians and other retrospective observers have tended to reify the rhetorical figure of "fashionable philosophy"—conjured up as a serviceable straw man by any number of defensive eighteenth-century polemicists, not only maligned Jews—into a historical fact. They have posited an airy, abstract Enlightenment on the basis of accusations made in the heat of contestation, then ventured to determine the effect of this object on the people allegedly subjected to it. Not surprisingly, this version of the Enlightenment has come up wanting, first by conservatives advocating greater respect for "traditional" institutions and religious orthodoxy, and in the twentieth century by postmodernists who have determined that totalizing abstractions such as those attributed to the Enlightenment skew the perception of chaotic reality and violate the "right to be different."

Not surprisingly, evaluations of the "Jewish question" during and following the eighteenth century have similarly been affected by the construction of the Enlightenment as abstract and rationalistic. Thus Arthur Hertzberg argues in *The French Enlightenment and the Jews* that the poison of modern anti-Semitism is a legacy of the Enlightenment. Similarly, though more radically and with greater philosophical sophistication, Horkheimer and Adorno in their *Dialectic of Enlightenment* found anti-Semitism to be paradigmatic of the Enlightenment's allegedly destructive and violent tendencies. These two books afford an opportunity to re-evaluate the relationship between the Enlightenment and the Jewish question, which in turn will permit a re-examination of the values of the Enlightenment.

Arthur Hertzberg's *French Enlightenment and the Jews* takes as its point of departure the chilling paradox that "[t]he era of Western history that began with the French Revolution ended in Auschwitz."[3] The author's explanation of this terrible reversal was not simply that Europeans had failed to live up to the liberal Enlightenment principles of the Revolution, or that the dark forces of reaction had won them over, but that the Enlightenment itself was in some significant measure inimical to Judaism and the Jews. Thus, "Modern, secular anti-Semitism was fashioned not as a reaction to the Enlightenment and the Revolution, but within the Enlightenment and Revolution themselves."[4] Hertzberg's critique does not extend to the Enlightenment as a whole. Montesquieu is exempt because his "relativism" favored the acceptance of difference among peoples, and Hertzberg claims that "pro-Jewish" commentators in the late eighteenth-century debates on the Jews' legal status "invariably quoted from Montesquieu."[5]

The primary culprit in Hertzberg's scheme is Voltaire, against whom the "friends of the Jews . . . did battle."[6] Hertzberg maintains that Voltaire, though often remembered as an apostle of tolerance, made an exception of the Jews, whom he denounced as "ignorant," "barbarian," "superstitious," "fanatical," and asocial, insults he supposedly derived from classical authors, especially Cicero. Moreover, he argues that Voltaire, unlike "pro-Jewish" commentators, did not expect the vices typically attributed to the Jews to disappear upon an improvement in their legal condition; rather he "ruled the Jew to be outside society and to be hopelessly alien even to the future age of enlightened men."[7] And though Voltaire's alleged bias against Jews was the source of controversy in his own day and the subject of historiographical debate since the nineteenth century, Hertzberg has raised the stakes by claiming that Voltaire established a model of modern anti-Semitism on which future anti-Semites would draw when seeking an "enlightened" justification for their prejudices.[8]

Whatever merit there is to Hertzberg's claims about the road from Voltaire to Auschwitz could only be established by a study of postrevolutionary anti-Semitism, though even that project would be of doubtful value, since it would have to reify anti-Jewish statements made in various contexts into a "unit-idea" in the fashion of Arthur Lovejoy's *Great Chain of Being*.[9] Hertzberg's failure even to attempt to show a connection between the anti-Jewish statements of eighteenth-century authors and those of later writers, however, constitutes a serious shortcoming, since it is this very thesis which distinguishes *The French Enlightenment and the Jews* from previous books that have posited an "enlightened" form of anti-Semitism, especially in the writings of Voltaire.[10] More seriously still, I would submit, and will try to demonstrate later in this essay, that Hertzberg is mistaken even in his claims about the relationship between Voltaire's statements about the Jews and those of other eighteenth-century authors.

Yet before critiquing the specifics of Hertzberg's argument, it is instructive to compare his discussion to that of a more famous treatment of the relationship between the Enlightenment and the Holocaust: namely *Dialectic of Enlightenment* (1944), by the German-Jewish philosophers Max Horkheimer and Theodor Adorno. To be sure, *Dialectic of Enlightenment* was written as a work of social theory and cultural criticism rather than historiography, and its treatment of "Enlightenment" extends far beyond the historical period traditionally known as the Age of the Enlightenment. For Horkheimer and Adorno, Enlightenment is a mode of thinking characterized by "instrumental reason" rather than an historical epoch per se. It is evident wherever a capitalist mode of production is in place. Enlightenment is already present in embryonic form in Homeric times, as the ingenious "proprietor" Odysseus reveals through his mastery of nature (i.e., his ability to restrain himself in the face of the sirens' temptation) and his deception of anyone still in the thrall of a pre-representational, mythic attitude toward language (i.e., his ability to trick the blind cyclops Polyphemus by calling himself "No one").[11] It remains in residual form as late as the era of fascism and monopoly capitalism, in other words the authors' own day, when its worst feature, domination, is all that survives, and a farcical version of liberal individualism barely conceals the eclipse of human agency, choice, and responsibility.[12] Yet the Enlightenment as an era or a historically bounded movement, which the authors tend to designate with a definite article—die Aufklärung as opposed to Aufklärung—gets considerable attention in the Dialectic, and indeed is the period in which Enlightenment as a mode of thinking, as the "disenchantment of the world," appears in its most unalloyed form.[13]

Moreover, Horkheimer and Adorno, like Hertzberg nearly a quarter century later, took as their central problem the paradox that the Enlightenment itself contained a virulence capable of producing the horrors of National Socialism. The authors of the Dialectic of Enlightenment did not reduce the phenomenon of National Socialism to the Holocaust, and considered fascism more broadly as a force affecting all of society; yet they unequivocally regarded anti-Semitism as central to the paranoiac ideology of the Nazis, the Jews as their primary victims, and the gas chamber as the symbol of their descent into barbarism. Although Horkheimer and Adorno devoted a chapter to the subject of anti-Semitism, which they subtitled "The Limits of Enlightenment," they hinted at the problem in their earlier chapter, "The Concept of Enlightenment." There they argued that with the "disenchantment of the world" and the "extirpation of animism," the Enlightenment came to reduce all particularities to instances of universal concepts. For the scientist this meant that every object had to fit into universal schemas of species and genera. For the moralist it meant that nothing was valuable—neither actions nor individuals—except insofar as it was valuable for something else, preferably a universal principle such as happiness or utility. Thus, "[f]or the Enlightenment, whatever does not conform to the rule of computation and utility is suspect." The increase in the activity of commodity exchange, whose dominant principle was fungibility, fed the habit of regularization, until "equivalence itself [had] become a fetish." As a result the Enlightenment "excise[d] the incommensurable. Not only [were] qualities dissolved in thought, but men [were] brought to actual conformity." Social distinctions were deemed absurd, but "under the leveling domination of abstraction" individuals formed what Hegel had called a "herd."[14]

With hindsight one can derive the implications of the Enlightenment mode of thought for the Jews. The Jews might be tolerated insofar as their presence is deemed useful—and indeed, as Hertzberg points out, the French monarchy tolerated the Jews precisely on the basis of utilitarian reasoning.[15] Yet they might be expelled, or worse, should their usefulness disappear. Their difference, their incommensurability, was a problem, and the undifferentiated herd viewed them as intolerable. Yet the question remains as to why the Jews should have received so much attention—as opposed to some other "other" such as Basques or Bretons. At one point Horkheimer and Adorno suggested that the "herd's" preoccupation with the Jews was accidental, and accordingly speculated, "The fact that anti-Semitism tends to occur only as part of an interchangeable program is sure hope that it will die out one day."[16] But the bulk of their analysis in the chapter, "Elements of Anti-Semitism," suggests the opposite: namely the historically necessary development of anti-Semitism.

From Roman times, according to this analysis, the Jews were forced into commerce, an activity which became "not their vocation but their fate," and consequently provoked the hostility of their impoverished customers.[17] Yet coexisting with this orthodox Marxian explanation—which made the Jews harbingers of modernity—was the more peculiar claim that, on the contrary, the Jews reminded moderns of the terrifying natural world from which Enlightenment had striven to liberate humanity. This "greater affinity to nature" was visible in "certain gestures and behavior patterns"—specifically flattery and entreaty—that society in the "bourgeois mode of production" wished to have "consigned to oblivion."[18]

There are important differences between Hertzberg's analysis of "enlightened anti-Semitism" and that of Horkheimer and Adorno. Specifically, as Gary Kates has noted, Hertzberg's argument contains a distinctly Zionist subtext.[19] By contrast, Horkheimer and Adorno maintained what Martin Jay has called an "indifference to Zionism as a solution to the plight of the Jews."[20] Moreover, in Hertzberg's account *laissez-faire* economists receive praise for viewing Jewish merchants as a counterforce to the restrictive trading practices of the guild system;[21] and "secular anti-Semitism" is identified exclusively with "the left," both before the Revolution, when Voltaire is improbably associated with that wing, and in the nineteenth century, when the main culprits are utopian socialists and Marx.[22] Horkheimer and Adorno, meanwhile, typically showed their Marxist colors by explaining ideas in terms of a materialist base and associating the worst type of thinking with capitalist mentalities.

Considering the differences between *The French Enlightenment and the Jews* and *Dialectic of Enlightenment*, one might question the wisdom of examining them together in an essay intended to contribute to a discussion on postmodernism. After all, postmodernism is usually associated with the left, and though Horkheimer and Adorno certainly fulfill that apparent prerequisite, Hertzberg's conservatism would seem to disqualify him, as would his Zionism, since the latter is intimately connected to the quintessentially modern project of nationalism. Moreover, Hertzberg's positivist method, which consists of finding quotations, lining them up as "pro-Jewish" or "anti-Semitic," judging their authors accordingly, and looking for the influence of ideas on thinkers, is hardly compatible with the postmodern suspicion of binary opposites, its skepticism regarding influences and coherent doctrines, and its emphasis on the relationship between language and cultural practices.

Yet if Hertzberg is not a self-conscious practitioner of postmodern scholarship, his principal theme—the destructive nature of hostility to difference—is quite compatible with the most characteristic goals of postmodernism. Jean-François Lyotard defines "postmodern knowledge" as "refin[ing] our sensitivity to differences and reinforc[ing] our ability to tolerate the incommensurable."[23] Similarly, Zygmunt Bauman argues that postmodern ethics require a respect of others "precisely in their otherness." He writes:

> One needs to honor the otherness in the other, the strangeness in the stranger, remembering—with Edmond Jabès—that "the unique is universal," that it is being different that makes us resemble each other and that I cannot respect my own difference but by respecting the difference of the other.[24]

In this context, Hertzberg's story of a people condemned for their supposed inability to conform to new universal standards of rationality and accepted only insofar as they rejected what made them different (i.e., their identity) can be seen as an object lesson in the abusive effects of Enlightenment universalism. Though the question of assimilation was relevant to Jews from the late eighteenth century—when enlightened Europeans first invited them to take part in their society on their terms—it acquired a new significance in the context of postmodern concerns. Just as liberal calls for the assimilation of immigrants and absorption of regional identities into a modernizing state were being challenged by those who invoked, in post-1968 fashion, the *droit à la différence*, Hertzberg's book, itself published in 1968, seems to have confirmed an increasing distaste for the ethos of assimilation.[25] And just as postmodern feminists proclaim the need to recognize women as fundamentally different from men rather than conflating the terms "equal" and "identical,"[26] Hertzberg notes the damage done to Jews by those who wished to deny their specificity.

In addition to addressing postmodern concerns more generally, Hertzberg's argument resembles that of Horkheimer and Adorno in some important specifics. Both Hertzberg and the authors of *Dialectic of Enlightenment* share the belief that it was the extreme rationalism of the Enlightenment that anti-Semites could use as a weapon against the Jews. In some cases this rationalism appears simply as the horror of and desire to eliminate difference. Thus Hertzberg sees the Jews as a problem to many *philosophes* and revolutionaries who mistrusted their alleged "particularism"; and Horkheimer and Adorno saw the Jews as an affront to anyone who employed abstract *Verstand*—the Enlightenment's favored mode of intellection—when attempting to make sense of reality. In other cases the menacing rationalism is depicted in the more mundane terms of "enlightened" thinkers denouncing the Jews as primitive. Thus Hertzberg refers to Voltaire's disparaging comments about the Jews' alleged "barbarism" and "superstition," while Horkheimer and Adorno hypothesized an urbane aversion to the "mimetic" gestures of insufficiently civilized Jews still in the thrall of "nature."

To what extent does this picture of the Jews in conflict with rationality correspond with eighteenth-century French texts on the "Jewish question"? There is a good deal of evidence for the first claim—that the Jews posed a problem to "enlightened" thinkers simply because they were different, particular, or "other." Yet it must be remembered that this discomfort is precisely what made the elimination of discriminatory laws possible. For Pierre-Louis Lacretelle, the barrister who in 1775 defended two Jewish merchants excluded from setting up a store in Thionville despite a 1767 royal decree permitting nonguild members to establish retail shops, the issue was not whether a specific law had been violated. Rather, "The real question of this case" was "to determine whether Jews are men."[27] Of course, the problem was purely rhetorical, since Lacretelle had no doubt that Jews were "men." But since he implicitly believed in the natural equality of all human beings and assumed his audience shared this belief,[28] his point was precisely that their exclusion from equal participation in society absurdly implied that they were outside the human race. Similarly, the Comte de Mirabeau claimed that reducing Jews to the label "Jew" suggested they were non-human, and in arguing for equal property rights wrote, "The Jew is still more a man than he is a Jew. . . . [H]ow could he not wish for a status in which he could become a landowner?"[29] Abbé Grégoire proved that the "regeneration" of the Jews was possible by noting, "[F]or a long time now it has been repeated that they are men like us, [that] they are [men] before they are Jews";[30] and a member of the Paris Commune countered opponents to the proposed revolutionary decree on Jewish equality by writing, "To say that the Jews are incapable of satisfying the duties of society is to sustain that the Jew is more Jew than he is man."[31] Examples such as these could be multiplied, but the point is clear: The denial of Jewish specificity was a crucial strategy in the struggle for civic and political equality.

Nevertheless, the denial of difference cut both ways, and if it facilitated legal equality it simultaneously did violence to any components of Jewish identity deemed "particularistic." In an oft-quoted statement, the Comte de Clermont-Tonnerre urged his fellow deputies in the Constituent Assembly, "One must refuse the Jews everything as a nation and give them everything as individuals. . . . They must form neither a political corporation nor an order in the state; they must be individual citizens."[32] Insofar as this exhortation pays homage to the individual, it appears to conform to a respect for difference. Yet it contained the hint of a threat, which Clermont-Tonnerre made explicit when he claimed that any Jews who did not wish to be citizens under the conditions laid out above should be "banished." He said, "It is repugnant that there should be a society of noncitizens in the state and a nation within the nation."[33] This was perhaps a rhetorical concession to opponents of his proposed legislation, since he went on to assure the assembly that Jews did indeed wish to be citizens. Yet the statement reflected a real tension in the contract between the representatives of the revolutionary state and the Jews, according to which legal equality entailed a change in habits and beliefs that deviated from some (admittedly fictional) norm, as well as the elimination of allegedly "antisocial" practices such as endogamy and dietary restrictions. In a word—assimilation. Clermont-Tonnerre himself did not believe that this assimilation had to go beyond submission to French law and the relinquishing of corporate privileges of self-governance, and asked rhetorically, "Is there a law obliging me to marry your daughter? Is there a law obliging me to eat hare, and to eat it with you?"[34] In this respect he deviated from Hertzberg's picture of revolutionaries who made "demands . . . on the inner spirit and religion of the Jews."[35] Yet other proponents of Jewish "regeneration," most famously Grégoire, proclaimed the need for the Jews to abandon the Talmud—which supposedly produced superstitious beliefs and an aversion to sociability—and for the state to oversee religious instruction to prevent rabbis from teaching such nonsense.[36] He proposed the forced re-education of Jews, their removal from miasmic ghettos to rural surroundings, where they would learn the morally salutary as well as physically healthful vocation of agriculture.[37]

Grégoire toned down his coercive program of 1787 when the Revolution broke out and he stood a realistic chance of enacting "regenerating" legislation. In his *Motion en faveur de Juifs*, published between mid-October and late December 1789, he simply called for the formal abolition of the legal difference between Jews and Christians. Perhaps he reasoned that any restrictive proposals would play into the hands of those deputies opposed to all reform in the Jews' legal status. He may also have been responding to the anti-Semitic violence that had gripped Alsace in the summer and fall of 1789. Yet he did not retract his earlier *Essai*, and even proudly referred readers to it.[38] Whether or not he changed his mind about the *Essai* or some components of it, however, is less important than the fact that it reflected the widely held belief that Jews would be better citizens to the extent they became more like their non-Jewish compatriots.

Even the Revolution's complete dismantling of Jewish communal autonomy, therefore, did not protect Jews from the accusation that they were a "nation within the nation." The persistence of this epithet is not surprising when one considers that it indicated less an institutional structure than an attitude of exclusiveness and even hostility which Christians repeatedly attributed to the Jews. This is what the Alsatian anti-Semite François Hell meant when in 1779 he denounced the Jews as "a nation in the nation" and a "powerful little state in a large state."[39] And Napoleon evidently had something similar in mind when in 1806 he responded to accusations of persistent Jewish usury in Alsace by declaring the Jews a "nation within a nation."[40] He could not have been referring to communal structures since these had been abolished with the Revolution, and indeed Napoleon himself quickly responded to the perceived problem by establishing a neocorporate system of consistories—without the legal autonomy of the *ci-devant* communities, to be sure—by which Jewish "notables" could enforce civic virtue.[41]

If the hostility to difference was pervasive both in undisguised libels and proposals for the legal and moral "regeneration" of the Jews, as Hertzberg suggests, it was not limited to the "Jewish question." Indeed, the very relevance of this discourse lies in its ability to reveal a larger animosity to difference which was, as Horkheimer and Adorno claimed, characteristic of the Enlightenment. Thus the tendency to regard Jews as actually or potentially a "nation within the nation" is symptomatic of a political philosophy that insists on the indivisibility of the body politic. It bears a striking resemblance to Sieyès's denunciation of the nobility as *imperium in imperio*, which itself evokes Rousseau's claim that sovereignty must remain undivided.[42] Moreover, these taboos against particularism—with their ethical overtones aligning civic virtue with conformity and civic vice with nonconformity—constitute the moral-political version of a taboo against alterity in general. With respect to the latter prohibition, Horkheimer and Adorno claimed that "the Enlightenment recognizes as being and occurrence only what can be apprehended in unity." And further, "To the Enlightenment, that which does not reduce to numbers, and ultimately to the one, becomes illusion."[43] In this respect, Jacobinism can be seen as merely the moralization of an epistemological principle. With it unity has been transformed from a condition of intelligibility to a moral imperative.

If the Enlightenment was inimical to the Jews insofar as they constituted an incommensurable "other," however, the second set of claims by Hertzberg and the authors of *Dialectic of Enlightenment*—namely that "enlightened" observers found the Jews insufficiently civilized, lacking in rationality, or overly proximate to nature—is less supportable.

For Hertzberg, Voltaire was the greatest and most influential of the "enlightened anti-Semites," and since this claim plays such a central role in the "enlightened anti-Semitism" thesis more generally, it is worth examining in some detail. As evidence of Voltaire's anti-Semitism, Hertzberg relies almost exclusively on biblical criticism and commentary on classical history, in which the *ancient* Hebrews are allegedly denounced as barbaric and superstitious. Thus the Jews of Abraham's time (!) are called "a small, new, ignorant, crude people."[44] Hertzberg alludes to "Voltaire's arguments against the Bible" as if biblical criticism were identical with anti-Semitism. He goes to great lengths to find in Bayle and the English Deists "the crucial sources" of this critique without considering that indignant remarks about Saul's treachery against David or David's murder of Naboth do not constitute anti-Semitism; indeed the behavior of both kings is denounced in the Old Testament itself.[45] Elsewhere, the perfectly accurate claim that the Bible depicts God commanding the Israelites to kill idolaters is a "slur."[46] More evidence of Voltaire's anti-Semitism is found in his distaste for the Hebrew language, which evidently showed that the ancient Israelites "had no idea of that which we call taste, delicacy, or proportion."[47] His belief that the Jews borrowed Bible stories from Greek myths is yet another telltale sign of his anti-Semitism, as is his praise of Grotius for "his opinion that Alexander and Aristotle were superior to the Jews" of the fourth century B.C.[48]

As to Voltaire's animosity toward contemporary Jews, Hertzberg provides a single letter, buried in the immense corpus of his correspondence, in which he wrote that the *converted* Jews in the English colonies were "the greatest scoundrels who have ever sullied the face of the globe."[49] In the face of this lack of evidence, Hertzberg uses comments by *other philosophes* to indict Voltaire. Anti-Jewish remarks by Diderot and Holbach are unearthed, though these too were primarily directed against the ancient Jews.[50] Even so, Voltaire is judged guilty by association with a "*coterie*" of *philosophes*, which he simultaneously is presumed to have led.

Hertzberg might have made a more convincing case had he refrained from prosecuting Voltaire as a kind of anti-Jewish ringleader and simply argued that a tendency to criticize the Jewish religion as irrational was present in a number of Enlightenment thinkers. Yet even this claim would be meaningless outside the polemical context of these "anti-Semitic" statements. As Peter Gay has convincingly argued, Voltaire's criticism of Judaism and the biblical Jews served the strategic purpose of defaming the Church, his real enemy, and that he "struck at the Jews to strike at the Christians."[51] One finds support for this position in the *Dictionnaire philosophique*, in which Voltaire depicted the "fanaticism," "ignorance," and "barbarity" of the ancient Jews, but then revealed his contemporary anticlerical agenda when he claimed that Christians "have imitated" the "cruelest and most intolerant people of all antiquity" in "their absurd furors."[52] Elsewhere, in a passage cited by Hertzberg, Voltaire insisted that the Christians were merely "uncircumcised Jews," the heirs to a religion they held in contempt. He wrote that the Jews of Roman times "kept all their customs, which are exactly the opposite of all proper social customs; they were therefore rightly treated as a people opposed to all others, whom they served, out of greed and hatred, out of fanaticism; they made usury into a sacred duty." Yet he went on to write a crucial addendum, "And these are our fathers."[53] This subtle mixture of humanism and calumny was meant to deflate a pretentious church by reminding it of its familial origins among a people it otherwise reviled and persecuted.

That Voltaire's strategy was not unique among the *philosophes* is evident from an examination of the writings of the baron d'Holbach, who similarly defamed the genealogy of *"l'infâme"* by associating it with its most celebrated adversary. Indeed, even the title of his principal work on Judaism, *L'Esprit du Judaïsme, ou examen raisonné de la loi de Moyse, et de son influence sur la religion chrétienne*, reveals his goal of determining the influence of the Judaism on Christianity. In this work Holbach summarized the history of the ancient Jews as the deeds of "a throng of people whom [a] healthy [sense of] morality would have us regard as monsters sullied by the most revolting cruelties and the most horrifying crimes."[54] The villain of the story is Moses, a cynical tyrant who has invented a religion for the sole purpose of enriching himself and his successors. Moses takes advantage of the credulity of the Jews, "this vulgar people, still incapable of reasoning."[55] He convinces them, through magic tricks that he learned in Egypt, of his special relationship to God. He invents the fable of Abraham and Isaac, since the barbarians he is trying to convince can only conceive of a God who demands blood sacrifices.[56] Moses and his successors the priests whip the common people into a "perpetual fanaticism" that enables them to conquer the territory of their neighbors.[57] Once established, the priests steal from the people on the pretext of requiring sacrifices for the expiation of their sins. They ally themselves with the monarchs, then attempt to usurp their authority, the result being a long and bloody series of civil wars that ends only with the destruction of Jerusalem and the dispersion of the Jews.

Throughout his narrative, Holbach makes it clear that his real enemy is the contemporary church. He treats the Jews as a dead people whose only significance lies in the lessons their history can teach contemporary Europeans.[58] Thus the priests of ancient Israel stand for the modern Catholic clergy, and the high priest of the temple represents the pope. Demands for agricultural sacrifices are likened to modern tithes and indulgences.[59] The fanaticism and barbarity of the ancient Jews is seen again in the Christian people, and the conception of a bloodthirsty God that produced the barbaric story of Abraham and Isaac also explains the Christian belief in a "cannibal God" who could only redeem his sinful creatures by spilling the blood of his son.[60] Holbach sees the dangerous alliance between priests and kings reproduced in his own day, as well as the dangers of their quarrels.[61] He sees almost no meaningful difference between Judaism and Christianity. The latter is only "a reformed Judaism," and its believers are, in language identical to that of Voltaire, merely "uncircumcised Jews."[62] The principal defect of ancient Judaism, the "spirit of priesthood," is the defining character of Christianity.[63] The only difference is that Christianity has done more damage. Whereas the "prophets of Judea" caused harm only to "a little corner of Asia," "the Christian Priests have covered immense empires with corpses and blood."[64]

Thus Voltaire participated in a larger campaign of anticlericalism in which "anti-Semitic" statements served the purpose of condemning the Church. None of this is meant to exculpate Voltaire, a project which would be as pointless as condemning him. For what it is worth, it is likely that Voltaire, like nearly all his contemporaries, "enlightened" or not, harbored prejudices against the Jews of his day. It may also be true that Voltaire "regarded the Jewish character as a continuity from ancient times to the present," a claim Hertzberg borrows from Hannah Emmrich's 1930 study, *Das Judentum bei Voltaire.*[65] That he considered Jews incapable of regeneration and "hopelessly alien even to the future age of enlightened men" is thoroughly unsubstantiated.[66]

More important than Voltaire's personal feelings, as Hertzberg acknowledges, is the reception of his statements by contemporaries and posterity. As noted above, Hertzberg does not even attempt to prove his assertion that Voltaire is "the major link in Western intellectual history between the anti-Semitism of classic paganism and the modern age," so there is little need to refute this claim.[67] As to the eighteenth-century reception of his statements, there is some support for the belief that contemporaries regarded Voltaire as hostile to Jews past and present. Thus Isaac de Pinto, taking offense to remarks in the *Dictionnaire philosophique,* defended the religion of his ancestors in a spirited rejoinder.[68] The Jansenist Abbé Guénée posed as a group of insulted Jews and undertook to disabuse Voltaire of his apparent misconceptions about the Jews and Judaism, clearly doing so because of outrage at what he rightly took as an attack on his own religion.[69]

Yet if Jews and defenders of the Bible took offense at Voltaire's statements about them, this does not mean that anti-Semites in eighteenth-century France drew much inspiration from him. The most infamous of these Jew-baiters was François Hell, an Alsatian bailiff who in the late 1770s organized the production of forged receipts to release Christians from loans owed to Jewish lenders; he then attempted to justify his action in a pamphlet entitled *Observations d'un Alsacien sur l'affaire présente des Juifs d'Alsace.* Yet Hell made no mention of Voltaire in his 86-page diatribe. Untroubled by this inconvenient omission, Hertzberg writes, "Though Hell never quoted Voltaire directly, it is clear from his book that he had read with great care the anti-Jewish pronouncements of the sage of Ferney."[70] In fact, this is not at all clear; and even if Hell had read Voltaire's writings on the Jews his own opinions were in direct opposition to them. While Voltaire saw the persecution of the Jews as evidence of a deplorable popular fanaticism, Hell saw it as the "just wrath of Heaven."[71] Whereas Voltaire denounced the belief that Jews crucified Christian children at Passover and poisoned wells from which Christians drank as outrageous libels, Hell repeated these very accusations and used them to justify anti-Semitic violence.[72] In style as well as the content of his writing Hell was the very opposite of Voltaire. Voltaire ironically mocked what he disliked; Hell was a student of *sensibilité*, relying on tear-jerking tropes and narratives of domestic tragedy—complete with weeping wives and children—brought on by Jewish usury. His defiant abhorrence of irony was reminiscent of Rousseau, Voltaire's rival in content and style, and he had a Rousseauian persecution complex as well. Both are evident in his prediction that his opponents, the "sectarian[s] of tolerance whose eye sees fanatics everywhere" (hardly the words of a disciple of Voltaire) and "the *bel esprit* who runs after brilliance"—would "pronounce an edict of proscription against me." Yet he defiantly wrote, "*Et qu'importe?* I will immediately call my heart, which will absolve me." Further along these lines, he confessed (i.e., boasted) that he was "a bit agitated by an excess of patriotism," but added, "my sentiments are pure." His only desire was to "unmask crime," that is the crime of Jewish usury that forced him to take the technically illegal but morally justifiable action of forging receipts.[73] The implications of Hell's style and the content of his claims will be considered later, but for now it is sufficient to note that Voltaire, far from being an influence or inspiration upon Hell, was on the contrary inimical to the anti-Semitic message he was trying to send.

By contrast, in 1786 the anti-Semitic libelist Latour-Foissac did refer to Voltaire when accusing the Jews of "ignorance," "superstition" "fanaticism," and "barbarism." Yet the bulk of his pamphlet, like that of Hell, was a sentimental tableau in which gullible yet virtuous Christians are duped by clever, evil Jews.[74] It thus clashed with the elitist contempt for the unlettered *canaille* suggested by the reference to Voltaire. Yet, aside from Latour-Foissac's reference to Voltaire, Hertzberg shows nothing else to suggest that he had any impact on any anti-Semitic authors or statements in eighteenth-century France.

This does not mean that rationalist language was never used in the discourse on the Jews and Judaism. Grégoire, for example, lamented what he saw as the Jews' "acquired ignorance, which has depraved their intellectual faculties." He did not consider the Jews incapable of genius, and like contemporaries interested in improving their condition cited the German-Jewish philosopher Moses Mendelssohn as proof that they harbored the potential for intellectual greatness if given the proper conditions. Mendelssohn, moreover, was a sign that the Jews were "at least at the dawn of reason." Grégoire nevertheless claimed that "since the historian Josephus it took seventeen centuries to produce a Mendelssohn." In the intervening time the Jews had allegedly only borrowed ideas from their neighbors, "and what ideas!" Alchemy and cabbala were what the Jews in Grégoire's view had found most appealing. Most irrational, according to the author, was the Jews' attachment to the Talmud, "this sewer in which the deliriums of the human mind are accumulated."[75] Similarly, Mirabeau envisaged intellectual improvement as crucial to the program of "regeneration," and in a eulogy for Mendelssohn he opposed the philosopher to his ignorant coreligionists, especially the rabbis who "could not see without indignation that humanity and truth seemed dearer to Mendelssohn than the dark dreams of the Talmudists."[76]

Yet if commentators occasionally criticized the Jews for being insufficiently rational, persistently primitive, or troublingly close to nature, the shortcomings much more often attributed to them were quite the opposite. Indeed, *pace* Hertzberg and the authors of the *Dialectic of Enlightenment*, they were denounced as *all too rational*, as overly cunning and calculating and in possession of the unnatural ability to conceal their thoughts and emotions. By contrast, their "victims," i.e., their debtors, were idealized as naïve innocents incapable of calculation, transparent in their emotional expression, but all the more virtuous for their natural simplicity. The binary opposition between the natural Christian and calculating Jew is unmistakable in the anti-Semitic pamphlets of the 1770s and 1780s. Specifically, Hell takes on the role of the simple citizen defending his compatriots from the depredations of clever Jews. As mentioned earlier, he "call[s] [his] heart" to prove his sincerity, which is apparently a rhetorical substitute for reason. This kind of cardiac language saturates his pamphlet, which he hopes will "reheat the hearts" of his compatriots, and if his "ideas [do] not appear . . . subtly fashioned enough or encased in a sufficiently elegant style," they have been "dictated by a patriotic heart."[77]

The dichotomy between "citizen" and "Jew" is clearest in Hell's representation of the paradigmatic fraudulent loan. The victim of usury is "the youth, in whom *reason is still weak* or bewildered by *the ardor of budding passions.*" He "cannot foresee," that is, cannot calculate, "the finesse of the fraud and the consequences of the commitment" to the loan.[78] In what amounts to a monetary seduction, the Jewish usurer repeatedly "offers his purse" to the "young man," who is naturally "susceptible to debauchery" (*enclin à la débauche*).[79] Each time the victim "avidly bites" at the contents of the purse, and his "passions, nourished by this food, grow." (*Les passions nourries par cet aliment croissent.*) "The prodigal son . . . returns," and "each time well-received, he receives" more money. But each time he must offer to pay a higher rate of interest. "The passions" of the young man "are kindled, the taste of dissipation is excited and quickly consumes" him. Yet the Jew, in contrast to the picture presented by Horkheimer and Adorno of a person in the thrall of natural or "mimetic" gestures, controls himself. He "seizes the moment at which [the young man] returns, "feigns an obdurate expression" (*fait mine d'être dur*), "refuses for a moment, but after prevailing upon the young man to sign IOUs the sum total of which is quadruple that of the loan, he gives in" and lends. Hell writes:

> It is thus that this young man of good family, corrupted by the fire of debauchery, drinking from the perfidious cup of usury, swallows in one gulp the patrimony that he does not yet have and the dowry of the woman to whom he is not yet engaged.[80]

For Hell, then, it is the "young man of good family" who is close to nature, as his uncontrollable "passions" and his penchant for corporeal satisfaction—expressed in the digestive language of biting, swallowing, and tasting—makes clear. It is the calculating Jew who controls his gestures and profits from the Christian's appetites. Yet Hell asks the reader to be sympathetic to the debauched young man, whose excesses should be forgiven—as the biblical metaphor of the prodigal son suggests—and whose errors are sentimentalized through their connection to domestic tragedy.

A strikingly similar rhetorical strategy is evident in Latour-Foissac's *Cri du citoyen*. Here the author recalls his experiences as a young officer away from home for the first time. Writing in the third person, he describes the naïve citizen, "[j]ust out of the hands of an instructor, under whom his petulant concern for liberty sighed." At this time "[his] open, honest and loyal heart is still in the heedlessness of a profound calm." Like the victim of usury in Hell's account, he is incapable of foreseeing the traps set by the calculating Jew. As soon as he arrives in the garrison town of Metz, he and his colleagues "become the object of the Synagogue's scrutiny." The Jewish moneylenders have already determined that this is one of the "opportune moments that can make seductive and pleasant the ruinous offers they make," presumably since the men are away from the supervision of their families and tempted to various forms of debauchery. In a revealing phrase the author claims that it is at precisely such "moments when *weakened reason becomes powerless*, that the Jews appear and deal their money." The officer tries to resist the temptation, but dissimulation triumphs over naïveté, and inevitably "the transaction will be completed, to the certain ruin of the unfortunate borrower."[81]

In addition to unequivocal anti-Semites such as Hell and Latour-Foissac, those who agitated for the legal improvement in the Jews' condition similarly considered them, in their unregenerated state, to be overly calculating and thus the opposite of natural, hence virtuous, citizens. Grégoire, although capable of denouncing the irrationality of the Talmud and rabbinical teaching, much more frequently accused the Jews of harboring a cold, commercial mentality and lacking the attachment to nature that would presumably increase their level of morality. He called rabbis "casuists," suggesting a hair-splitting rationality on their part, and claimed that "a multitude" of them "authorize . . . bad faith, equivocation, mental restrictions, hypocrisy." "Is it true," he asked, reserving judgment on the answer, "that, according to the Talmud, a Jew must . . . wish [a Christian] a *bon voyage* while adding, under his breath, 'like that of Pharaoh in the sea . . .?'"[82] Thus he attributed a kind of duplicitous irony to Jews that would be seen as "aristocratic" during the Revolution. That irony, absent from the unambiguous, straightforward citizen, was a sign of the corruption of civilization, not a proximity to primitive "nature." Indeed, in his claim that Jews were not to blame for their decadent morality, Grégoire opposed them to the "peaceable Tahitians" presumed to be superior in morality not only to Jews, but to Europeans in general. He proposed a thought experiment: "bring [the Tahitians] on the scene . . . forbid them all means of subsistence except a retail commerce whose gains are precarious and small, sometimes nonexistent when agility and activity do not suffice to support imperious and ever reappearing needs," and "soon they will call to their aid cunning and trickery."[83] "Cunning and trickery," then, were absent from the moral economy of the noble savage; they were conditions that only obtained in a civilized, capitalist economy.

On those few occasions when Grégoire praised the Jews of his day, moreover, he did not praise their rationality, but their "natural" virtues. He noted that certain vices of civilization, such as drinking, libertinage, pornography, and adultery, were not common among Jews. They were frugal, charitable to their poor, and respectful of their elders, and Grégoire noted with Rousseauian approval that Jewish mothers breastfed their children.[84] In other words, he praised their simple, natural affections, and hoped that someday these would not be limited to their domestic relations, but would extend toward their relations with Christians. Thus it was possible for him to predict that with regeneration they "would acquire sociability, sentiments, virtues, without losing the antique simplicity of their morals."[85] For that transformation to take place, the Jews would have to abandon the decadent occupation of commerce and return to the pastoral existence that Grégoire believed they had led in biblical times. At that time, Grégoire prophesied:

> The rustic tasks will then call the Hebrew to our fields, once watered by the blood of his forefathers, and which at that time will be watered by his sweat; he will leave his manor to breathe the pure air of the hills: soon stimulated by interest, his once-soft arms will be strengthened by exercise, and this physical improvement will bring moral improvement too, for the first of arts is also the first in virtue.[86]

Grégoire also considered traditional crafts as regenerative work, but his main requirements were that the work be simple, traditional and, in keeping with physiocratic doctrine, productive.

Mirabeau similarly conceived of Jewish vice and the possibilities of regeneration in terms of an opposition between decadent commerce and virtuous work, especially agriculture. He had apparently inherited anti-commercial ideas from his father, one of the founders of physiocracy, and disparaged trade not only as economically sterile, but morally degrading as well. He idealized the farmer, writing, "The simple morals of the countryside, the regular diligence that [the farmers'] work requires, preserve his innocence and hospitable morality."[87] The merchant, by contrast, had "different habits, different principles, a completely different spirit." In a kind of psychopathology of commerce he wrote:

> Continually occupied with making a profit, avoiding losses, fighting foreign interests, consulting, provoking, tampering with his fortune, [the merchant] is incessantly agitated by restless activity. . . . The habit of seeing everything from the point of view of gain must naturally tighten his feelings; temptations are too frequent; overpricing is too hard to distinguish from taking prudent advantage of circumstances. The merchant, even an honest one, might eventually deceive himself and take the one for the other. He always stands to lose or gain in his relations with other men; insensibly he accustoms himself to regarding them as adversaries or rivals; his soul contracts, his sensitivity is deadened, sordid interest or ostentatious luxury too often take its place.[88]

If the ordinary merchant was subjected to such assaults on his morality, Mirabeau argued, then *a fortiori* the Jew, who saw nothing but contempt from his Christian neighbors, would be even less inclined to act honestly. It was not about the Jew's rationality that Mirabeau expressed concern, but his "sensitivity," which would be "deadened" by the effects of incessant calculation. His intellect operated effectively, even too effectively; it was his "feelings" that were "tighten[ed]" and his "soul" which was "contract[ed]."

The texts on the Jewish question in eighteenth-century France call for a re-evaluation of the relationship between the Enlightenment and the Jews. If Enlightenment rationality made it difficult to accept the Jews as an incommensurable other, rationality as a value in and of itself was rarely invoked in evaluations of the Jews and their level of morality. On the contrary, the Jews tended to receive praise insofar as they appeared "natural" and "sensitive" and criticism insofar as observers judged them to be calculating and clever. In the latter case they were typically opposed to an ideal Christian "citizen," either a peasant or a soldier, who embodied the qualities necessary for civic virtue: visible, affective (yet unaffected) intensity and proximity to nature.

It would be difficult to overstate the significance of this re-evaluation of "enlightened anti-Semitism," as it sheds light on the much larger question of just what the values of the Enlightenment were. Indeed, if Hertzberg and the authors of *Dialectic of Enlightenment* were mistaken about the relationship between the Enlightenment and the Jews, it is because they were mistaken about the respective value the Enlightenment placed on reason and "nature," rationality and sensitivity, or (to borrow a dichotomy from Jane Austen) sense and sensibility.

This is a very large claim, one that the eighteenth-century French literature on the Jewish question alone cannot prove. Yet other tendencies in eighteenth-century thought tend to corroborate the hypothesis that the Enlightenment placed a greater value on the senses and the emotions than is typically assumed. The most obvious piece of evidence in this respect is the corpus of sentimental literature that flourished in eighteenth-century Europe. Tear-jerking authors, from Richardson to Rousseau to Goethe, aimed not at the head but the heart, as did genre painters such as Greuze, upon whom Diderot famously lavished praise.[89] The valorization of sensation was not limited to art and novels. It was crucial to the century's most favored epistemology, known significantly as sensationalism. From Locke to Condillac to Hume, theorists of knowledge rejected the rationalism of Descartes in favor of a system in which feeling preceded both knowing and thinking. Even Kant's greatest work was, revealingly, *A Critique of Pure Reason*, a book that rejected the "dogmatic" belief that the understanding alone could know the thing-in-itself.

In the philosophical subfield of ethics, sensation was again indispensable. Not only was "*un coeur sensible . . .* the precondition for morality."[90] In Hume's philosophy ethics derived from sensation, and in the *Preliminary Discourse* to the *Encyclopédie* d'Alembert argued that it was the prior sensation of injustice, either direct or indirect, that made knowledge of right and wrong possible.[91] To be sure, Kant had hoped to derive an ethics from rationality alone, i.e., from *a priori* principles without the aid of experience, and Horkheimer and Adorno made much of his failure to do so. They argued devastatingly that the autonomous individual postulated in the categorical imperative could just as easily (and justifiably) behave like a character invented by the Marquis de Sade as a restrained moralist such as Kant himself.[92] The failure itself is nevertheless indicative—as is Kant's desperate recourse to "practical reason"—of the Enlightenment's prior success (with Kant's help) at lowering philosophical expectations about the power of unaided reason. Sade's pornographic burlesque of philosophy, moreover, is itself evidence that the mind was not the summa for Enlightenment thinkers.

Horkheimer and Adorno used Sade as evidence that the Enlightenment had rationalized (in both senses of the word) vice and crime, but did not appreciate the implications of just what kind of vice and crime was being rationalized. The single-minded determination with which Sade's characters attempt to reduce sexual activity to a dispassionate, mechanical activity reveals the dangerous power the author attributed to the senses, which needed to be dominated if they were not to dominate their subjects. In a less overtly sexual way, the moral and political philosophers of the eighteenth century problematized the human will as a set of drives that conflicted with those of fellow human beings in civil society. Thus Kant, in his categorical imperative, wished to rationalize the will by requiring it to be fairly and feasibly universalized, and Rousseau, in his *Social Contract*, sought to domesticate it by making it conform to the consent of public-spirited citizens. In both cases the will was potentially dangerous—though elsewhere in Rousseau's writings strong desires are themselves evidence of virtue. But by recognizing that danger, Kant and Rousseau, like Sade, showed their belief in the power of a force, the senses, which could with only great difficulty be governed by reason.

Even the Rousseauian-Jacobin fear of "particularism," which translated into a contempt for dissenting individuals and Jewish or noble "nations within the nation," can be seen as a kind of irrationalist organicism. Although Horkheimer and Adorno attributed the Enlightenment disdain for the incommensurable to its fetishistic need to "reduce to numbers, and ultimately to the one,"[93] when seen in the context of nascent nationalism this tendency appears to confirm Durkheim's claim that Rousseau (as well as Montesquieu) viewed society as an organism, as having a living identity irreducible to the sum of its parts.[94] Thus Rousseau, Sieyès, and the republican nationalists of the revolutionary era were closer to animism than they were to the preferred rationalist physics of mechanism.

Of course, it would be wrong to deny that rationalism and the ethos of rationality played significant roles in the Enlightenment. Certainly *philosophes* were capable of singing reason's praises, and the desire of thinkers to understand both the natural and human world in terms of predictable laws is undeniable—though again it should be emphasized that these laws, according to empirical epistemology and the scientific method, could not be derived without the data of experience, and ultimately of the senses. But even this modified rationalism competed with a valorization of the senses as vehicles of knowledge, both physical and moral, and indeed as guarantors of ethically correct behavior. The tension between reason and sensation, the mind and the body, the head and the heart provided the stuff of philosophical speculation as well as imaginative literature throughout the century, as is evident in Hume, Rousseau, Kant, and Sade. It is perhaps here, at the intersection of thinking and feeling, rather than the crossroads of myth and disenchantment, that one should locate the dialectic of Enlightenment.

Yet what explains the error made by Hertzberg and the authors of *Dialectic of Enlightenment?* To be fair, it is an old mistake which does not belong to them alone. For more than two centuries critics have conjured up a largely fictitious image of a cold, dispassionate, bloodless Enlightenment. This essay began with a description of how Isaiah Berr Bing exaggerated the rationalist, materialist tendencies of "fashionable philosophy" for polemical purposes. Those who opposed the French Revolution—which had sought its justifying heritage in the philosophy of the eighteenth century—would have other reasons for presenting the Enlightenment as the apotheosis of rationalism.

For example, Edmund Burke was an heir to Enlightenment empiricism, which he consecrated in his paeans to human experience. His reluctance to alter established institutions, though later consecrated "conservative," does not mean that he was anti-Enlightenment, since the Enlightenment thinkers were themselves, as empiricists, respectful of human experience and reluctant to change institutions on the basis of abstract models. Thus Burke's defiant acclaim for the "prejudices" of peoples was not so different from Montesquieu's reverence for the "genius of the nation" and his caution with respect to altering institutions.[95] Yet the Revolution's appropriation of the *philosophes* made it desirable for Burke, as an opponent of the revolutionary program, to distance himself from the Enlightenment Pantheon. Thus he criticized the revolutionaries as abstract system builders and "metaphysicians," though it should not be forgotten that this was precisely the language that Voltaire had used to deride his adversaries.[96]

Similarly, Hegel viewed the Enlightenment through the prism of the Revolution, which for him took the form of Napoleon and the battle of Jena. He too critiqued the Enlightenment as an abstract, "gaseous" movement that fetishized the universal and ignored the particular.[97] This analysis, on which Horkheimer and Adorno would later rely and which conforms to Lyotard's and Bauman's conceptions of postmodernism as discussed earlier, bears more than a little resemblance to that of Burke, especially insofar as it justified Hegel's reputedly conservative call for the preservation of established institutions, however irrational.

Thus an overly rationalized, insufficiently sensitized Enlightenment was fabricated by Enlightenment thinkers themselves, for polemical and political reasons, then bequeathed to historians and philosophers as an object for evaluation. Some would reject it, others would embrace it, merely placing a positive spin on its fabled rationalism.[98] But in the process of judging the Enlightenment they would forget the extent to which it valued sensation, emotions, and displayed an arational or even irrational reverence for nature, both in its order and its chaos.

NOTES

1. I wish to thank Daniel Gordon for his encouragement and judicious suggestions for revising this article. I also wish to thank the College of William and Mary for the Faculty Summer Grant that made this essay possible.
2. *Lettre du Sr.I[saïah] B[err] B[ing], Juif de Metz, à l'auteur anonyme d'un écrit intitulé: Le Cri du citoyen contre les Juifs* (Metz, 1787), pp. 29–30; repr. in *Révolution française et l'émancipation des Juifs* (Paris: EdHis, 1968), vol. 8. Cf. Ronald Schechter, "Translating the 'Marseillaise': Biblical Republicanism and the Emancipation of Jews in Revolutionary France," *Past and Present* 143 (May 1994): 131.
3. Arthur Hertzberg, *The French Enlightenment and the Jews* (New York, 1968), p. 5.
4. Hertzberg, *French Enlightenment*, p. 7.
5. Ibid., p. 10.
6. Ibid.
7. Ibid.
8. On Voltaire's relationship to the Jews and Judaism see Heinrich Graetz, "Voltaire und die Juden," *Monatsschrift für die Geschichte und Wissenschaft des Judentums* XVI (1867): 321–30; Herbert Solow, "Voltaire and Some Jews," *Menorah Journal* XIII (1927): 186–97; Hanna Emmrich, *Das Judentum bei Voltaire* (Breslau, 1930); Pierre Aubery, "Voltaire et les Juifs," *Studies on Voltaire and the Eighteenth Century* XXIV (1963): 67–79; and Peter Gay, *The Party of Humanity: Essays in the French Enlightenment* (New York, 1964), pp. 97–108.
9. Arthur O. Lovejoy, *The Great Chain of Being* (Cambridge, MA, 1936 and 1964), pp. 3–23. For a powerful critique of Lovejoy's approach see Quentin Skinner, "Meaning and Understanding in the History of Ideas," *History and Theory* 8 (1969): 3–53.
10. See note 8 above.

11. Max Horkheimer and Theodor W. Adorno, *Dialectic of Enlightenment*, trans. John Cumming (New York, 1972), pp. 43–80.

12. Horkheimer and Adorno, *Dialectic*, passim.

13. Ibid., p. 3.

14. Ibid., pp. 6, 12–13, 17.

15. Hertzberg, *French Enlightenment*, pp. 12–28, 64–71 passim.

16. Horkheimer and Adorno, *Dialectic*, p. 207. Elsewhere they wrote that "victims [of persecution] are interchangeable according to circumstances—gypsies, Jews, Protestants, Catholics, and so on." *Dialectic*, p. 171.

17. Ibid., pp. 174–75.

18. Ibid., pp. 112, 181–82.

19. Gary Kates, "Jews into Frenchmen: Nationality and Representation in Revolutionary France" in Ferenc Fehér, ed., *The French Revolution and the Birth of Modernity* (Berkeley, 1990), pp. 103–16. Hertzberg reveals his sympathies when he writes that the Zionist founders Leo Pinsker and Theodor Herzl "both independently *recognized that* modern anti-Semitism was . . . a new, secular, and continuing phenomenon." By implication, only a coherent and self-conscious Jewish nation, or nation-state, could protect the Jews from the hatred of non-Jews. Hertzberg, *French Enlightenment*, p. 5. Emphasis added.

20. Martin Jay, *The Dialectical Imagination: A History of the Frankfurt School and the Institute of Social Research, 1923–1950* (Boston and Toronto, 1973), p. 32.

21. Hertzberg, *French Enlightenment*, pp. 12–28, 64–71 passim.

22. Ibid., pp. 10–11, 357.

23. Jean-François Lyotard, "Excerpts from *The Postmodern Condition: A Report on Knowledge*" in Joseph Natoli and Linda Hutcheon, eds., *A Postmodern Reader* (Albany, 1993), p. 73.

24. Zygmunt Bauman, "Postmodernity, or Living with Ambivalence" in Natoli and Hutcheon, *Postmodern Reader*, p. 14.

25. On the assertion of the "right to be different" among Jews and regional minorities in post-1968 France, see Judith Friedlander, *Vilna on the Seine: Jewish Intellectuals in France since 1968* (New Haven, 1990), pp. 38–64.

26. On the division of feminists between advocates of "sameness" and "difference" see Carol Lee Bacchi, *Same Difference: Feminism and Sexual Difference* (Sydney, 1990).

27. "LVIIIe cause. Question d'état sur les Juifs de Metz," *Causes célèbres, curieuses et intéressantes, de toutes les cours souveraines du royaume, avec les jugemens qui les ont décidées*, vol. 23 (Paris, 1776), p. 65. Published separately as *Plaidoyer pour Moyse May, Godechaux et Abraham Lévy, Juifs de Metz. Contre l'hôtel-de-ville de Thionville et le Corps des Marchands de cette ville* (Bruxelles, 1775). On Lacretelle see David A. Bell, *Lawyers and Citizens: The Making of a Political Elite in Old Regime France* (New York, 1994), pp. 164–67, 175–80.

28. The "audience" did not merely include the court, but the reading public for whom legal briefs such as Lacretelle's were extraordinarily popular. On this phenomenon see Sarah Maza, *Private Lives and Public Affairs: The Causes Célèbres of Prerevolutionary France* (Berkeley, 1993).

29. Honoré Gabriel de Riquetti, Comte de Mirabeau, *Sur Moses Mendelssohn, sur la réforme politique des Juifs: et en particulier sur la révolution tentée en leur faveur en 1753 dans la grande Bretagne* (London, 1787), p. 66, repr. in *Révolution française et l'émancipation des Juifs* (Paris, 1968), vol. 1.

30. Abbé Henri Grégoire, *Essai sur la régénération physique, morale et politique des Juifs* (Paris, 1789), p. 118, repr. in *Révolution française et l'émancipation des Juifs* (Paris, 1968), vol. 3.

31. [Jean Debourge], *Lettre au comité de constitution sur l'affaire des Juifs; par M. de Bourge, représentant de la commune de Paris* (Paris, 1790), p. 31.

32. *Opinion de M. le comte de Clermont-Tonnerre, député de Paris. Le 23 décembre 1789* (Paris, 1789), p. 13. Cf. *Archives parlementaires*, vol. 10, pp. 754–56.

33. *Opinion de M. le comte*, p. 13.
34. *Opinion de M. le comte*, p. 12.
35. Hertzberg, *French Enlightenment*, p. 364.
36. Grégoire, *Essai*, p. 87.
37. Ibid., p. 124.
38. *Motion en faveur des Juifs, par M. Grégoire, curé d'Embermenil, député de Nancy; précédée d'une notice historique, sur les persécutions qu'ils viennent d'essuyer en divers lieux, notamment en Alsace, et sur l'admission de leurs députés à la barre de l'Assemblée nationale* (Paris, 1789), repr. in *Révolution française et l'émancipation des Juifs* (Paris, 1968), vol. 7.
39. François Hell, *Observations d'un Alsacien sur l'affaire présente des Juifs d'Alsace* (Frankfurt, 1779), p. 66.
40. Simon Schwarzfuchs, *Napoleon, the Jews, and the Sanhedrin* (London, 1979), p. 49.
41. On the Jewish consistories in France see Phyllis Cohen Albert, *The Modernization of French Jewry: Consistory and Community in the Nineteenth Century* (Hanover, N.H., 1977).
42. Abbé Emmanuel Joseph Sieyès, *Qu'est-ce que le tiers-état?* (1789; reprint Paris: Société de l'Histoire de la Révolution Française, 1888), p. 31. Cf. Jean-Jacques Rousseau, *On the Social Contract*, book II, ch. 2.
43. Horkheimer and Adorno, *Dialectic*, p. 7.
44. Hertzberg, *French Enlightenment*, p. 303.
45. Ibid., p. 39, 39n.
46. Ibid., p. 304.
47. Ibid., p. 301.
48. Ibid., p. 303.
49. Ibid., p. 284.
50. Ibid., pp. 281–82, 308–12.
51. Peter Gay, *The Party of Humanity: Essays in the French Enlightenment* (New York, 1964), p. 103.
52. Voltaire, *Dictionnaire philosophique* (1764; reprint Paris, 1954), p. 402.
53. Hertzberg, *French Enlightenment*, pp. 302–3.
54. Paul Henri Thiry, baron d'Holbach, *L'Esprit du Judaïsme, ou examen raisonné de la loi de Moyse, et de son influence sur la religion chrétienne* (London [i.e. Amsterdam], 1770), pp. viii, ix.
55. Ibid., p. xiv.
56. Ibid., pp. 7–8.
57. Ibid., p. xv.
58. Though he mentions the modern Jews and even professes sympathy for their suffering, Holbach revealingly entitles his penultimate chapter, "The conduct and fate of the Jews from their captivity to their total destruction." This conceit is necessary for him to predict that Christianity will ultimately be destroyed as well.
59. Holbach, *L'Esprit du Judaïsme*, pp. 49–65.
60. Ibid, pp. xxi–xxii, 7–8, 176.
61. Ibid., pp. xv, 96.
62. Ibid., pp. i, 182.
63. Ibid., p. 56.
64. Ibid., p. 97.
65. Hertzberg, *French Enlightenment*, p. 300. Cf. Hannah Emmrich, *Das Judentum bei Voltaire* (Breslau, 1930).
66. Hertzberg, *French Enlightenment*, p. 10.
67. Ibid.
68. [Isaac de Pinto], *Apologie pour la nation juive, où réflexions critiques sur le premier chapitre du VIIe tome des oeuvres de M. de Voltaire au sujet des Juifs. Par l'auteur de "l'Essai sur le luxe"* (Amsterdam, 1762).

69. Abbé Antoine Guenée, *Lettres de quelques Juifs portugais et allemands à M. de Voltaire: avec des réflexions critiques, &c: et un petit commentaire extrait d'un plus grand* (Paris, 1769).

70. Hertzberg, *French Enlightenment*, p. 288.

71. Hell, *Observations*, p. 11.

72. Ibid., pp. 11–18. For Voltaire's denunciation of medieval anti-Jewish fanaticism and false beliefs regarding alleged ritual crimes, see *Essai sur l'histoire générale* (Geneva, 1756), 343; and "Le philosophe ignorant" in J. Van Den Heuvel, Ed., *Mélanges* (Paris, 1961), p. 929.

73. Hell, *Observations*, pp. 3–4. On Rousseau's preoccupation with "unmasking," see Jean Starobinski, *J.-J. Rousseau: la transparence et l'obstacle* (Paris, 1971), esp. pp. 84–101.

74. [Philippe-François de Latour-Foissac], *Le Cri du citoyen contre les Juifs de Metz. Par un capitaine d'infanterie* (Lausanne [Metz], 1786).

75. Grégoire, *Essai*, pp. 87, 116, 161–63.

76. Mirabeau, *Sur Moses Mendelssohn*, p. 28.

77. Hell, *Observations*, pp. 3–4.

78. Ibid., p. 40.

79. Whether "susceptible to debauchery" means desiring the sex money will presumably buy or defenseless in the face of the Jew's monetary debauchery of the young man is (perhaps deliberately) ambiguous.

80. Hell, *Observations*, pp. 40–41.

81. Latour-Foissac, *Cri du citoyen*, pp. 5–24. Emphasis added.

82. Grégoire, *Essai*, pp. 87–88.

83. Ibid., p. 67.

84. Ibid., pp. 65–67, 80–81.

85. Ibid., p. 139.

86. Ibid., p. 124. Cf. Schechter, "Translating the 'Marseillaise,'" p. 121.

87. Mirabeau, *Sur Moses Mendelssohn*, p. 86.

88. Ibid., p. 87.

89. Simon Schama, *Citizens: A Chronicle of the French Revolution* (New York, 1989), pp. 145–62; and Anita Brookner, *Greuze: The Rise and Fall of an Eighteenth-Century Phenomenon* (Greenwich, CT, 1972).

90. Schama, *Citizens*, p. 149.

91. David Hume, *An Enquiry Concerning the Principles of Morals* (London, 1751), esp. section 1; and Jean Le Rond d'Alembert, *Preliminary Discourse to the Encyclopedia of Diderot*, trans. and intro. Richard N. Schwab (Chicago, 1995), pp. 12–13.

92. Horkheimer and Adorno, *Dialectic*, pp. 81–119.

93. Ibid., p. 7.

94. Emile Durkheim, *Montesquieu and Rousseau: Forerunners of Sociology*, trans. Ralph Manheim, foreword Henri Peyre (Ann Arbor, 1960).

95. Burke, *Reflections on the Revolution in France* (London, 1790). Cf. Montesquieu, *De l'esprit des loix*, esp. pt. 6, bk. 31, ch. 4.

96. Burke, *Reflections*, passim. I have found 25 variations on the term "metaphysics" and 15 on "abstract," all of them pejorative, in the *Reflections*.

97. Hegel, *Phenomenology*, §488–595. On the "gaseous" nature of Enlightenment religion see §586. Similarly, Burke referred to the "spirit of liberty" as a "wild gas." *Reflections*, ed. Conor Cruise O'Brien (Harmondsworth, 1969), p. 90.

98. Most recently, Jürgen Habermas has praised the Enlightenment as a period during which rational individuals could discuss issues dispassionately in the "political public sphere," and lamented the replacement of this golden age by a late-capitalist culture of public opinion management. *The Structural Transformation of the Public Sphere: An Inquiry into a Category of Bourgeois Society*, trans. Thomas Burger and Frederick Lawrence (Cambridge, MA, 1991).

WRITING THE HISTORY OF CENSORSHIP IN THE AGE OF ENLIGHTENMENT

SOPHIA ROSENFELD

Censorship is not an easy topic to discuss at present. Both in the academy and in the larger American public sphere, the term is frequently and widely bandied about. But in this era of advanced capitalism, identity politics, and postmodern thought, all of the old certainties about censorship's value, meaning, and relation to its traditional opposite—freedom of expression—have come under repeated attack.[1] In the political realm, advocates for such diverse causes as the prohibition of "hate speech," the restriction of access to pornography, and the reform of campaign financing and broadcasting laws have opened up important questions about whether certain forms of censorship can actually serve rather than impinge upon the goals of a democratic society. Moreover, in the realm of theory, there seems no longer to be any consensus about what censorship is; both its characteristic forms and identifying markers have become subjects of dispute in courtrooms and classrooms alike, especially as a result of poststructuralist critiques of its binary relation to free speech. The only real point of agreement is that these varied efforts to rethink the established parameters of censorship and freedom of expression pose a fundamental challenge to modern liberalism and, more broadly, to the "enlightened" humanist philosophical tradition, with its emphasis on inalienable and natural rights, upon which this political ideology rests.

But how should contemporary debates about the nature of censorship affect the way we write the history of the Enlightenment itself? The purpose of this chapter is to argue that scholars of eighteenth-century

France have much to gain from taking seriously these recent challenges to the liberal conception of the ongoing contest between censorship and free speech. The pages that follow lay particular stress on the postmodern concept of "constitutive" censorship, a generic term for the kind of invisible, socially constituted thought control that has tended to flourish, some poststructuralists claim, in precisely those modern societies that have been most invested in the notion of a free market of ideas. However, the theory of "constitutive" censorship is employed in this article neither to condemn the shortsightedness of Enlightenment *philosophes* nor to expose the limitations of their nascent liberal vision. Rather, it is appropriated as a heuristic device to help bring to light the complexity of late-eighteenth-century French thinking about questions of language, liberty, and social control.

Now, some historians might well object to this endeavor from the start and respond that the intellectual formulations of our time can and should have no bearing on eighteenth-century Europe. Indeed, many scholars would posit that the primary task of the historian is precisely to distinguish our current understanding of the world from that of people who lived in eras past. Yet where the historiography of the French Enlightenment is concerned, it is especially difficult to insist upon the importance of maintaining clear-cut distinctions between past and present. The relationship between the French *philosophes* and the absolutist Old Regime state has long been explained in ways that have served the cause of modern liberalism, and modern liberal positions on individual rights and autonomy have frequently been justified by reference to their Enlightenment roots. Students of the French Enlightenment have often, in fact, worked in tandem with modern defenders of the principle of free speech to provide them with concepts, heroes, enemies, and landmarks. Thus, before we tackle the question of how postmodernist thought can or cannot help us to better understand the Enlightenment battle over censorship and free expression, we must first address the issue of how this subject has been discussed before and, especially, of how past historians' interpretations of this fundamental eighteenth-century struggle have traditionally been implicated in a larger project: the promotion of a liberal worldview.

I.

Let me start with an example. One book makes especially evident how twentieth-century Enlightenment historiography has worked to bolster and to give an intellectual genealogy to what might be called, in the American context, First Amendment liberalism. That book is Peter Gay's classic *Voltaire's Politics: The Poet as Realist*, which first appeared in

1959. Gay's Voltaire, it must be noted, is a complex figure; he is personally difficult, self-protective, and shrewd. But Gay insists on dramatizing the life of Voltaire as, first and foremost, the story of a lone and righteous individual who deliberately and repeatedly confronted the established—and in many ways oppressive—institutions and customs of eighteenth-century Europe. In this regard, the chapter heading "Voltaire against the Censors" is emblematic of the way Gay's narrative plays itself out.

Voltaire, according to Gay, was not simply a victim of the abusive censorship policies of Old Regime France, which were designed to control the flow of ideas both prior to publication (by weeding out manuscripts containing statements offensive to the state, church, or common decency and refusing to grant them a royal *privilège*) and after publication (by penalizing the bodies or texts of persons who had violated the law by producing unauthorized publications). The Voltaire of this account was also a long-standing champion of the highly subversive idea of freedom of thought and expression. Rather than change his ways after early experiences with imprisonment in the Bastille, forced exile, and the burning of his published work, Voltaire continued to challenge the authorities at every turn, alternately trying to co-opt, to trick, or to circumvent them. Furthermore, he made free speech one of the chief causes of his political writings, from his famous tribute to the freedom of English writers, in his *Lettres philosophiques* of 1734, to his unabashed insistence on the importance of liberty of expression in his "liberal" pamphlets and *Dictionnaire philosophique* of the mid-1760s. Gay quotes admiringly from Voltaire's 1765 *Idées républicaines* ("In a republic worthy of its name, the liberty to publish one's thoughts is the natural right of the citizen . . . it should no more be forbidden to write than to talk") and from his contemporaneous *Questions sur les miracles* ("There are two important things that people never talk about in slave countries, and which all citizens should discuss in free countries: one is government, the other is religion.").[2] Gay uses these examples to make the point that Voltaire's strongly worded defenses of free speech amounted to more than a selfish quest to ensure that his own writing saw the light of day. Voltaire's faith in freedom of opinion was, according to Gay, the centerpiece of his "platform for social reform."[3] For Voltaire believed that only with the liberty to read, hear, and discuss challenging ideas (such as those of the *philosophes*) could enlightenment ever become generalized and create a foundation for the liberation of the population as a whole. Voltaire assumes a heroic profile in this book because, as the introduction makes clear, he can be seen as the prototypical *engagé* intellectual, the man who succeeded in laying the groundwork for those freedoms now widely enjoyed by modern writers in all liberal, democratic societies.

Indeed, Gay's view of Voltaire, and of the eighteenth-century *philosophes* more generally, implicitly links the French Enlightenment to a progressive, humanist conception of modernity. And many other historians have traced the long struggle against royal or clerical monopolies on ideas and their expression forward to the "age of democratic revolutions" (to borrow R. R. Palmer's famous term), suggesting how the values specific to Voltaire's beloved Republic of Letters were gradually publicized, democratized, and finally enshrined in law. One can easily identify key markers—thinkers, texts, events—in this story. By the 1760s, the idea that the *homme de lettres* required freedom from government or church interference had already become something of an intellectual cliché in France; Antoine-Léonard Thomas's 1767 reception speech at the Académie Française made the case that independence for this "class" of men would ultimately aid in enlightening both those who governed and the abstraction he called "public opinion."[4] *Le Mariage de Figaro*, Beaumarchais's sensational play in which the lead character himself ridicules the censors, then helped transform the struggle against state censorship into a popular cause. The *cahiers de doléances* of the late 1780s indicate that by the time the royal system for policing ideas began to unravel on the eve of the Revolution, the desire for greater expressive liberty had already become widespread in urban France.[5] Finally, in the summer of 1789, in the context of the Declaration of the Rights of Man and of the Citizen, the *parti des Lumières*, following the American example, succeeded in establishing freedom of speech, along with freedom of conscience, as an inalienable right of citizenship. Article 11 of this foundational text in the battle against absolutism reads, "The free expression of thought and opinions is one of the most precious rights of man: thus every citizen may freely speak, write, and print, subject to accountability for abuse of this freedom in the cases determined by law."[6] Of course, Voltaire was no longer alive at the time these sentences were composed. But for Ernst Cassirer, the great German historian of the Enlightenment, not simply this statement but the whole "literature of the French Revolution" had to be seen as the inevitable outcome of the redefinition of freedom, beginning with freedom of expression, inaugurated by Voltaire more than fifty years earlier.[7] And in the wake of the judicial revolution of 1789, these ideas did not lose their force. Limiting or overturning official censorship policies became a priority of almost all nineteenth-century European revolutionary movements, and French-style declarations of human rights, including protections of free speech, came to be widely seen as prerequisites for the foundation of liberal states. In fact, though much has changed in the way "liberalism" is understood today, freedom of thought and expression remains what the major late-twentieth-century theorist of liberalism, John Rawls calls a "basic liberty," a fundamental civil and political freedom that must be protected in any democratic state that aims to conduct its political affairs in a rational and just (or perhaps we can say *enlightened*) rather than arbitrary and tyrannical fashion.[8]

It is, however, essential to point out that our traditional understanding of the relationship between the opposing sides at the origins of this struggle—the repressive, censoring Old Regime state and its rational, liberal, and ultimately successful challengers, eager for intellectual and political freedom—has by now been considerably modified by several decades of revisionist scholarship, much of it growing out of a field known as "the history of the book." Gay, writing in the late 1950s, was already able to offer his readers a good sense of the complexity of the dealings between censorship authorities and controversial writers like Voltaire, even as he took pains to challenge "those who think of the Bastille as a kind of Guggenheim fellowship."[9] Then, following pioneering collaborative studies by Henri-Jean Martin and various members of the Annales school, who made the study of print culture a key component of a new kind of sociocultural history in the 1960s and 1970s,[10] numerous historians on both sides of the Atlantic began to interest themselves in the intricate details of composing, publishing, distributing, reading, and, especially, censoring the written word in late Old Regime France. Taken together, these more recent studies have forced us to see that the business of censorship in the eighteenth century depended above all upon collusion between two supposedly opposing sides.[11]

On the surface, eighteenth-century records suggest that regulatory censorship and the persecution of writers actually increased in France during the years of the Enlightenment. The number of government-appointed censors rose steadily in the course of the century, and works that passed by the royal censors still ran the risk of additional challenges from the Parlement de Paris, the French church, the Université de Paris, or other bodies with an overlapping authority to censor materials that they considered to be dangerous or offensive. At the same time, the number of authors jailed for violating the publishing laws mounted (witness, in particular, the increase in writers serving time in the Bastille between 1750 and 1780). And the severity of the penalties that subversive writers faced grew as well. Following an attempt on Louis XV's life in 1757, authors or publishers of unauthorized works were henceforth potentially punishable by death. Moreover, royal efforts to protect against the informal, verbal circulation of seditious opinions or terms led to a simultaneous crackdown on so-called *mauvais discours*.[12]

Nevertheless, in recent decades historians have tended to emphasize not so much the repressiveness of the Old Regime censorship system but, rather, its extraordinary ineffectiveness and laxity in controlling the flood of novel, heterodox ideas coursing through eighteenth-century France. Furthermore, many of these scholars have convincingly demonstrated the state's complicity in making sure that the *philosophes*—despite (or perhaps as a result of) a few notorious cases to the contrary and the harsh laws on the books—generally escaped prosecution or punishment and were allowed to continue with their activities relatively unimpeded. After all, the absolutist state also actively supported the work of many controversial Enlightenment figures: from Voltaire, who ended his years as a member of that prestigious royal institution known as the Académie Française, to Beaumarchais, who found himself compensated with both a generous indemnity and a request to stage *Le Mariage de Figaro* at court soon after his well-publicized troubles with the censors. In addition, there were many royal officials, not least the chief royal censor Lamoignon de Malesherbes, who were themselves sympathetic to the message of the *philosophes* and made a point of helping them circumvent the law. During the 1750s and early 1760s, Malesherbes institutionalized the practice of issuing *permissions tacites*—assurances that neither authors nor publishers of controversial works would be prosecuted—for manuscripts that could not, because of their content, officially be given a royal endorsement. Historians have found that over the last four decades of the Old Regime, almost as many books were printed with various informal forms of permission, from verbal police permits to tacit permissions, as with the royal *privilège*.[13]

Indeed, a complementary area of scholarship has demonstrated the success of the *philosophes* in working within, as well as around, the royal censorship apparatus. By cultivating the right patrons and protectors and by employing clever literary techniques for cloaking their dissident opinions, enlightened *gens de lettres* often succeeded in seeing even their most heterodox works published in France. And following several decades of research by Robert Darnton, we know that when these strategies failed, eighteenth-century writers (and readers) had recourse to an extensive clandestine French-language publishing world that operated largely outside the hexagon's borders and beyond the reaches of French authorities.[14]

Contemporary historians have thus tended to focus their attention on a different question than that which fascinated Gay: Why did the eighteenth-century monarchical state engage in official censorship and unofficial toleration, routinely (if irregularly) permitting everyone from censors to police spies to look the other way? Traditionally, it was argued that the crown had no other choice. In the age of Enlightenment, the flow of ideas and the demand for print were simply too extensive for the state to check, and the censorship bureaucracy, which involved several often hostile bodies with frequently conflicting goals, was ill-equipped for its task. Gay, for example, regarding the eighteenth-century trend toward the de facto relaxation of censorship, stated plainly: "It was less a policy than a symptom—a symptom of the declining authority of the Old Regime."[15] But recently, others have proposed that at the height of the Enlightenment, the French censorship system depended upon a careful and deliberate blend of efficiency and failure that actually served the state's purposes. Barbara de Negroni, for example, has pointed out that an unrigorous procedure for policing texts still gave both the government and the church the opportunity to articulate their official line and to affirm their power over ideas.[16] Roger Chartier has emphasized the way that the flexibility of the censorship apparatus ultimately protected the economic interests of the French publishing industry.[17] Others have noted that even the *philosophes* benefited to some extent; for if we are to believe Diderot, the texts that sold on the underground market might have been unusually costly, but their notoriety as forbidden books gave them a cachet that more than compensated for their high price.[18]

Yet even as they have put new emphasis upon collusion and shared interests, revisionist historians have, in the end, left undisturbed the traditional image of the Enlightenment as a critical turning point in the history of the struggle to free ideas and their exponents from the stranglehold of political and religious censorship. For these same contemporary scholars have also tended to insist (following Tocqueville's nineteenth-century lead) that the long-term effects of this only occasionally punitive censorship apparatus were "paradoxical."[19] The system might well have become more flexible in an effort to shore up the status quo. But, according to this argument, its unsystematic combination of repressiveness and pliancy ultimately helped to do the opposite: to stir up the resentments of *gens de lettres*, to sustain an underground publishing industry built around works critical of the government, and to publicize rather than suppress the controversial ideas—including the concept of freedom of speech—contained therein. Indeed, if anything, revisionist historians of the eighteenth century have succeeded in magnifying the significance of the *philosophes'* interactions with censorship authorities by making them central to the story of the emergence of an autonomous, rational "public sphere" during the late stages of absolutism and thus to accounts of the "cultural" origins of the Revolution.[20] In the final analysis, the old liberal conception of the *philosophes* as tireless, pathbreaking champions of individual self-expression and the eighteenth century as a watershed in the long story of the demise of state censorship remains well preserved in French Enlightenment historiography to this day.

By and large, the critique of the liberal account of the gradual triumph of free speech has come in recent years from thinkers outside the history profession. These challenges have not generally been directed at the research findings of historians of print culture. Rather, they have been leveled at the very terms and ethical assumptions that have long governed this historical discussion. The key questions include: Have twentieth-century liberal historians and political theorists taken the binary and value-laden rhetoric of the eighteenth-century debate—free speech versus censorship, liberty versus prohibition or repression—too much at face value? Can we really ever make such absolute distinctions between these terms? Or are these oppositions themselves in need of destabilization? In a well-known collection of essays entitled *There's No Such Thing as Free Speech, and It's a Good Thing, Too*, the literary critic Stanley Fish rejects the very possibility of truly free speech, insisting that the force of the idea always depends upon certain exceptions or "originary exclusions" that "carve out the space in which expression can emerge." For as he puts it, "Without restriction, without an inbuilt sense of what it would be meaningless to say or wrong to say, there could be no assertion and no reason for asserting it."[21] Conversely, other theorists writing against the liberal tradition dispute what constitutes censorship, asking not only whether formal political or religious injunctions against certain kinds of expression are the only ways that the dissemination of ideas and information can be inhibited but also whether the complete absence of censorship is ever possible. At stake in this debate are not the details but the broad contours of the familiar emancipatory story generally told about the expansion of the right to free speech in the modern age.

One fundamental locus of criticism of the liberal approach has long been Marxist theory. Marx himself, despite being a vocal advocate of the deregulation of the press, laid the groundwork for a materialist counter-reading of enlightened claims for liberty of self-expression as a human right.[22] His argument took off from the premise that demands for press freedom, while admirable in the abstract, cannot be analyzed apart from the economic and social context in which they are formulated. For in a society in which, in practice, press access is only accorded to the wealthy, the powerful, or their spokesmen, the press—no matter how legally "free" or unregulated—will ultimately represent only moneyed or ruling-class interests. In other words, the market will exercise its own kind of "material censorship," simply replacing the state in stifling the expression of controversial or subversive ideas. Indeed, in an unjust society (such as the bourgeois, capitalist order just taking shape in late–Old Regime France), calls for freedom of expression as a natural right belonging to all individuals actually work to cover over and thus to legitimate (bourgeois) class domination rather than to liberate the citizenry from oppression. Consequently, in much subsequent Marxist writing, the standard binary opposition between censorship and freedom, the repressive state and enlightened *philosophes*, takes on a different cast. State censorship can be viewed as a potentially liberatory rather than oppressive force if it can be shown to help counteract or prevent the tyranny of the market; Herbert Marcuse, for example, in a famous essay entitled "Repressive Tolerance" (1965), endorsed the ideal of free speech in the abstract but insisted on the need in capitalist societies for the state to limit this freedom in order for unpopular and progressive voices to be heard.[23] Alternately, enlightened rhetoric about toleration, pluralism, liberty, and natural rights—despite its claims to universality—comes in much Marxist theory to look contingent and self-interested, in need of unmasking so that its true socioeconomic rationale and effects can be exposed.

But Marxist theory has not been the only important source of critiques of the liberal, humanist understanding of censorship or the accompanying story of historical progress. Some structuralist and poststructuralist theorists, influenced by Freudian psychoanalytic investigations of psychical censorship as well as Marxism, have further expanded the definition of censorship by emphasizing other forms of intellectual domination that are "constitutive" in nature rather than regulative and state-generated.[24] What interests these theorists are restrictions on thought and expression that are not exceptional (like a jail term) but constant and unavoidable, not explicit or spectacular (like a book burning) but invisible because they arise spontaneously out of ordinary social forces. But whereas Marxists look to the market, both structuralists and poststructuralist most frequently look to the constraints exercised by a different, even if often related, social structure: discourse, or language itself, insofar as language is understood to be a historical construct that determines what constitutes knowledge or truth in any given culture. In each and every society, the argument goes, there is a dominant way of speaking about any subject, and this discourse compels people to say (and mean) certain things and makes it impossible for them to say (and mean) others. Thus, discourse or language can be understood to exercise a censoring, as well as generative, function. In a 1988 book entitled *Censorship: The Knot that Binds Power and Knowledge*, Sue Curry Jansen refers to both the precondition and the effect of this kind of linguistic censorship as "socially structured silences."[25]

Two key French thinkers of the post-1968 era have been especially important in fostering this innovative way of thinking about the problem of censorship. Both are fundamentally interested in the connections between language and the operations of power. Both see "the

Enlightenment project," or modernity, as entailing inexplicit and novel forms of domination alongside guarantees of freedom. And though neither is a historian in a conventional sense, both have suggested that constitutive censorship, while a factor in all societies, has been particularly efficacious in those societies where regulative censorship has declined in force—in other words, in the liberal, post-Enlightenment nation-states of the modern West.

For historians of eighteenth-century France, the more familiar of these figures is, of course, Michel Foucault, whose work was so centrally concerned with exploring hidden forms of power and domination. During the mid-1970s, Foucault dedicated much of his intellectual energy to demonstrating that the exercise of power cannot be and has never been limited to a "juridical-political" conception of sovereignty: "the prince who formulates rights . . . the father who forbids . . . the censor who enforces silence."[26] Power is also, according to Foucault, always constituted and exercised by normative discourses or "discursive formations," Foucault's term for the sum total of statements that define an object (such as sexuality or punishment) and supply the concepts that are used to analyze it.[27] For Foucault insisted that dominant discourses, while productive insofar as they generate knowledge or what appears to be "truth," also always act in subtly coercive ways, eliminating other possibilities in terms of what can be said and by whom, in order to assure the cohesion of the social body. In particular, he emphasized the increasing "disciplinary" effect of those discourses rooted in the eighteenth century "science of man." Indeed, as Foucault attempted to demonstrate through historical example in such key works such as *Discipline and Punish* and *History of Sexuality*, it was the universalizing, quasi-scientific, and emancipatory claims—including the idea of the liberation of the autonomous individual subject—belonging to the chief discourses and institutions of the post-Enlightenment liberal state, which also turned out to be the primary (and generally unacknowledged) mechanisms of domination in the modern world.[28]

Foucault, however, shied away from labeling as "censorship" those kinds of social and ideological control exercised by discourse, perhaps because of the overwhelmingly negative connotations traditionally accorded to the term. Furthermore, in advancing his counter-myth of modernity, he paid little attention to the socioeconomic or political conditions under which the discourses he studied were constituted or enacted their hegemonic, censoring function. Here the sociologist Pierre Bourdieu, a thinker less often cited by historians in the United States, offers a potentially more helpful model to those interested in rethinking the history of censorship and free speech, especially in the Age of Enlightenment.

Bourdieu directly took on the issue of constitutive or "structural" (to use his term) censorship in some of his chief works of the 1970s and early 1980s, including his *Outline of a Theory of Practice*. In this 1972 text, he maintained that "the manifest censorship imposed by orthodox discourse, the official way of speaking and thinking about the world, conceals another, more radical censorship."[29] Bourdieu associated this "more radical" and yet intractable censorship with the language of the *doxa*, those ways of speaking about a subject that are taken for granted as common sense or beyond dispute—and thus act to ensure that a whole other universe of things cannot be stated and, consequently, thought. According to Bourdieu, this nonregulative form of structural censorship (rather than the obvious contest between the orthodox and the heterodox) is the more profound form of domination within modern society because it results in largely unconscious self-censorship. For as Bourdieu put it in an essay of 1982 entitled "Censorship and the Imposition of Form," "Censorship is never quite as perfect or as invisible as when each agent has nothing to say apart from what he is objectively authorized to say." In contrast to the individual who is subject to regulative censorship, the individual confronted with structural censorship "is, in a way, censored once and for all, through the forms of perception and expression that he has internalized and which impose their form on all his expressions."[30]

Here, Bourdieu sounds very close to Roland Barthes, who memorably insisted in *Sade/Fourier/Loyola* that language exercises a form of thought control that is much more invidious than regulatory or punitive censorship precisely because it unwittingly forces every speaker to reproduce a particular version of common sense. Barthes states, "The real instrument of censorship is not the police, it is the *endoxa*. Just as a language is better defined by what it obliges to be said (its obligatory rubrics) than by what it forbids to be said (its rhetorical rules), so social censorship is not found where speech is hindered, but where it is constrained."[31] But Barthes does not explain these constraints in sociological or historical terms; his concern is with the internal workings of texts alone. Bourdieu, in contrast, interests himself specifically in the question of how to identify the particular social, economic, political, and cultural conditions that make possible and then limit the production, content, and reception of texts. Drawing on Marxism as well as structuralism, Bourdieu maintains that there is always a "censorship constituted by the very structure of the field in which the discourse is produced and circulates."[32] Analyzing the form and content of any text or statement depends in good part on understanding not only the rules of access within that field but also which expressions and ways of speaking are valued—both materially and symbolically—over others within the specific field to which the text or statement belongs. In other words, he insists that "structural censorship" depends on the conjunction, within any field, of market conditions with formal norms. Moreover, he emphasizes the varied implications of this kind of censorship for different social groups within a hierarchical society; as a result of "structural censorship," the dominated classes—those who should necessarily have an interest in "pushing back the limits of *doxa* and exposing the arbitrariness of the taken for granted"—are, in one of his more felicitous phrases, "condemned [either] to silence or shocking outspokenness."[33]

Surprisingly, Bourdieu also gives a temporal dimension to his discussion of the varieties of censorship. Unlike Foucault, Bourdieu does not directly address either the Enlightenment ("classical") origins of the modern discourse of individual rights or the transformation in the nature of power that is generally thought to have occurred in the late eighteenth century in the West. The focus of Bourdieu's most important statement on the question of censorship ("Censorship and the Imposition of Form") is the language of the German philosopher Heidegger, a thoroughly twentieth-century topic. Yet the decision to open this essay with a long quote from a definition of the term *louche* (skewed) written by the eighteenth-century grammarian Beauzée for the *Encyclopédie méthodique* encourages the reader to draw a connection between Bourdieu's approach to Heidegger's writing and Enlightenment strategies of textual analysis. Bourdieu's evidently sees in Beauzée an early awareness of the discursive "euphemization" that the sociologist considers an unavoidable result of structural censorship. And in this same essay, Bourdieu goes on to posit a dialectical and ultimately historical relationship between structural and regulative censorship in the governing of expression; as the effectiveness of structural censorship grows, according to Bourdieu, so does "the need for censorship to manifest itself in the form of explicit prohibitions, imposed and sanctioned by an institutionalized authority" diminish. The chief implication of this statement is that our commonplace explanations for the demise of regulative censorship with the advent of modernity (read: the late eighteenth century) need to be rethought. Perhaps, Bourdieu suggests, this development should not be attributed to some extraordinary shift in the nature of governing, such as the change from absolutism to popular sovereignty predicated on the protection of the natural rights of individuals, but instead to inexplicit forms of censorship finally becoming so effective in the modern age.

III.

Bourdieu's remarks on the relationship between regulatory and structural censorship draw us back to our initial question: What have historians of the French Enlightenment and Revolution to gain from this postmodernist rewriting of the story of censorship? Can—and should— these suggestions of an alternative way of seeing the eighteenth-century struggle for freedom of expression be used to generate a more rounded and accurate account of the aspirations and achievements of the French *philosophes* than that traditionally offered by historians?

I argue that postmodernist reassessments of the nature and evolution of censorship offer historians a useful set of warnings. At the very least, the writings of Bourdieu and Foucault should spur students of eighteenth-century France to work against any easy acceptance of the distinctions common to enlightened rhetoric and help prevent scholars from simply reproducing the Enlightenment's explicit logic in an effort to explain its cause and effects. Like Marxist theorists before them, postmodernists rightly insist that historians read the universalist and emancipatory claims of the French *philosophes* (such as the idea of free speech as a natural right) in terms of what these claims ignore or even disguise (such as unequal rights to property) as well as in terms of what they make evident. But this is not the only possible gain. The history of the Enlightenment also needs a theory of "constitutive," "social," or "structural" censorship that will lead historians to pay greater attention to the constraints exercised by the structures of a wide variety of "fields" (to use Bourdieu's term), from the economy to the field of literature itself, that existed alongside regulative censorship during the Old Regime and Revolution. These hidden forms of intellectual pressure shape how Enlightenment writers framed texts and contemporary readers understood them, especially as the literary world became more subject to market conditions. Foucault and Bourdieu can thus remind us that various kinds of structural censorship were developed and employed in the eighteenth century as part and parcel of the contest between the punitive regulation of expression and the principle of free speech.

However, some aspects of the postmodernist censorship paradigm pose real problems when applied to Enlightenment France. First and foremost, this model entails a danger common to all post-Foucauldian discussions of power: if domination turns out to be everywhere, then all forms of repression—from that which results in murder to that which produces social conformity—can come to seem equivalent. It remains very important in writing the history of censorship to distinguish carefully between different kinds and forms of power belonging to different political and cultural moments so as to avoid either downplaying instances of overt persecution or, in the fashion of Barthes, needlessly minimizing the dangers associated with the official censorship of the police as somehow less "real."[34] One might well argue that, in general, the postmodern use of the term "censorship," or *censure*, to cover so many different kinds of constraints on expression makes these distinctions excessively difficult to maintain.

Postmodernist theory can also be misleading in a more specific way when it comes to discussions of the conditions governing the decline in the legitimacy of state censorship in Enlightenment France. In postmodernist accounts, the French *philosophes*, in their attack on regulative censorship and their defense of freedom of expression as well as commerce, generally assume one of two possible unflattering roles. In one version they come across as naifs who believed wholeheartedly in their own utopian, emancipatory rhetoric and refused to see the need for any checks on their vision of unfettered communication. In another they turn out to be crypto-censors themselves, eager to mask their true (bourgeois or hegemonic) motives by insisting that the real battle was limited to what Bourdieu describes as the comparatively insignificant struggle between orthodoxy and heterodoxy. Yet when one looks more carefully at the full range of rhetorical pronouncements and actions common to the *philosophes* in the second half of the eighteenth century—indeed, when one considers their advocacy of freedom of expression in conjunction with their broader sense of mission—neither seems to have been precisely the case.

First of all, we must avoid the temptation (which both liberal defenders of free speech and the postmodernists who attack them often do not) to caricature the chief *philosophes* as true believers in a complete free market of ideas, eager to do away with all kinds of ideational control as a result of their absolute commitment to the principle of unregulated speech. Surely men like Voltaire and Diderot wanted to open up space for their more iconoclastic notions to acquire an audience and, consequently, legitimacy. But in fact, the members of this small coterie, like both Locke and Milton before them in the list of great advocates of freedom of speech, were always interested in qualifying the nature of the legal liberty that they demanded, and they repeatedly maintained that exceptions and limits to individual freedom of expression were essential both for public security and for the ultimate triumph of enlightened values. At the height of the French Enlightenment, calls for the police or even royal censors to intervene in literary fights were commonplace (witness, for example, the well-known stories of the *philosophes* themselves demanding that the unenlightened ideas of Elie Fréron be censored), and opponents in debate who appeared to have violated the Republic of Letters' spirit of *politesse* were regularly threatened with libel charges. As the historian Dena Goodman notes, the *philosophes* did not confuse liberty with license.[35] More obviously, when the framers of the Declaration of the Rights of Man, whose ranks included many of the second- and third-generation *philosophes*, came to write a constitutional protection for freedom of expression, they were almost unanimous in insisting (in marked contrast to the American framers of the Bill of Rights) on the need to make this freedom dependent on and subordinate to the law. Only Robespierre, ironically, argued for establishing an unqualified right.[36] The other framers had in mind a system very similar to the English one, where prior restraint had been abolished but where subsequent prosecution—for libel, blasphemy, or obscenity—was always possible. And in practice this guarantee, with its public safety clause, did not even last through the "liberal" phase of the Revolution; royalist pamphlets were made illegal by the Commune in August 1792 and the range of acceptable opinions, both spoken and printed, was continually narrowed up through the Terror, when the Constitution's protections were suspended entirely. Indeed, partially because it was framed in a spirit of ideological compromise, the Declaration's initial guarantee has, from the Revolution to the present, been open in France to numerous reinterpretations and limitations based on the perceived importance of balancing individual liberty with public needs and security.[37] Clearly, total or "absolute" freedom of speech was never imagined to be desirable or possible by either the *philosophes* or their modern followers.

But to consider the other side of the coin, the French *philosophes* do not appear to have been hypocrites either, promising one thing and secretly doing or encouraging another when it came to questions of freedom of speech. They never pretended that their intentions were either democratic or populist in nature. They never sought diversity of opinion as a goal unto itself. On the contrary, what needs to be emphasized is that eighteenth-century *gens de lettres* were often explicit not only about the importance of dismantling aspects of the regulative censorship apparatus of the church and absolutist state but also about the moral necessity of substituting other constitutive or social types of censorship in their place. They even developed a neologism with a very similar ring to postmodernist terminology to make this point. Right alongside their pleas for the deregulation of the press and the importance of intellectual independence, a small number of radical writers, including Mercier, Helvétius, and the Baron d'Holbach, began in the 1770s to speak longingly of a time when "the public" or its representatives might exercise what they called *la censure publique.*[38]

In making sense of this neologism, it is important to keep in mind that the French noun *censure* refers both to censorship and to censure, two concepts that the English language distinguishes.[39] For in this case, these dual meanings clearly coexisted and overlapped. On the one hand, the term *censure publique* could suggest something potentially inquisitorial and punitive insofar as it could be taken to mean the public assumption of the power of the state or the church in the area of moral policing and punishment. In his utopian novel *L'An deux mille quatre cent quarante*, Mercier, for example, employed this expression to refer to a future moment when representatives of "the public" would routinely force writers of immoral books to see the error of their ways and to recant.[40] But on the other hand, the expression *la censure publique* was also used in the 1770s in ways closely related to *l'opinion publique*, a contemporaneous concept in which historians have been very interested as of late because of its seeming connection with the rise of an independent public sphere marked by unrestricted critical debate.[41] In *De l'Homme*, to take a different example, Helvétius waxed nostalgic about the Roman custom of exposing potential laws to *la censure publique* for an entire year so as to make sure that they were formulated with concern for what he called *le bien publique*.[42] In this case, the term was intended to suggest a publicly agreed upon judgment, destined to play an important role in regulating public behavior and thought and formed as a result of individual citizens' freedom to make decisions based on reason and consideration of the public good. Here, in other words, the principle of freedom of expression existed not in opposition to but rather as a precondition for public censure or censorship—and vice versa. And a rereading of the Enlightenment debate around these questions suggests that the French *philosophes* saw the creation of a limited "free market" of ideas only as a beginning. What these writers sought, above all, was a way to turn this abstract entity, "the public," into an enlightened and consensual moral watchdog, a substitute for punitive state censorship, with the *philosophes* as its master and guide.

One approach was to rely upon the regulatory effects of postpublication criticism based on the community standards operative in the Republic of Letters. The *philosophes*, after all, had reason to view criticism as an alternative form of censorship in which they could potentially play a large role; Robert Darnton has pointed out that Old Regime censors often acted like literary critics, commenting on matters of style and quality as well as content, and Ann Goldgar has drawn our attention to the self-conscious assumption of a censoring function on the part of many eighteenth-century literary journalists, whose ranks often overlapped with those of royal censors.[43] The idea was that inferior or unenlightened works, once condemned by enlightened judges, would simply languish on the shelf. But this solution never seemed to be entirely satisfactory by itself. A second and more far-reaching idea was to find a means by which to make all subsequent forms of explicit *censure* largely unnecessary. In other words, the *philosophes* also sought to establish a new version of popular opinion or *doxa* that would require "the public" to act and think in an enlightened fashion as a matter of course. They attempted to satisfy this ambition first and foremost by seizing control of the French language and replanning it in reason's (which is also to say their own) interest.

Here, in fact, is where Bourdieu can help the historian—and the historian can offer a corrective to the postmodernist understanding of the Enlightenment. Bourdieu and Barthes both urge us to look at the maintenance of the language of the existing *doxa* as "the ultimate censorship," and to view the invention of a truly new language—"a paradoxical (pure of any *doxa*) discourse," in Barthes's terms—as "the ultimate subversion (contra-censorship)."[44] But what neither acknowledges is that the eighteenth-century French *philosophes* (and not just the Marquis de Sade, to cite Barthes's exceptional case) already thought about and acted upon language in a similar way. Enlightenment thinkers were, as a rule, acutely aware of the need not only to challenge prevailing opinion on specific subjects but to create new discourses that would change the very terms in which public discussion took place. They also understood that the success of their project would depend upon their ability to remake and control everyday language so as to render what they took to be obsolete, distasteful, subversive, or contrary ideas outside the acceptable realm of debate. Eighteenth-century French *philosophes*, in other words, commonly treated language as an instrument of both liberation and social control. Revealing the importance of efforts to institute new kinds of constitutive censorship in eighteenth-century France does not make the *philosophes* into hypocrites or expose their "doublespeak"; it brings into focus an important—and comparatively neglected—part of the Enlightenment story. The final purpose of this essay is to suggest how a historian of the late eighteenth century, working both within and against the postmodernist paradigm, might integrate the well-known tale of the rise of the right to individual self-expression with the lesser-known story of the rise of constitutive or social censorship, especially in relation to language politics and planning.

IV.

One way to illustrate the relationship between the two halves of this complicated story is to start at its conclusion: the few short years between 9 Thermidor Year II and the triumph of Napoleon, or the last moments of the French Enlightenment. The trajectory of anticensorship agitation has, as we have seen, its established eighteenth-century landmarks, from Voltaire to the Declaration of Rights. But the contours and markers of this tale's other side, the part concentrated on alternative modes of constitutive censorship, have still to be uncovered and integrated into the larger narrative of the Enlightenment. In this pursuit, the Ideologues, those moderate republican intellectuals who tried so hard in the late 1790s both to uphold the basic tenets of the liberal, sensationalist Enlightenment and to compensate for what had gone wrong with these ideas in practice in the course of the revolutionary struggle, provide us with an especially good beginning.

For 9 Thermidor left the last of the Enlightenment-style *philosophes* with a dilemma. On the one hand, the chief Ideologues, including Cabanis and Destutt de Tracy, rejected the idea that the liberation of speech in 1789 had been an error. On the contrary, most of them viewed the gradual erosion of civil liberties and the return of punitive censorship to have been one of the key disappointments of the Revolution, a reversal and betrayal of the values of the Enlightenment and especially its beloved Republic of Letters. And now that they finally found themselves at the center of power, they remained committed to the idea that the state needed to protect the basic "rights" of citizenship.

But on the other hand, even as they endorsed that key Enlightenment idea of a free market of ideas, these same moderate republican thinkers who congregated in the new Institut National and the post-Thermidorean government still felt threatened by the extraordinary ideological diversity that the Revolution's initial deregulation and democratization of speech had unleashed. Indeed, they continued to believe in another fundamental Revolutionary idea: that a single, individual sovereign nation required a single general will and a way to curtail truly dissident or erroneous points of view for the sake of social and political stability. Thus the Ideologues, along with the various political figures who supported them, found themselves in the difficult position of seeking simultaneously to dismantle what Mercier memorably called the revolutionary "logomachy" or "tower of Babel" and to impose their own moral and social values on the nation—without compromising their liberal principles.[45]

As a solution, late-eighteenth-century republican intellectuals looked in two directions. Almost immediately, they challenged the punitive censorship laws of the recent as well as distant past by writing a broad protection for free speech. The new Constitution of Year III (1795) explicitly preserved most of the "liberal" principles of 1789, including the idea that "no one can be prevented from speaking, writing, printing and publishing his thoughts" (though the ominous new clause "except when circumstances make it necessary" was added).[46] In this sense, the early Ideologues picked up where Voltaire left off, hoping that freedom of speech would ultimately lead to general enlightenment. But at the same time, these same men also began exploring the possibility of expanding what poststructuralists would label "constitutive" or "structural" censorship. More specifically, based on the common idea that it was not freedom of speech per se but the explosion of multiple and variable meanings attached to political concepts that had helped push the Revolution off its course, the Thermidorean and then Directorial intellectual elite became convinced that it needed to develop more effective control over the language of politics and morality. In order to establish its own moderate republican belief system in the public consciousness as a stable, incontestable *doxa* (to return to Bourdieu's term), this new elite needed to "fix" its own conceptions of the significance of words as the common sense of the day.

Some might see this dual emphasis on liberty and language control as an intellectual contradiction. To others, it might appear as a form of hypocrisy on the part of those who professed to be "liberals." But I argue that the Ideologues' preoccupation with linguistic *planification* or *dirigisme* belonged to a long, enlightened intellectual tradition that cannot be dissociated from the *philosophes*' emancipatory claims.[47] After all, during the last half-century of the Old Regime, an idea derived from Locke—that the imprecise use of ambiguous and multivalent expressions, or what was known as the "abuse of words," constituted the chief source of most intellectual disagreements—had permeated Enlightenment culture.[48] And at the same time the *philosophes* had proclaimed the need for greater freedom of expression, they had also become obsessed with efforts to seize control of quotidian language and hence meaning, usually with the justification that they were clearing up past "abuses." Indeed, it is no exaggeration to say that much of the French Enlightenment was directed toward changing the way that the public understood the words it used on a daily basis. Consider the emphasis that key eighteenth-century intellectuals placed on grammatical reform and standardization, on the analytic method, on questions of language origins and development, on new forms of pedagogy, all designed to change the manner in which words were comprehended and conveyed. Consider, too, the constant attention to semantics or redefinitions of the meaning of controversial terms. From this vantage point, it is no coincidence that many of the great books of the Enlightenment were written in the form of dictionaries. The creation of the Académie Française in the seventeenth century had already made manifest the importance of linguistic *dirigisme* to the expansion of power. In the next century, the *philosophes* tried to appropriate this authority over language from within the state apparatus by taking over the membership of the Académie. They also tried to accomplish the same thing from outside royal institutions; Voltaire's *Dictionnaire philosophique* (1764) and Diderot and D'Alembert's *Encyclopédie, ou Dictionnaire raisonné des sciences, des arts et des métiers* (1751–65) are only two of the best-known examples.

Both dictionaries can, of course, be seen as monuments in a liberatory struggle against censors, in part because of their boldly unorthodox contents, in part because both ran into serious trouble (not surprisingly, given their totalizing ambitions) with authorities. But from another perspective, these two dictionaries can also be understood as signifying their authors' efforts to replace the existing censors, to do their job in a different manner with a different agenda—in short, to redefine the language of the *doxa* on their authors' own terms. Sensationalism, with its insistence on the symbiotic relationship among social developments, ideas, and language, fostered the notion that the precise meaning of words can never be sure, that unfixability and mutability are built into the very nature of language. However, this epistemological theory also suggested to its adherents that any linguistic system could be altered deliberately in order to modify ideas. Indeed, language could become a tool through which the members of the Republic of Letters might liberate the public from older prejudices and superstitions embedded in traditional usage and then determine and limit what these same people could convey, mean, or even think in the future. All that was required for the establishment of this new normativity, with its justifications based on reason and nature, was the freedom to spread the message.

But if the Ideologues were determined to follow a decidedly enlightened course in attempting to use language as an instrument of social control, they also confronted the problem that they would have to succeed where their revolutionary predecessors—men such as Condorcet and Sieyès, who had continued to uphold the Enlightenment tradition of lexicography as political practice after 1789—had not. And in this context, an old question often associated with the philosophy of the previous century, though this time inflected with the mid-eighteenth-century sensationalism of Condillac and the political concerns of the late 1790s, was broached anew. Might it be possible not simply to redefine but actually to remake the language of politics and of daily affairs so that the *abus des mots* became a thing of the past? In other words, could a radical change in the material form of written language provide the means by which to overcome political discord stemming from linguistic ambiguity and variability and to cement the ideas of the postrevolutionary ruling class as incontestable truths?

It is from this perspective that we must consider the efforts of the Ideologues to promote and encourage a whole range of extraordinarily strange forms of communication during the very last years of the eighteenth century. The half-decade immediately following the end of the Terror saw a wave of interest not only in language teaching and reform but in the construction of novel and specifically nonverbal sign systems: gestural languages for communicating with the deaf and mute, telegraphic and marine signals, stenographies, shorthands, and pasigraphies, as universal written languages were then known.[49] Indeed, anyone who reads newspapers from the era of the Directory will quickly notice the considerable attention paid to experiments with visual and often ideographic languages, especially in republican intellectual and political circles. Inventors trumpeted plans for iconic forms of notation with names like vigigraphies and polygraphies, insisting that they could function as substitutes or supplements for equivocal and cumbersome words. Crowds flocked to see such unusual spectacles as a new form of telegraphy at the Lycée Républicain or an improved stenography at the Société Philotechnique, as demonstrated by the deaf and mute.[50] Most conspicuously, new systems for notating and transmitting ideas were discussed in all three classes of the Institut National[51] and lauded in the councils of the Directory government,[52] where some prominent commentators even brashly declared these projects to be the hallmark of the new enlightened age ushered in by the demise of Robespierre. In 1797 the political economist Pierre-Louis Roederer, speaking at the Institut, characterized his present moment as one "when all minds are turned towards the perfecting of means of communication among men . . . when men vie with one another in order to form a universal language or mode of writing . . . when the signs of writing have, as a consequence, become a special object of zealous interest for the sciences."[53] Two years later, an anonymous writer in the *Magasin encyclopédique* asked rhetorically what Cicero might have said had he lived to witness such developments as "our telegraphy at the point where it is a perfected pasigraphy [and] finally the new stenography, which must take its place among the admirable inventions of the human mind."[54]

What should we make of these numerous tributes and claims regarding such seemingly marginal systems of communication? Moreover, what do they have to do with the politics of censorship and free speech in the immediate aftermath of the Terror? The answer is not immediately obvious. For late-twentieth-century historians of eighteenth-century France, these linguistic experiments and the commentary that they generated have generally registered only as curiosities, odd by-products of an age enamored of science and its myriad applications. However, in the context of this chapter, I aim to emphasize a different aspect of these plans to construct novel semiotic systems: their status as deliberate responses to the language politics of the Revolution. I propose, in short, that the support given to these projects by the intellectuals who dominated the government and its key pedagogical institutions during the Directory and early Consulate makes sense only in light of the significance that these men attached to two distinct principles in their efforts to craft a stable, moderate republic: the enlightened ideal of freedom of expression *and* the perceived need to stem the war of words or "logomachy" of the recent past. For what these experiments offered the new intellectual establishment of the late 1790s was the possibility of a new way of controlling language and, hence, of controlling meaning so as finally to create a new, incontestable *doxa* based upon their own enlightened revolutionary values. In effect, the Ideologues' advocacy of these experiments can be said to have constituted the Enlightenment's most ambitious and explicit effort to institute the type of constitutive censorship that eventually became a common characteristic of all modern liberal societies, even (or especially) as these societies continued officially to employ an enlightened anticensorship rhetoric.

Now, it goes without saying that the men who designed these new sign systems never talked about their projects as mechanisms of constitutive censorship or, for that matter, as in any way related to the promotion of a particular political perspective or social cohort. On the contrary, capitalizing on the mood of linguistic caution and restraint that followed the end of the Terror, almost all of these language theorists, from the Abbé Sicard to Zalkind Hourwitz, touted their inventions as ways of freeing the French nation from the thrall of equivocal and easily manipulable words associated with partisan declarations. They sold their plans as antidotes to dangerous "verbiage" (as Hourwitz put it) and as means to thwart the nefarious effects of "shameful and maliciously shallow rhetoricians" (in the words of an inventor named Joseph De Maimieux).[55] And each of them promised that his visual sign system—because it separated *la langue* from *la parole*—would convey only fixed, objective, univocal meanings, indeed, that his system would be impossible to employ without understanding exactly what one wished to say and impossible to misconstrue. If the whole world were to adopt his pasigraphy, de Maimieux claimed, "alphabetic chaos" would disappear, the exact signification of all ideas would become clear, and writing would once again become "the image of thought itself."[56]

Yet the celebration of an inviolable science of signs at a moment of great unhappiness about the variable use and misuse of ordinary language should not be taken to mean that these projects constituted a postrevolutionary attempt to decouple language and power. Of course, statements such as that of De Maimieux might appear to be merely the residue of an earlier Enlightenment fascination with transparency or the restoration of a lost isomorphism between representative signs and ideas. Or such boasts might seem simply to indicate the popularity of the idea of scientific objectivity after the perceived irrationality of the previous few years. But there was a second, related claim that was essential to the promotion of all of these plans. Their authors also insisted that ideographic signs could be used not only to "fix" but first to clarify how abstract moral or metaphysical ideas were understood. "The rectification of ideas through the perfecting of language" was how the historian of the Institut's Second Class described this goal.[57] Indirectly, in other words, the creators of these pasigraphies, okygraphies, and the like promised the members of the new class of late Enlightenment *philosophe*-legislators, who now found themselves part of the establishment rather than outside agitators, that language could be used to satisfy their chief political ambitions. And in many cases, the Ideologues and their sympathizers were persuaded of the possibility.

First, late-eighteenth-century advocates of extreme experiments in linguistic *dirigisme* hoped that by adopting a nominalist approach to language, they might be able to institute a new *doxa* that was actually reflective of their own values. Second, by coding this *doxa* in ways that made its contents appear universal, objective, and thus incontestable, these same men thought that they might be able to stem all dissent or subsequent challenges to this new status quo and in this manner bring the logomachy characteristic of the Revolution to a permanent close—without having to resort to explicitly coercive measures another time. Here, Roederer again provides us with an example. In holding up these experiments as potentially effective means of social control for the postrevolutionary French, Roederer even went so far as to evoke the precedent of Chinese characters. Contrary to the long-standing European prejudice that held this form of notation as a major cause of the intellectual backwardness of that nation's population, Roederer insisted that the ancient institution of fixed, ideographic characters was a principal reason why China had existed "strong, peaceful, happy and always the same for 4,000 years."[58] The ultimate promise of the language planning efforts of the Directory and the first years of the Consulate was that they would function not only as antidotes to past abuses of words but as a means of staving off the threat of a truly contestatory democracy and securing a new form of hegemony within an ostensibly liberal, rights-oriented order.

Of course, from the perspective of successes and failures, historians are justified in paying little attention to these efforts or the support that they generated at the close of the eighteenth century. None of these new semiotic systems ever became widely used outside of highly specialized domains, and both the political and the philosophical positions implied by these experiments always had their outspoken opponents, even among supporters of the Directory. Mercier, for example, despite his insistence on the Revolution as logomachy, repeatedly argued, both in the Institut and in the Directory's Council of 500, for the preservation of individual choice in the employment of words and against any kind of linguistic *dirigisme*.[59] Furthermore, the moment of enthusiasm for these pasigraphies was extremely short lived. By the turn of the new century, it had already become clear that not only had these projects garnered little support outside of Paris, but even many of the Ideologues had lost their faith in the efficacy or desirability of such effort to control ideas. Both Joseph-Marie Degérando's prize-winning *Des Signes et l'art de pensée considérés dans leurs rapports mutuels* of 1800 and Destutt de Tracy's *Elémens d'Idéologie*, the summation of the Ideologue movement published shortly after, contained sustained challenges to these language-planning experiments. Both men believed that visual ideograms stirred the passions in ways inimical to clear thought, promoted the development of scientific elites instead of fostering universality and in the end were powerless against inevitable changes in ideas.[60] Degérando argued further that the moral and social sciences could never be the equivalent of the physical or natural ones because truths were constituted in distinct ways in different domains. In the political realm, it was the prerogative of the strongest, not philosophers, to determine the form and content of the language. But after the turn of the new century, such arguments were already well on their way to becoming moot. For after power was once again concentrated in the hands of one ruler—in this case, Napoleon Bonaparte—there was no longer any need to think of the French language as a mechanism for solidifying or maintaining the current sociopolitical order. Napoleon, even while paying lip service to the liberal idea of the freedom of ideas, quickly curtailed this revolutionary right. By 1810, France's censorship policies recalled those of the monarchy during the Old Regime, and all talk of controlling ideas by controlling the signs for them appeared to be the residue of another era.

Still, these late-eighteenth-century semiotic experiments, undertaken at a vital moment of transition for the first self-consciously postrevolutionary and "enlightened" European republic, can also be said to have set an important precedent. For the enthusiasm with which these plans were met within key late-eighteenth-century republican institutions was based upon an idea that subsequently became characteristic of postrevolutionary "enlightened" states in general. This idea is that liberal societies, whose key principles supposedly guarantee and are guaranteed by freedom of expression, must also actively respond to the threat of linguistic anarchy that this same freedom generates in order to preserve their status as liberal societies. And this has meant that modern, liberal democracies have commonly replicated the rhetoric of free speech while also attempting, through constitutive means, to make regulative censorship superfluous. Ultimately, in other words, the French Revolution of the 1790s marked the conscious intensification of an Enlightenment dualism—the search for means both to liberate the individual and to foster social cohesion and conformity—that has continued into the modern era. Pasigraphies and the like are admittedly extreme examples of this latter pursuit; certainly, we no longer look to sign language or telegraphy for models for the normative discourse of politics. But recognizing these experiments as early examples of efforts to develop a form of sign-based constitutive or social censorship does more than complicate our understanding of the values held by those late-Enlightenment thinkers known as the Ideologues. It forces us to see the eighteenth-century obsession with language politics and planning as an essential, if often neglected, part of the larger and much better-known story of the modern struggle to free ideas and their expression.

NOTES

1. I use the terms "freedom of expression" and "free speech" interchangeably in this chapter. Both are umbrella terms generally taken to include a number of different freedoms, including freedom of thought or opinion, freedom of discussion, freedom of the press or publication, artistic freedom, and freedom to participate in political meetings or demonstrations. See Alan Haworth, *Free Speech* (New York, 1998), p. 8. Most eighteenth-century debate concentrated on the first three freedoms listed above and, consequently, this chapter will as well.

2. Peter Gay, *Voltaire's Politics: The Poet as Realist* (New Haven, 1988; first published in 1959), pp. 215 and 217n, respectively.

3. Gay, *Voltaire's Politics*, p. 32.

4. Antoine-Léonard Thomas, *Discours prononcé, dans l'Académie françoise, le jeudi, 22 janvier 1767, à la reception de M. Thomas* (Paris, 1767).

5. Georges Minois, *Censure et culture sous l'Ancien Régime* (Paris, 1995), pp. 276–77.

6. "Declaration of the Rights of Man and of the Citizen," reproduced in translation in *Readings in Western Civilization*, vol. 7, *The Old Regime and the French Revolution*, ed. Keith Michael Baker (Chicago, 1987), pp. 237–239.

7. Ernst Cassirer, *The Philosophy of the Enlightenment*, trans. Fritz C. A. Koelln and James P. Pettegrove (Princeton, 1951; first published in 1932), pp. 251–52.

8. John Rawls, *A Theory of Justice* (Cambridge MA, 1971), pp. 201–205, 225.

9. Gay, *Voltaire's Politics*, p. 374. See also Gay's comments on eighteenth-century European censorship in his subsequent *The Enlightenment: An Interpretation*, vol. 2, *The Science of Freedom* (New York, 1969), pp. 69–79.

10. For the eighteenth century, see François Furet et al., eds., *Livre et société, dans la France du XVIIIe siècle* (Paris, 1965–70) and, more recently, Henri-Jean Martin, Roger Chartier, and Jean-Pierre Vivet, eds., *Histoire de l'édition française*, vol. 2, *Le Livre triomphant, 1660–1830* (Paris, 1983).

11. See especially, William Hanley, "The Policing of Thought: Censorship in Eighteenth-Century France," *Studies on Voltaire and the Eighteenth Century* 183 (1980) 265–295; Nicole Hermann-Mascard, *La Censure des livres à la fin de l'Ancien Régime, 1750–1789* (Paris, 1986); Daniel Roche, "Censorship and the Publishing Industry," in *Revolution in Print: The Press in France, 1775–1800*, eds. Daniel Roche and Robert Darnton (Berkeley, 1989), pp. 3–26; Christiane Schroeder-Angermund, *Von der Zensur zur Pressefreiheit: das absolutistische Zensursystem in der 2. Hälfte des 18. Jahrhunderts: eine Innensicht* (Pfaffenweiler, 1993); Georges Minois, *Censure et culture sous l'Ancien Régime* (1995); and Barbara de Negroni, *Lectures interdites: le travail des censeurs au XVIIIe siècle, 1723–1774* (Paris, 1995).

12. Lisa Jane Graham, "Crimes of Opinion: Policing the Public in Eighteenth-Century Paris," in *Visions and Revisions of Eighteenth-Century France*, eds. Christine Adams, Jack Censer and Lisa Jane Graham (University Park, PA, 1997), especially pp. 84–88.

13. Raymond Birn, "Religious Toleration and Freedom of Expression," in *The French Idea of Freedom: The Old Regime and the Declaration of Rights of 1789*, ed. Dale Van Kley (Stanford, 1994), p. 275.

14. See Robert Darnton, *The Literary Underground of the Old Regime* (Cambridge, 1982); *Edition et sédition: l'univers de la littérature clandestine au XVIIIe siècle* (Paris, 1991); and *The Forbidden Best-Sellers of Pre-Revolutionary France* (New York, 1995).

15. Gay, *Voltaire's Politics*, p. 87.

16. Barbara de Negroni, *Lectures interdites*, especially chapter 1.

17. Roger Chartier, *The Cultural Origins of the French Revolution*, trans. Lydia G. Cochrane (Durham, 1991), chapter 3.

18. Diderot, "Lettre sur le commerce de la librairie" (1763), published as *Sur la liberté de la presse*, ed. Jacques Proust (Paris, 1964), pp. 81–83.

19. Tocqueville is quoted by Gay in *Voltaire's Politics* to the effect: "Authors were [in the reign of Louis XV] harried to an extent that won them sympathy, but not enough to inspire them with any real fear. They were, in fact, subjected to the petty persecutions that spur men to revolt, but not the steady pressure that breaks their spirit" (77). A similar and explicit emphasis on the "paradoxical" nature and effects of the eighteenth-century censorship system can be found in the more recent accounts of Roger Chartier, Robert Darnton, Isser Woloch, Barbara de Negroni, and Georges Minois.

20. See, for example, how Roger Chartier in chapters 2–4 of *The Cultural Origins of the French Revolution* uses the findings of French historians of the book to bolster a Habermasian account of the rise of a "bourgeois public sphere" all in service of a "cultural" explanation for the origins of the French Revolution.

21. Stanley Fish, *There's No Such Thing as Free Speech, and It's a Good Thing, Too* (Oxford, 1994), p. 103.

22. See the *Karl Marx Library*, vol. 4, *On Freedom of the Press and Censorship*, ed. Saul K. Padover (New York, 1974), especially "Debates on the Freedom of the Press and Publication" (1842).

23. Herbert Marcuse, "Repressive Tolerance," in Robert Paul Wolff, Barrington Moore Jr., and Herbert Marcuse, *A Critique of Pure Tolerance* (Boston, 1965), pp. 81–117.

24. It is important to note that the Freudian notion of psychical censorship or repression, while outside the scope of this paper as a subject of discussion, has played an important role along with Marxism in encouraging poststructuralist thinkers to turn their attention toward invisible and omnipresent forms of thought control and, especially, mechanisms of self-censorship. Freud uses the term "censorship" in *The Interpretation of Dreams* (1900), "The Unconscious" (1915), and *Introductory Lectures on Psycho-Analysis* (1916–17) to refer to that permanent function which acts as a barrier or guardian and prohibits unconscious wishes and the formations deriving from them from gaining access to the preconscious-conscious system. See the entry "Censorship" in J. Laplanche and J.-B. Pontalis, *The Language of Psycho-Analysis*, trans. Donald Nicholson-Smith (London, 1973; first published in 1967), pp. 65–66.

25. Sue Curry Jansen, *Censorship: The Knot that Binds Power and Knowledge* (Oxford, 1988), p. 9.

26. Michel Foucault, *History of Sexuality, Vol. I: An Introduction*, trans. Robert Hurley (New York, 1978; first published in 1976), p. 85.

27. Foucault uses the term "discursive formations" in *The Archeology of Knowledge*, trans. Alan Sheridan (New York, 1972; first published in 1969). On the relations between discourse and power, see also Foucault, *Discipline and Punish: Birth of the Prison*, trans. Alan Sheridan (New York, 1977; first published in 1975).

28. Foucault summarized his thoughts on the modern state in "Two lectures," in *Power/Knowledge: Selected Interviews and Other Writings, 1972–1977*, ed. C. Gordon, trans. C. Gordon, L. Marshall, J. Mepham, and K. Soper (New York, 1980), especially pp. 103-108.

29. Pierre Bourdieu, *Outline of a Theory of Practice*, trans. Richard Nice (Cambridge, 1977; first published in 1972), p. 169.

30. Pierre Bourdieu, "Censorship and the Imposition of Form" (1982), in *Language and Symbolic Power*, ed. John B. Thompson, trans. Gino Raymond and Matthew Adamson (Cambridge MA, 1991), pp. 137–59 (see especially p. 138).

31. Roland Barthes, "Censorship, Invention" in *Sade/Fourier/Loyola*, trans. Richard Miller (New York, 1976; first published in 1971), p. 126.
32. Bourdieu, "Censorship and the Imposition of Form," p. 137.
33. Bourdieu, *Outline of a Theory of Practice*, p. 169; and "Censorship and the Imposition of Form," p. 138, respectively.
34. This point is clearly articulated in Robert Post, "Censorship and Silencing" in *Censorship and Silencing: Practices of Cultural Regulation*, ed. Robert Post (Los Angeles, 1998), pp. 1–12.
35. Dena Goodman, *The Republic of Letters: A Cultural History of the French Enlightenment* (Ithaca, 1994), especially pp. 201–203, 217.
36. On this debate and, specifically, Robespierre's unpopular contention that "Il faut bien distinguer *le droit* en lui-même de l'abus . . . La Déclaration des droits de l'homme doit être franche, décisive et sans aucune modification" see Marcel Gauchet, *La Révolution des droits de l'homme* (Paris, 1989), pp. 174–78.
37. See Richard Mowery Andrews, "Boundaries of Citizenship: The Penal Regulation of Speech in Revolutionary France," *French Politics and Society* 7, no. 3 (summer 1989): 90–109; Nicholas Harrison, *Circles of Censorship: Censorship and its Metaphors in French History, Literature, and Theory* (Oxford, 1995); and Pascal Ory, ed., *La Censure en France à l'ère démocratique* (Bruxelles, 1997).
38. See, as examples, Louis-Sébastien Mercier, *L'An deux mille quatre cent quarante, rêve s'il en fût jamais* (London, 1774); Claude-Adrien Helvétius, *De l'Homme* (London, 1773); and Baron d'Holbach, *La Morale universelle* (Amsterdam, 1776). Note that all of the above works, each of which also openly advocated greater freedom for the press, were printed anonymously and outside of France so as to avoid official pre-publication censorship.
39. In the *Dictionnaire de l'Académie française* of both 1694 and 1798, the first meaning of *censure* is given as "correction, répréhension" (as in "soumettre ses écrits à la censure de quelqu'un" or "subir la censure de quelqu'un"). The second meaning in both cases is "le jugement et la condamnation d'un livre" (as in "la censure que la Sorbonne a faite d'un tel livre"). The later edition of the *Dictionnaire* adds that in speaking of the ancient Romans, one also uses the term *censure* to refer to "la dignité, et la fonction de Censeur," meaning the official (censor) who both drew up a census of citizens and oversaw public morality.
40. Mercier, *L'An deux mille quatre cent quarante*, p. 51. The passage in question is briefly discussed and reproduced in translation in Darnton, *The Forbidden Bestsellers*, pp. 135–36, 311–13.
41. See especially Mona Ozouf, "'Public Opinion' at the End of the Old Regime." *Journal of Modern History* 60 (September 1988): S1–21; and Keith Michael Baker, "Public Opinion as Political Invention," in *Inventing the French Revolution: Essays on French Political Culture in the Eighteenth Century* (Cambridge, 1990), pp. 167–99.
42. Helvétius, *De l'Homme*, p. 191.
43. Robert Darnton, "A Police Inspector Sorts His Files: The Anatomy of the Republic of Letters," in *The Great Cat Massacre and Other Episodes in French Cultural History* (New York, 1984), pp. 144–89; and Anne Goldgar, "The Absolutism of Taste: Journalists as Censors in Eighteenth-Century Paris," in *Censorship and the Control of Print in England and France, 1600–1910*, ed. Robin Myers and Michael Harris (Winchester, 1992), pp. 87–110. On the theoretical connections between criticism and censorship, see also Michael Holquist, "Corrupt Originals: The Paradox of Censorship," *PMLA* 109, no. 1 (January 1994): 14–25, which argues that censorship involves a form of prepublication editing; and Richard Burt, "Introduction: The 'New' Censorship," in *The Administration of Aesthetics: Censorship, Political Criticism, and the Public Sphere*, ed. Richard Burt (Minneapolis, 1994), pp. xi–xxix, which argues that censorship and criticism are related ways of regulating aesthetic consumption.

44. Barthes, *Sade/Fourier/Loyola*, p. 126. On Barthes's conception of the relationship between doxa and paradox, see also *Roland Barthes par Roland Barthes* (Paris, 1975), p. 75.

45. Louis-Sébastien Mercier, *Le Nouveau Paris*, ed. J.-C. Bonnet (Paris, 1994; first published in 1798), vol. 2, p. 3.

46. On the Constitution of Year III's protection of speech, as well as the exceptional clause that led to the law of 27 Germinal Year IV imposing the death penalty for advocacy of changes in the Constitution itself, see Jeremy Popkin, *Revolutionary News: The Press in France, 1789–1799* (Durham, 1998), pp. 38, 173–95.

47. For a more expansive discussion of the sources, effects, and nature of Enlightenment and revolutionary language-planning efforts, including those of the Ideologues, see my forthcoming book, *A Revolution in Language: The Problem of Signs in Late Eighteenth-Century France*.

48. See the following important article: Ulrich Ricken, "Réflexions du XVIIIe siècle sur 'l'abus des mots'," *Mots* 4 (1982): 29–84.

49. As far as I am aware, no comprehensive listing of these projects exists. Numerous references to both manuscript and published plans can be found in Rosenfeld, *A Revolution in Language*, as well as the pages of *La Décade philosophique*, the *Magasin encyclopédique*, and other contemporary journals.

50. See the Lycée Républicain's register (ms. 920, Bibliothèque Historique de la Ville de Paris) and correspondence (American Philosophical Society, Papers of the Athenée de Paris, 506.44/At4) for February 1800, and the Société Philotechnique's minutes for February 1801 (ms. 1938, Papers of the Société Philotechnique, Archives of the Sorbonne).

51. Plans for new sign systems sent to the Institut National in the late 1790s, and well as the reports of commissions established to review these projects and related discussion can be found today in the Archives of the Institut de France. See especially the Archives de l'Institut National, Classe des Sciences morales st Politiques (AISMP): A1–A10 (registers, reports, etc.) and B1–2 (responses to the prize contest on "the influence of signs on the formation of ideas").

52. Tributes in the Directory include: Guillaume-François Charles Goupil de Préfelne, *Corps législatif. Conseil des Anciens. Discours prononcé dans la séance du Conseil des Anciens, le 18 pluviôse de l'an VI de la République française . . . en présentant au Conseil l'hommage de la Pasigraphie, nouvel art littéraire inventé, par le citoyen Jean [sic] de Maimieux* (Paris: Imprimerie nationale, Year VI); and Dominique-Joseph Garat, *Corps législatif. Conseil des Anciens. Discours de Garat sur l'hommage fait au Conseil des Anciens des premières strophes du 'Chant du Départ' écrites avec les caractères pasigraphiques. Séance du 13 nivôse an VII* (Paris, Year VII).

53. P. L. Roederer, "Mémoires sur le gouvernement de la Chine, sur la langue des chinois et particulièrement sur leur écriture," in *Oeuvres du Comte P. L. Roederer*, ed. Baron A. M. Roederer (Paris, 1856), vol. 8, p. 129.

54. An anonymous review of Adrien Pront's *Elémens d'une Typographie qui réduit au tiers celle dont on se sert, et d'une Ecriture qui gagne près de trois quarts sur l'Ecriture françoise* (1797) in the *Magasin encyclopédique*, no. 10 (Year VIII), quoted in Charles-Claude Montigny, *Alphabet universel, ou Sténographie méthodique* (Paris: Ballard, 1799), p. 50.

55. Zalkind Hourwitz, *Polygraphie, ou l'art de correspondre à l'aide d'un dictionnaire, dans toutes les langues* (Paris, Year IX), 33; and Joseph de Maimieux, *Epître familière au sens-commun, sur la pasigraphie et la pasilalie* (Paris, Year X), 9.

56. [J. de Maimieux], *Pasigraphie* (Paris, 1797), pp. 5 and 1 respectively.

57. See the "Histoire abrégée des travaux de la Classe des Sciences Morales et Politiques," in *Mémoires de l'Institut National des Sciences et Arts*, vol. 3 (Paris, Year IX), p. 4.

58. Roederer, "Mémoires sur le gouvernement de la Chine," p. 98.

59. See, for example, the following works by Mercier: *Corps législatif. Conseil des Cinq-Cents. Rapport fait par L. S. Mercier au nom d'une commission spéciale, sur l'enseignement des langues vivantes. Séance du 22 messidor an IV* (Paris, Year IV); *Néologie, ou Vocabulaire de mots nouveaux, à renouveller ou pris dans des acceptions nouvelles* (Paris, Year IX); and "De la Supériorité du langage sur la langue" (memoir read at the Institut in Year X) in Bibliothèque de l'Arsenal, Papiers of Mercier, ms. 15081 (1d), ff. 262–67.

60. See Joseph-Marie Degérando, *Des Signes et l'art de la pensée considérés dans leurs rapports mutuels* (Paris, 1800), especially vol. 4, chap. 11; Antoine Louis Claude Destutt de Tracy, *Elémens d'Idéologie. Seconde Partie. Grammaire* (Paris, 1803), especially chap. 6; Destutt de Tracy, "Réflexions sur les projets de pasigraphie" (Year VIII), in *Mémoires des l'Institut*, vol. 3, pp. 535–51; and the ms. summary of Degérando's report on De Maimieux's pasigraphy in "Travaux de la classe des sciences morales et politiques de l'Institut National, pendant l'an VIII de la République" (AI-SMP, A7).

REPRODUCING UTOPIA

Jeanne-Marie Leprince de Beaumont's
The New Clarissa

ALESSA JOHNS

Utopia would appear to be incompatible with postmodernism. Its universalism contradicts postmodern pluralism; its totalizing runs counter to postmodern emphases on heterogeneity and difference. Literary utopias often take the form of blueprints for ideal societies, and blueprints, with their fixed forms, smack of coercion and totalitarian regimentation. Enlightenment utopianism in particular, echoing the confident, progress-oriented strains of the Age of Reason, has suffered from postmodern critiques of the Enlightenment project in general. However, if some scholars second Horkheimer's and Adorno's dismal appraisal of the Enlightenment project, others, following Jürgen Habermas, have argued its continuing relevance. Seyla Benhabib, foremost a student of Habermas's work, has taken account of postmodernist critiques to insist that feminism needs Enlightenment ideas if it is to remain viable. Utopia in particular, she argues, is a concept that must be embraced; it is a "practical-moral imperative":

> Postmodernism can teach us the theoretical and political traps of why utopias and foundational thinking can go wrong, but it should not lead to a retreat from utopia altogether. For we, as women, have much to lose by giving up the utopian hope in the wholly other.[1]

With a look at literary texts, Angelika Bammer argues that women's utopianism has indeed remained a viable political and intellectual force even in a postmodern age. Feminist writing in the 1970s, she claims, was sustained by utopian thought even when utopia was declared dead. She suggests that female utopian authors figured their feminist challenge to the status quo in a novel way, as a "partial vision": one that eschewed a comprehensive, totalizing plan, insisting on its partiality by being both fragmentary and overtly partisan, by refusing to mystify or obscure its political intentions. Even though Bammer's work focuses on the 1970s, her argument is nonetheless helpful in looking at eighteenth-century women's utopianism.[2]

In particular, Bammer's thesis can be applied to Jeanne-Marie Leprince de Beaumont's novel *The New Clarissa*, published in 1767 as a response to Samuel Richardson's acclaimed *Clarissa*, which appeared in London in 1747–48. Leprince de Beaumont's novel contains a female-centered utopia that in the end leaves its heroine alive within a burgeoning family, very much in control of her fate and community, a counter to Richardson's protagonist who, unable to attach herself to any community or enlist the aid of relatives or female friends, is raped and dies alone.

Leprince de Beaumont, I will argue, offers a partial vision that insists upon its universality; she takes advantage of woman's indeterminate political position to articulate local reforms with global repercussions. Patriotically seeking to solve France's depopulation problem, Leprince de Beaumont envisages sociopolitical changes that will increase fertility and strengthen France's economic and military might. Yet, one of her female characters justifies her political goals by claiming she is "a citizen of the universe"; though Leprince de Beaumont's suggested reforms are intended to strengthen France's power after setbacks following the Seven Years' War, these improvements will at the same time create a place for women as citizen-reformers of nations in the process of finding their orbit in a harmonious universe.

Bammer points out that women's utopian visions during the 1970s transformed the very notions of "revolution" and "utopia": "Revolution was defined in terms of process. And the concept of utopia became concrete."[3] That is, substitutional revolutionary values gave way to a pragmatic, reformist model, while "abstract utopia," a term coined by Ernst Bloch denoting the immaterial, ethereal quality of some visions utopias, was overtaken by the material realities and anticipatory work accomplished by "concrete utopia."[4] Leprince de Beaumont's utopian vision represents this transformation in the eighteenth century. By means of a utopian development Leprince de Beaumont's community materially models a utopian solution designed to ripple out and alter global conditions; she offers an imagined cure for concrete local *and* distant international injustices, economic imbalances, and political ills. An early feminist text, though not a radical one, *The New Clarissa* paradoxically privileges women's nationlessness and simultaneously justifies their instrumentality as citizens, inscribing for them a political domicile in whichever nation they see fit to ensconce themselves.

Details about Jeanne-Marie Leprince de Beaumont's life are scarce. She was born in Rouen in 1711 and died in Annecy in 1780. A marriage to an irresponsible and inconstant husband was annulled in 1745, and thereafter Leprince de Beaumont was forced to earn her own support. From 1748 to 1762 she lived in England, working as governess for several aristocratic families as well as the household of the Prince of Wales.[5] She enjoyed moving in elite circles; Madame du Boccage, who visited London, commented on Leprince de Beaumont's opportunity to discuss metaphysical subjects with Lord Chesterfield.[6]

During her English sojourn she began to write seriously. Her best-known publication is a periodical, *Le Magasin des enfans* (1758), which actually first appeared in English as the *Young Misses' Magazine* (1757) and was written with an English audience in mind. "Beauty and the Beast" is the most famous story from the *Magasin des enfans*; it is not the first extant version of the tale, but it is the one which became popular and was most often reprinted.[7]

Le Magasin des enfans was succeeded by *Le Magasin des adolescents* (1760), *Instructions pour les jeunes dames* (1764), and *Les Américaines* (1770). In addition Leprince de Beaumont wrote educational works for boys, as well as for artisans, country people, and the poor: *Le Mentor moderne* (1772) and *Le Magasin des pauvres, des artisans, des domestiques et des gens de campagne* (1768). Her novels also proved popular: *Lettres de Madame du Montier* (1756), *Mémoires de Madame la Baronne de Batteville* (1756), *Civan, roi de Bungo, histoire japonnoise ou tableau de l'éducation d'un prince* (1758), and *Lettres d'Emerance à Lucie* (1774).

The New Clarissa may follow Richardson's tale in inscribing bourgeois values and using the epistolary form to depict the fate of a moral heroine seeking to escape an undesirable marriage, but it nevertheless offers a plot in which the heroine need not die passively and unprotected. Instead, Clarissa comes to enjoy the sanctuary of a superlative mother-in-law who enlists her energies in creating a utopian community. Leprince de Beaumont's Clarissa, unlike Richardson's, takes stock of her unlucky situation, chooses her own husband—a disguised French baron—and settles in the Bordeaux region with her mother-in-law, the Baroness d'Astie. Clarissa, thrilled by the baroness's improvements to the countryside, describes her reforms in letters to her mother and her lively friend Harriet.[8]

Since Clarissa has been taken in as a daughter by her mother-in-law, and since her mother, Mrs. Darby, comes to Paris and for vague reasons adopts Harriet, the women create a supportive familial community characterized by the epistolary exchange of moral and utopian ideas. It is a situation meant to oppose the quandary of Richardson's lonely protagonist, vainly seeking shelter and protection, forever unable to act on her own behalf let alone the behalf of others. In their letters the women applaud the baroness's innovations; she has studied agricultural methods, livestock diseases, and remedies, and has increased the area's productivity by introducing new ways of fertilizing, composting, and irrigating. Each poor family is given a cow, and the baroness ensures that babies can be fed the milk—thereby "freeing" the mothers for agricultural labor—by fashioning ceramic nipples for baby bottles. The Baroness d'Astie develops incubators for chickens; she organizes dairy and cattle cooperatives. The latter allow more people to remain home at work, as only one representative, rather than one from every family, need make the long trip to market. These innovations enhance productivity, lessen poverty, improve nutrition, and thus increase population. The enthused farmers praise and bless their benefactress (II 14 ff). The Baroness d'Astie has thus organized and managed the countryside to bring it to an optimal productive state.

Leprince de Beaumont makes clear the impact the baroness's example should have on the reader. Harriet and Mrs. Darby model this response as they study the baroness's projects and attempt to initiate their own reforms. "You have reconciled me to the right path," writes Harriet, who is setting up spinning in her house, "and, if God has not found me worthy to become legislator of a whole village, I am, at least, determined to play this part in my family; and on my estate when my affairs are finished [in Paris]" (II 64). Mrs. Darby, for her part, visits the General Hospital in the city and offers ideas about caring for orphans, educating girls, getting people to work, and rehabilitating fallen women (II 160).

If Harriet's and Mrs. Darby's proposals appear conservative and modest, Clarissa counters with a radical plan. She hopes to found a Christian Union,

> where these words [*meum* and *tuum*] should never enter, and of
> whose happy inhabitants, it might be said as of primitive
> Christians, their goods were in common, they had but one mind,
> one heart. (II 76–77)

She imagines herself and her husband at the head of this community of sixty families where meals—mostly vegetarian—are taken in common, clothing is uniform, the sick are cared for in a sanatorium, and aged women play a major part by running an infirmary, cooking, and mending and distributing clothing.

The plan reveals the novel's central aim: to outline conditions that will augment the country's population. This demographic theme places Leprince de Beaumont's novel in the middle of eighteenth-century debates over France's perceived demographic decline; her project participates in the "useful and public discourses," described by Foucault in his *History of Sexuality*, that in the eighteenth century worked to manage sex in the interest of the state.[9] However, while Leprince de Beaumont's arguments second many of those proffered by the *philosophes*, they focus on women's political instrumentality and ultimately create a space for women as citizen-reformers. To that end, Mrs. Darby points out that Clarissa's Christian Unions would be preferable to unproductive monasteries:

> I should like every village to have an hamlet of Christian union, where those who were desirous of practising the gospel literally, might retire: these would be true monasteries useful to the state. These people would furnish an healthy numerous race, for fruitfulness and health are the consequence of labor and a sober way of life. Their children, by entering into society, would bring there virtues which would change the face of the earth; our country places would become an heaven. (II 93)

Christian Unions will produce ideal citizens whose migration to other regions will ensure the expansion of utopia.

Real limits, however, restrict the text's proposed reforms. Because the scant nutrition and excessive labor of peasant life would endanger Clarissa's fertility, Mrs. Darby and the baroness insist that she retain the amenities of rank to which she was born and had become accustomed. "God has made different conditions in life, and wills that each should live according to his station" (II 94); "it would be contrary to the order of Providence to live as peasants do" (II 129–130). Consequently Clarissa must be satisfied with three-course meals (two courses of meat, one vegetable); plain clothing; decent, not spartan lodging; eight hours of sleep; and only a few servants.

The text, then, flirts with radical ideas but finally buttresses the class system and glorifies bourgeois virtues. Indeed, when Clarissa is about to marry the penniless Baron d'Astie posing as a wigmaker's assistant, she decides that, "We shall live in the mediocrity which nourishes virtue, preserves it, and produces happiness," for in the middle class "one generally finds people of better morals, than among those in more exalted stations" (I 192, I 176). The comment suggests that all should work, contributing according to their capacities; farmers must engage in vigorous manual labor, while the wealthy and the high-ranking, with their supposedly superior education, organize the lives of workers and set an example. The Baroness d'Astie provides one successful model, having organized her village in the most efficient and cost-effective way; the Christian Unions too—even as they incorporate established class and rank hierarchies—will help to "furnish an healthy numerous race" (II 93). Unproductive social elements must be eradicated: the monasteries in France have devolved and disintegrated, Mrs. Darby argues, partly because the monks have given up manual labor; they no longer fulfill "the duties . . . owed society" (II 92, 90). No place exists for such people in Leprince de Beaumont's vision, and no room is provided for those who seek to live meditatively or economically apart from the rest of society. Leprince de Beaumont's active interest in contemporary debates is evident in her antimonasticism and her emphasis on trade, but these issues, including her conservative views about class, serve to further her arguments about population.

Leprince de Beaumont's intervention in contemporary debates about depopulation included a patriotic call for empowering France after its defeat in the Seven Years' War. That conflict (1756–63) with Britain, Prussia, and Hanover stripped France of its most substantial overseas colonies and led to urgent calls for national reform. Proposals for improvements included fundamental change in laws, taxation, trade, tariffs, and financial institutions. Though concerns over depopulation had been raised years earlier, the postwar situation brought those fears to a new level. And while that worry had earlier been framed as a global problem, it now came to be seen, as Leprince de Beaumont's text demonstrates, as a national imperative.[10]

Indeed, for some time depopulation had been ascribed to moral decay, and Leprince de Beaumont's project tackles the problem accordingly. She agrees with Montesquieu's *Lettres persanes* (1721), which argued for remedying French depopulation through social and political reforms. These reforms included abolishing primogeniture; promoting commerce; limiting permanent immigration to foreign colonies; and doing away with monasteries and priestly celibacy. Since Leprince de Beaumont raises the depopulation issue and places some of her solutions in precisely the same framework, she could well have been responding to Montesquieu's arguments.[11]

Leprince de Beaumont entered the Enlightenment debate about depopulation, but she also modified its terms. In *The New Clarissa*, her concerns about French vigor are bound up with questions of woman's social weakness and the dearth of Christian values. Her contribution to depopulationist discourse is complicated by her gender identification and religious idealism, both of which move her beyond Montesquieu and the concern for national boundaries. Thus the text exhibits an unusual blend of specificity and generality, of ideas for practical and local reform with an eye to universal change.

That Leprince de Beaumont spent the period of the Seven Years' War in England may explain why *The New Clarissa* demonstrates a fascinating combination of respect for British ways and a desperate faith in France's potential ascendancy. The utopia takes on British characteristics even though the author's goal is to refashion France into the "first nation in the universe."

> Cities would be desolated to the advantage of the provinces; the rich and the nobility would drive from their antechambers three parts of the idle fellows whom they detain from labour: France would become the treasury, the magazine, the granary of Europe; not an inch of ground would be left uncultivated. Population would be doubled with labour, and produce for the king a numerous people, hardened by labour, fit for the fatigues of war. Plenty would take the place of poverty, always dreadful when it is the consequence of sloth: in a word, we should become the first nation in the universe, without exciting the envy of our neighbours. (II 152–53)

Given her experience in England, Leprince de Beaumont likely witnessed the early effects of Britain's industrial revolution and the impact of new agricultural techniques, which involved reorganizing the land and improving methods of cultivation to enhance productivity. She also may have sought to initiate similar reforms without causing the displacement enclosures forced on English peasants, given the plan she outlines in the novel. A passage from the preface to the French edition of the *Magasin des enfans*—a passage that does not appear in the earlier English version—confirms her view of English economic development and its moral effects:

> To what should we attribute the progress of commerce in England? To the destruction of that prejudice which makes one regard commerce as a profession unworthy of the nobility. An honest and productive merchant can aspire to any honor. Dukes and Counts are not embarrassed to associate with him, to treat him with distinction, to show him respect. The most powerful influences upon the human mind, interest and self-love, thus combine to make commerce flourish. Commerce leads to wealth and esteem. But the English go further: agriculture too is a path to distinction for anyone who excels in making it flourish. A farmer able to enrich himself through his industry take his place among the gentlemen; the lord admits him to his table, to his friendship,

to his amusements. If I were the distributor of signs of honor, I would not hesitate to erect a statue to the first person who had the courage to rise above the ridiculous prejudice which makes one disdain commerce and agriculture. This person did more for his country than he would have done by winning ten battles: he unblocked the fertile springs of true wealth.[12]

Impatient with the aristocracy yet bound to the notion of social hierarchy, Leprince de Beaumont postulates for France a gentrification of the farmer and the industrialist as well as the aristocrat. England may be leading the way, but France need not remain behind.

Indeed, France should overtake her rival and become dominant, and at the same time, oddly enough, avoid Britain's envy. Leprince de Beaumont's nationalism proves strangely internationalist. For example, France's strength depends not on expanding beyond its borders to colonize other regions, but on retaining and multiplying its own population. Rather than view the acquisition of foreign territories as increasing the scope of the nation and the number of its subjects, Leprince de Beaumont—like Montesquieu—judges such developments a burden. Anticipating the argument of Oliver Goldsmith's *Deserted Village* (1770), which contrasts the simple joys of England's "Sweet Auburn! Loveliest village of the plain" with the "various terrors of that horrid shore" in America, Leprince de Beaumont has Clarissa declare that, "We are eager to find islands in the new world at a great expence, France is depopulated to people these climes; and we have, in the very centre of the kingdom, desert places which might be rendered fertile" (II 218). Agricultural and procreative fecundity are thus inextricably linked, while centrifugal colonial movement disperses national resources; a strong France can only emerge if its inhabitants muster and extend their rural productive and reproductive forces and set aside colonial rivalries with Britain.

The New Clarissa addresses issues concerning international politics even as it concentrates on national strength, and it not only looks to contemporary issues but also critiques past positions. In particular, the novel points to the damaging consequences of the revocation of the Edict of Nantes in 1685, when over 400,000 Huguenots emigrated to Britain, Prussia, Holland, Switzerland, and America. A strong advocate of religious tolerance, Leprince de Beaumont calls for toleration of Protestants within France and asks English readers to grant the same for Catholics across the Channel. Yet, tolerance is not her primary aim; it remains secondary to demographic concerns. Although emigrating Huguenots represented less than 2 percent of France's population in the late seventeenth century, the revocation nonetheless worked against population growth. And characteristically, Leprince de Beaumont offers a solution: children of beggars and orphans should not be neglected or sent off to monasteries. Instead they should be nurtured by French society, educated and encouraged to marry and have children. She even projects forward the positive results of such a policy: it would produce 128,000 families, and if each family averaged four children, France would have 512,000 additional inhabitants in twenty years (II 176). In one generation, therefore, the revocation's harm could be undone.

Impelled by these hopeful numbers, Clarissa details what type of education might bring about desired change. "Colleges of husbandmen" should be established where orphans could live in common and thereby save expenses. The increase in trained agricultural workers would raise productivity, lower prices, and free others to engage in manufacturing. As a result, France would produce all its own necessities, which would increase exports, decrease imports, and ensure that "the French would become the purveyors of all Europe" (II 178–79). Leprince de Beaumont's largely agricultural image of France comes to include industrial activity at the novel's end, confirming that the economic comparison with Britain remains constantly in mind.

Women's special reproductive and maternal role in increasing France's population thus gives way in *The New Clarissa* to concern about the instrumentality of women in discourses of national reform and international exchange. Leprince de Beaumont's situation could be said to parallel that of her contemporary Madame du Coudray, the "king's midwife," who was appointed to lecture on obstetrics in the countryside in order to increase rural birthrates. Du Coudray's lectures and writings on prenatal care, labor, and delivery, and her invention of a "machine"—a kind of mannequin—on which to teach her principles, reveal another instance of female intervention in France's eighteenth-century "pronatalist program." Nina Rattner Gelbart, in her recent biography, reflects on Madame du Coudray in relation to the medical and political establishment, and she implies that she herself assumes an analogous position as historian vis-à-vis established historiographical practices, one that requires her to invent a new method of conveying historiographical principles:

> If we acknowledge that our understanding is at best partial, that our views, far from being objective, are inescapably colored by the concerns of our present vantage point, that evidence itself is subjective, serendipitous, and fragmentary, that our pictures of the past are incurably approximate and full of artifice, that they are

constructed by us and not found or given ready-made, *how* then can we distinguish history from fable? How can we convince ourselves that our research leads to anything sound, trustworthy, or accurate? . . . I realized I could make a virtue of necessity by using Mme du Coudray's case to illustrate these larger issues: the spotty, opaque, incomplete record that all historians have to work with, the tentativeness of answers, the impossibility of closure, and the opportunity for useful storytelling anyway. I want to show the process, not just the product, the recognition that many of the pieces are missing, that the puzzle will be full of holes.[13]

Gelbart, the late-twentieth-century historian, and Leprince de Beaumont, the eighteenth-century writer, face a similar predicament; they must forge a new method that will demonstrate how their partial and incomplete materials can nonetheless issue in a story worth telling and reading.

Leprince de Beaumont's text, like Gelbart's biography, is a "partial vision" in Angelika Bammer's sense; it reveals the extent to which customs and social institutions limit women's activities and consequently the records of their lives, forcing their texts to be "partial"—fragmentary or incomplete. At the same time it is "partial" in its interested aims, seeking changes in the very customs and institutions that beget the limitations.

Leprince de Beaumont thematizes this sentiment; her novel reflects on its own reformist goals as Mrs. Darby considers the status of a woman's views on social change. The mother cheers on Clarissa's plans for increasing population and hopes that those in power will recognize their value and implement them. "But, as this is not to be expected, do yourself in miniature, what you could wish was done in great; perhaps, your good example will excite some rich persons to second you" (II 192). She says that she too will aid in the process: "if you cannot engage others to execute in great your good projects, we will endeavour to offer models of them in miniature" (II 159). Leprince de Beaumont thus inscribes a hopeful gradualism rather than revolutionary substitution, where a local model, capable of universal application, will point the way to national and international reform.

To this extent, then, Leprince de Beaumont surrenders to the necessity of a woman's "partiality," her need to attempt social change "in miniature." Nevertheless, these small attempts are complete ones; Leprince de Beaumont's innovations may begin in the provinces, but they have the potential, she insists, to transform the nation and even to have international impact. In this respect her utopian project is not "partial," a plan that demonstrates its "feminine" quality by refusing universalizing or totalizing strategies. Quite the contrary, while she avoids a totalizing approach or method, Leprince de Beaumont still imagines an ambitious community offering a model that will cure social injustices, economic imbalances and political ills. Reflecting on how some might think it silly for uninfluential women to "set themselves up for reformers," especially women who are not natives—they are English, not French—Mrs. Darby counters by concluding:

> Ah! I feel, from the emotions of my heart, that I am a citizen of
> the universe; and all mankind, whatever they are, are my brethren.
> (II 165–166)

Leprince de Beaumont recognizes women's predicament; whether English or French, they are not citizens, and, like the poor, might well feel no connection to their country (II 172). They possess little power or capacity for effecting substantial change. Yet, women's lack of citizenship in a particular nation means that they can claim a greater loyalty to humankind in general.[14]

The condition of nationlessness thus paradoxically offers women a place from which to articulate their ideas for national reform. These concrete ideas for social change, in turn, demonstrate why women should be taken seriously by those in power and why they should therefore in fact be viewed as active subjects. Further, Leprince de Beaumont suggests, women's ideas for reform offer a model of conditions under which women would want to become citizens in the first place. Rampant colonial ambitions, an idle aristocracy, unproductive cities exploiting underpaid and overworked country laborers—all of these forces are working, according to Leprince de Beaumont, to weaken France's demographic, economic, military, and moral force. Citizenship can only be meaningful if these wrongs are righted, and undoing them will reconcile other women to the nation so that they too will energetically participate in its growth and improvement. Leprince de Beaumont's *New Clarissa* therefore simultaneously argues that the cosmic outlook of women—whether they be French or English—can fashion a nation that will set an example to be copied by all others, *and* that France in particular will become the "first nation in the universe," a singular model country in which all people will desire to participate—even Englishwomen such as Clarissa, Mrs. Darby, and Harriet—and to which all will wish to contribute. Leprince de Beaumont thus expresses a feminist utopianism—one foreshadowing the "partial visions" of later women writers—that will both counter France's unique setbacks after the Seven Years' War and create a space for women as citizen-reformers of whatever country they inhabit.

Therefore, while *The New Clarissa*'s "partiality," its novel method, allies it with what we today perceive as postmodern practice and feminist discourse, it nonetheless reinscribes Enlightenment values. In so

ALESSA JOHNS

doing it provides an example of an attempt to alter "the semantic horizon" of the Enlightenment narrative even as that narrative was being written. According to Seyla Benhabib:

> Revealing the gender subtext of the ideals of reason and the Enlightenment compromises the assumed universality of these ideals. Nonetheless, they should not be thrown aside altogether. Instead we can ask what these categories have meant for the actual lives of women in certain historical periods, and how, if women are to be thought of as subjects and not just as fulfillers of certain functions, the semantic horizon of these categories is transformed. Once we approach the tradition to recover from it women's subjectivity and their lives and activities, we hear contradictory voices, competing claims, and see that so-called "descriptive" discourses about the sexes are but "legitimizations" of male power. The traditional view of gender differences is the discourse of those who have won out and who have codified history as we know it. But what would the history of ideas look like from the standpoint of the victims? What ideals, aspirations and utopias of the past ran into a dead-end? Can we recapture their memory from the battleground of history?[15]

Benhabib forcefully articulates feminism's need for utopian historiography, the inscription of a story that simultaneously accounts for individual desire as well as women's larger goals in the interest of transforming the categories within which we labor. *The New Clarissa* both recognizes its partiality and at the same time offers a utopian plan that, leaning on Enlightenment ideals, seeks to improve the lives of the rural poor and create the possibility for women to become active reformers and political subjects. Thus the contradictions of *The New Clarissa* shed light not only on Leprince de Beaumont's conflicted position as a patriotic woman writer seeking to draw attention to her female-centered visions for reform, but also on the problems postmodernist thought faces when confronted with substantial expressions of utopian dreams.

NOTES

1. Seyla Benhabib, *Situating the Self: Gender, Community, and Postmodernism in Contemporary Ethics* (Cambridge, 1992) p. 230. See also Max Horkheimer and Theodor W. Adorno, *Dialektik der Aufklärung* (Frankfurt, 1969); and Jürgen Habermas, *Der Philosophische Diskurs der Moderne* (Frankfurt, 1985).
2. Angelika Bammer, *Partial Visions: Feminism and Utopianism in the 1970s* (New York, 1991).
3. Ibid., p. 2.
4. Ernst Bloch, *Das Prinzip Hoffnung* (Frankfurt, 1959); see also *The Utopian Function of Art and Literature: Selected Essays*, trans. Jack Zipes and Frank Mecklenburg (Cambridge, MA, 1988).

5. She must have been well-respected and well-liked, as a number of girls she instructed, among them Sophie Carteret, later made her a surprise visit in France for her sixtieth birthday. Leprince de Beaumont's life is not well documented; information can be found in Patricia A. Clancy, "A French Writer and Educator in England: Mme Le Prince de Beaumont," *Studies on Voltaire and the Eighteenth Century* 201 (1982): 195–208; and Alix Deguise, "Madame Leprince de Beaumont: Conteuse ou moraliste?" in *Femmes savantes et femmes d'esprit: Women Intellectuals of the French Eighteenth Century*, ed. Roland Bonnel and Catherine Rubinger (New York, 1994), pp. 155–82.

6. Deguise, "Madame Leprince de Beaumont," p. 164; quoting Grace Gill-Mark, *Une femme de lettres au XVIIIe siècle, Anne-Marie du Boccage*, Bibliothèque de la Revue de Littérature Comparée, vol. 41 (Paris, 1927), p. 62.

7. Jacques Barchilon, "A Note on the Original Text of 'Beauty and the Beast'," *MLR* 56 (1961): 81–82.

8. Jeanne-Marie Leprince de Beaumont, *The New Clarissa: A True History*, 2 vols. (London, 1768). The novel was first published in French a year earlier by the same bookseller: *La Nouvelle Clarice, histoire véritable*, 2 vols. (Londres, 1767). I would like to thank Anna Striedter for informing me about this text; she discusses it in her dissertation, "Women Writers and the Epistolary Novel: Gender, Genre, and Ideology in Eighteenth-Century Fiction" (PhD dissertation, University of California, San Diego, 1994), pp. 57–61. Further citations to the English edition of the text will appear parenthetically, with page numbers preceded by volume numbers in Roman numerals.

9. Michel Foucault, *The History of Sexuality: Volume I*, trans. Robert Hurley (New York, 1990), pp. 23ff.

10. James C. Riley, *The Seven Years War and the Old Regime in France* (Princeton, 1986), pp. 192ff.; see also his *Population Thought in the Age of the Demographic Revolution* (Durham, 1985). However, and contrary to conventional wisdom at the time, France's population was actually increasing in the late eighteenth century; estimates suggest France enjoyed a populace three to four times that of its rival, Britain. The misperception of demographic numbers and the ensuing debate underscore France's compromised self-image, in particular its sense of impotence and moral weakness in relation to its cross-Channel competitor.

11. She may also have been responding to followers of Montesquieu, such as Étienne Noël Damilaville, who composed the *Encyclopédie* essay on "Population" [XIII, pp. 88–103]. Other followers on this issue include Mirabeau, the Physiocratic writers, the Abbé Coyer, Jean Auffray, Rousseau, and Maurice de Saxe; see Riley, *Population Thought*, p. 53.

12. Madame Leprince de Beaumont, *Le Magasin des enfans* (Paris, n.d. [ca. 1800]), "Avertissement" pp. 15–16.

13. Nina Rattner Gelbart, *The King's Midwife: A History and Mystery of Madame du Coudray* (Berkeley, 1998), pp. 9–10, 11.

14. This feminist response remains even a hundred and fifty years later; see Virginia Woolf in *Three Guineas* (1938): "As a woman, I have no country. As a woman I want no country. As a woman my country is the whole world."

15. Benhabib, *Situating the Self*, p. 243.

THE PRE-POSTMODERNISM OF
CARL BECKER

JOHNSON KENT WRIGHT

One of the more striking features of the postmodern "turn" is the extent to which its leading proponents have been willing to focus their critical energies on a single polemical target—the European Enlightenment, held to be the first source of the illusions of modernity from which postmodernism promises release.[1] There is, of course, nothing particularly novel about this choice of target. On the Right an uninterrupted tradition of invective, descending from Burke and Maistre, has condemned the Enlightenment for its destructive radicalism—the intellectual terrain recently surveyed to brilliant effect in Hirschman's *The Rhetoric of Reaction*. On the Left, where the political sympathies of postmodernism are more generally presumed to lie—even if, in the eyes of not a few of its theorists, the distinction between Right and Left is itself a token of eighteenth-century thought now destined for the dustbin of history—the repudiation of the Enlightenment is a much more recent phenomenon. But there are distinguished antecedents here as well, chiefly within specific currents of Western Marxism: the early Lukács, in the first instance, but above all the Frankfurt School, whose critical interrogation of the legacy of the Enlightenment had no parallels in earlier Marxist thought. Amid these grand instances, however, there is one other curious precedent—if unlikely source—for the postmodern critique of the Enlightenment, one that seems to have gone largely unremarked in recent discussion.

Surprisingly enough, it comes from the Center rather than the Right or the Left of the political spectrum. This is Carl Becker's sparkling set of lectures, *The Heavenly City of the Eighteenth-Century Philosophers*, which has maintained its place as a classic in the field for nearly seventy years. Becker wrote as a principled liberal—one of the gallery of Progressive historians who remade the profession in the first half of the century. Yet in some respects *The Heavenly City* presents an almost uncanny anticipation of the postmodern "reading" of the eighteenth century. A half-century before Lyotard or Rorty, Becker declared the Enlightenment obsolete, and for similar reasons; he did so in a prose—alternately playful and cynical, mordant and melancholy—that captures the characteristic postmodern tone with remarkable accuracy. This is not to say that Becker should be seen as a postmodernist before the fact—indeed, *The Heavenly City* can far more accurately be described as a quintessentially *modernist* meditation on the Enlightenment. But this is just one more reason for revisiting the book today. Paradoxically, or logically, *The Heavenly City of the Eighteenth-Century Philosophers* has a good deal to teach us about the specificity and novelty of the postmodern critique.

1.

Becker wrote *The Heavenly City of the Eighteenth-Century Philosophers*—it was delivered first as the Storrs Lectures at the Yale School of Law in April 1931 and published the following year—at the peak of a distinguished career. Formed under Frederick Jackson Turner at Wisconsin and James Harvey Robinson at Columbia, he proved to be the most versatile of the Progressive historians, equally at home in American and European historiography. The acknowledged literary artist among his peers, Becker was also the most politically aloof, his relative detachment from political engagement a far cry from the inveterate activism of Charles Beard, to whom he was otherwise intellectually close. In fact, a temporary loss of direction and intellectual energy, prompted in part by dismay over the settlement at Versailles and its sequels, seem to have overtaken Becker in the wake of the First World War; this was further compounded by illness in the 1920s. But Becker's creative powers were certainly fully restored by 1931. Later in the same year he delivered his famous Presidential Address to the American Historical Association, "Everyman His Own Historian," now often seen as a landmark in American intellectual history.

In the meantime, the lectures at Yale permitted Becker to make an elegantly compressed statement of favorite themes on familiar terrain. He began *The Heavenly City* with a characteristic rhetorical move, by pointing to a paradox familiar from everyday life—the fact that genuine disagreement can occur only where there exists a deeper fund of shared concepts and beliefs. Nothing would be more absurd, for example, than a contemporary attempt to contest St. Thomas's definition of natural law, or to debate the League of Nations with Dante. For the medieval "climate of opinion"—the phrase was borrowed from Whitehead—was simply too remote from our own to permit any real *disagreement* with these figures. The medieval outlook, "deriving from Greek logic and the Christian story," presupposed an orderly, hierarchical cosmos, product of a benevolent creator and scene of a divine drama whose end—the advent of a providential heavenly city—was known in advance; intellectually, the age was equally rationalist and fideist, its characteristic philosophical method the dialectic of St. Thomas, its deepest artistic expression the four-level interpretative schema of Dante. As for the twentieth century—"Whirl is king, having deposed Zeus," Becker declared, echoing Aristophanes. The contemporary world looked out at a universe that lacked both divine authority and hierarchical order—indeed, order of any kind beyond the certainty of a final, meaningless extinction; faith persisted, if at all, only as a kind of private hobby, and reason was reduced to a mere instrumental tool; both were wholly subordinate to the brute "fact" whose own ultimate horizon was no longer truth, but practice. Having drawn this stark contrast between the medieval and the modern, Becker then introduced the theme of his lectures. His goal was to overturn a common assumption about the eighteenth century. Conventional opinion held that the Enlightenment was fundamentally modern, indeed the first source of the twentieth-century "climate of opinion." Becker's purpose was to demonstrate that, on the contrary, the eighteenth century was infinitely closer to the thirteenth—that "there is more of Christian philosophy in the writings of the *Philosophes* than has yet been dreamt of in our histories," that the *philosophes* "demolished the Heavenly City of St. Augustine only to rebuild it with more up-to-date materials."[2]

Such was the memorable thesis of *The Heavenly City of the Eighteenth-Century Philosophers*—familiar to every student of the Enlightenment. Less familiar than the thesis itself, perhaps, is Becker's demonstration of it, which assumed a specific narrative shape. He began his second lecture by insisting that the ironic detachment and hostility toward "enthusiasm" often ascribed to the Enlightenment were entirely superficial. In fact, what the leading *philosophes* really shared was a profound didactic zeal and passion for improvement, both clearly secularizations of the Christian ideal of service. What inspired these commitments? Their ground was metaphysical—the keynote of the age was a specific conception of *nature*, joining the descriptive and the normative in a harmonious whole. As in the thirteenth century, faith and reason went hand in hand: a profound credence in a natural order made possible a complementary rationalism. For all of its obvious debts to Greek and Christian models, however, the new naturalism of the eighteenth century was "less ghostly" than its medieval predecessor—its concept of "natural law," after all, was Newtonian, and its most characteristic expression came from the pen of the atheist David Hume. Indeed, the turn toward immanence heightened, rather than resolved, what was already an acute problem for Christian naturalism. This was the issue of theodicy, with its attendant moral dilemmas: "if nature is good, then there is no evil in the world; if there was evil in the world, then nature is so far not good." In these circumstances, the *philosophes* appealed to naturalist reason—a goddess, apparently—in vain: "She is pointing in two directions: back toward Christian faith; forward toward atheism. Which way will they choose? It does not really matter much, since in either case she will vanish at last, leaving them to face existence with no other support than hope, or indifference, or despair."[3]

In the event, the *philosophes* themselves chose hope, in the form of a secularized version of Christian providential history. In his third lecture Becker explained how a general crisis of confidence in reason provoked by the theodicy problem was resolved, after midcentury, by a turn from the laws of nature to the record of history. "Nature" was not banished from the field altogether, however. For the common goal of the "new history" of the eighteenth century was the search for the constants of *human* nature—in effect, the "innate ideas" proscribed by Locke were reinstated here, suitably historicized. Whatever their differences, Hume and Mably, Raynal and Gibbon, even Montesquieu, shared a common faith, whose "essential articles" Becker listed thus: "that (1) man is not natively depraved; (2) the end of life is life itself, the good life on earth instead of the beatific life after death; (3) man is capable, guided solely by the light of reason and experience, of perfecting the good life on earth; and (4) the first and essential condition of the good life on earth is the freeing of men's minds from the bonds of ignorance and superstition, and of their bodies from the arbitrary oppression of the constituted social authorities."[4] On this basis, the theodicy problem proved easy to solve. Evil was effectively consigned to the past—or what Becker termed the "specious present," borrowing another philosophical phrase in order to draw attention to the arbitrary character of all historical periodization. History, for the *philosophes*, thus became a book of virtues and vices in vignette—the record of the Manichean struggle between the forces arrayed for, and against, ignorance, superstition and oppression.

Not that the outcome of the struggle was ever in doubt, Becker assured his readers in his last lecture. For the "specious present" of Enlightenment historiography extended to the future as well, to a utopian horizon—the advent of St. Augustine's Heavenly City, in the form of an earthly paradise. The development of the modern ideas of "posterity" and "progress," from Bacon to Condorcet, amounted to turning the

Christian model of redemptive history against itself, echoing the original Christian attack on the pessimism of Greco-Roman cyclical history. History thus repeated itself—but as tragedy or as farce? Becker did not put the question in quite those terms, but his conclusions left his answer in no doubt. Tocqueville had already recognized that the French Revolution, first child of the Enlightenment, was fundamentally *religious* in character. By the end of nineteenth century, its aspirations had, in a sense, come to terrestrial fruition—but in so compromised and shabby a fashion as to dismay even its truest believers. Meanwhile, the same epoch had seen the advent of a second and seemingly very different "social religion," formed on behalf of the modern working classes out of an admixture of Hegel and Darwin. Now that its first "historical act" had been accomplished in the October Revolution, however, what struck one was not the differences from the French Revolution, but the similarities. The spectacle of a calendar full of revolutionary festivals prompted Becker to conclude on a Laodicean note: "What, then, are we to think of all these 'great days,' these intimations of utopia? Are we to suppose that the Russian Revolution of the twentieth century, like the French Revolution of the eighteenth, is but another stage in the progress of mankind toward perfection? Or should we think, with Marcus Aurelius, that 'the man of forty years, if he have a grain of sense, in view of this sameness has seen all that has been and all that shall be'?"[5]

These concluding cadences give only a hint of the literary character of *The Heavenly City of the Eighteenth-Century Philosophers*, which no summary can adequately convey. Becker's writing in the lectures has attracted the admiration of several generations of readers. But the elegant surface of his prose conceals a fundamental ambiguity. Exactly how seriously should the argument of *The Heavenly City* be taken? On one reading, the book was itself an exercise in Voltairean irony, meant to please rather than persuade, by means of the witty exaggeration of a simple and familiar point—the *philosophes'* debt to their Christian forebears, which they were the first to acknowledge. On another, the upshot of Becker's claims, whatever his intentions, was very serious indeed—in effect, to declare the fundamental illegitimacy of the modern age, suggesting a lapse into a pessimism not far from that of another famous text of the same year, Freud's *Civilization and Its Discontents*—and seemed closer, one might say, to Weber than to Voltaire. Becker himself, along with the bulk of his initial readers, seems to have inclined to the first of these views. "This certainly isn't history," he wrote of the book to a friend, in a famously playful inscription, "I hope it's philosophy, because if it's not it's probably moonshine:—or would you say the distinction is over subtle?"[6] Over time, however, Becker's irony seems to have been increasingly lost on readers. When a symposium of distinguished scholars was convened to "revisit" *The Heavenly City* on the twenty-fifth anniversary of its publication, it was a tribute to its unflagging popularity. But along with the usual praise for the "charm" and "wit" of his prose, the symposium also generated by far the harshest critical judgments ever meted out to Becker. Peter Gay, in his contribution to the collection, concluded his sober demolition of *The Heavenly City* on a strikingly humorless note: "It is time we admitted that Carl Becker's critique of the *philosophes*, like Samuel Johnson's critique of Shakespeare, had every virtue save one, the virtue of being right."[7]

The reasons for this rough handling of Becker are not hard to see. For whatever the pleasures of the text, *The Heavenly City*'s thesis itself does indeed seem strangely out of tune with the times. To see how far, it is necessary only to turn to the *other* classic on the eighteenth century published in 1932, also the work of a great liberal thinker, famous for his Olympian rather than ironic detachment from active politics. Ernst Cassirer's *The Philosophy of the Enlightenment*, written on the eve of his exile from Nazi Germany, made virtually the opposite case about the eighteenth century from Becker's. Where the latter sought to demonstrate the "pre-modern" character of eighteenth-century thought, by showing its debts to medieval Christianity, Cassirer set out to establish the essential *modernity* of the Enlightenment, stressing its novelty and actuality at every turn. Far from being in thrall to Christian concepts of nature and natural law, the naturalism of the eighteenth century was an unprecedented formation, having broken decisively with the great metaphysical "systems" of the seventeenth century; there was all the difference in the world between Thomist natural law and modern conceptions of individualist natural right. Far from rehearsing Christian providential history in a "secularized" form, Enlightenment historiography was born from its frontal rejection, paving the way for the legitimate social *science* of the modern world; its aspirations for the future were founded not on utopian expectations of an essentially theological nature, but on confidence in the power of human beings to alter the world as they saw fit. The eighteenth century was indeed an "age of reason," but its rationalism was completely different from that of earlier epochs, scientific rather than religious, activist rather than contemplative, practical rather than utopian—in a word, *modern*. Cassirer allowed that the darkness of the first third of the twentieth century had indeed made the Enlightenment seem remote from our time. The proper response, however, was not to declare its superannuation, but to reactivate its powers: "The age which venerated reason and science as man's highest faculty cannot and must not be lost even for us. We must find a way not only to see that age in its own shape but to release again those original forces which brought forth and molded this shape."[8]

Cassirer's political sympathies were not far from those of Becker; they shared a familiar liberal humanism. But history had driven the two thinkers very far apart, at what proved to be the moment of liberal civilization's greatest emergency. Becker, writing from the relative security of Ithaca, could look back at the historical origins of liberalism itself with a teasing irony. Cassirer had no such luxury. He wrote in a vastly different intellectual and political context, against antagonists with whom Becker, comparatively uninterested in German intellectual culture, never had to contend—in the foreground, reactionary nationalists contemptuous of Anglo-French *Civilization,* and in the background the far more considerable figure of Heidegger, with whom Cassirer had already sparred over Kant. When liberal civilization had made its full recovery in the decades just after the Second World War, it was *The Philosophy of the Enlightenment* that did more than any other book to inspire and mold scholarly work on its subject. What remains the major American synthesis on the Enlightenment, published in the mid-1960s, was explicitly presented as an extension of Cassirer's perspective. Peter Gay's *The Enlightenment: An Interpretation* sought to restore anti-Christianism to the very center of the movement, describing the Enlightenment as a whole as a form of "modern paganism." Gay was now able to treat Becker's heterodoxy as a back number to be dismissed in a few curt lines.[9]

2.

In the thirty years since Gay wrote, however, the intellectual scene has again altered dramatically. Surely Becker himself would have been surprised to find, among other things, that a view of the Enlightenment not far from that of *The Heavenly City of the Eighteenth-Century Philosophers* has now become a kind of prevailing wisdom in contemporary intellectual culture. There is, of course, no single source for the postmodern critique of the Enlightenment, which has been the work of many hands, coming from a variety of different intellectual horizons. But among a large number of contemporary *doxa* about eighteenth-century thought, two claims in particular stand out as the objects of widest consensus. The first, focusing on philosophy, asserts that the Enlightenment was committed above all to a search for absolute "foundations," natural or supernatural, in metaphysics and epistemology; the second, looking at social thought, maintains that the Enlightenment fostered a credence in "grand narratives" of universal progress and emancipation. The claims are separable, deriving from different sources. The first is the more diffuse, given the large number of potential "foundational" targets in eighteenth-century thought; its most attractive version probably comes in the work of Richard Rorty, whose antifoundationalism appeals equally to pragmatist and deconstructivist arguments. The second has something closer to a single authority behind it. The end of the "grand narratives" descending from the Enlightenment was announced by Jean-François Lyotard at the end of the 1970s in one of the founding texts of the postmodern "turn." There are, of course, other, more political charges in the postmodern indictment of the Enlightenment—including giving succor to misogyny, racism, imperialism—but they have tended to be explained in terms of these first two. The result of their amalgamation over the past two decades, in any case, has been a view of the Enlightenment that amounts to the obverse of the long-standing attack from the Right: here its "project" stands condemned not for its all-too-modern radicalism, but rather for its all-too-backward—or perhaps, all-too-"modernist"—conservatism.

It would be wrong to claim that the postmodern critique of the Enlightenment has swept all opinion before it—but it would also be a mistake to underestimate its impact in informing contemporary attitudes about its subject. As for *The Heavenly City of the Eighteenth-Century Philosophers*, meanwhile, it seems to have played very little role in discussions of postmodernism and the Enlightenment beyond a few fleeting references. Yet what must surely strike any contemporary reader of Becker's text is how closely it anticipates the shape of the postmodern critique as a whole. Indeed, at first glance, the major differences seem to come down to little more than the shifting of chronological markers. For the unforgettable evocation of the *modern* "climate of opinion" with which Becker opened his lectures could serve equally well as a rendering of our "postmodern condition," à la Rorty or Lyotard—describing, in effect, an intellectual climate of positivism and nominalism, in equal parts postreligious and postrationalist. As for the Enlightenment, we have seen that Becker's arguments for its "medieval" character focused unerringly on what have been the two chief features of "modernity" in the eyes of postmodern theorists, metaphysical foundations and progressive philosophies of history. Fredric Jameson has recently suggested that the real target of the whole range of antifoundationalisms and anti-essentialisms that dominate our intellectual scene is none other than *nature* itself—precisely the metaphysical "foundation" that Becker placed at the center of eighteenth-century thought.[10] The latter's analysis of Enlightenment philosophies of history, meanwhile, yields nothing to Lyotard's exposure of "grand narratives." Indeed, it is here that Becker's anticipation of the postmodern critique of the Enlightenment is closest. For it is often forgotten that Lyotard's analysis includes not just a denunciation of totalizing narratives for their destructive political effects, but also an explanation of their origins—a variant of exactly the same "secularization" thesis sponsored in *The Heavenly City*, a point to which we will return below. Lyotard famously defined postmodernism itself as "incredulity towards metanarratives."[11] Who would deny that Becker's conclusions to his lectures, with their world-weary assimilation of the French and Russian Revolutions and coy gesture in the direction of a cyclical theory of history, convey something of the same kind of incredulity?

None of this is to suggest that a reader is likely to mistake *The Heavenly City of the Eighteenth-Century Philosophers* for anything other than a text written in 1931. The fact remains that the chronological markers count for something, and that Becker was denying a recognizably *modernist* modernity to the Enlightenment. Still the presentiment of postmodernism in *The Heavenly City* is striking enough to pose the question of its explanation. How was it possible for Becker to discover the obsolescence of the Enlightenment—or in a more contemporary idiom, the fact that "the Enlightenment is over"—so far in advance of his time? Here postmodernism has perhaps something to teach us about Becker. For all of the contention over its origins as an intellectual movement, virtually every account of postmodernism focuses on two kinds of condition of possibility for its emergence—a specific philosophical inheritance and a unique political conjuncture. Becker, owing to the exceptionalism of his American perch, seems to have arrived at versions of both fifty years or so early. On the one hand, the chief philosophical inspiration for postmodernism is, of course, typically traced to the critique of Western metaphysics and morality originating in Nietzsche and descending down through the phenomenological tradition, Heidegger above all. But the ease with which a thinker such as Rorty blends themes from Nietzsche and Heidegger with appeals to Pierce, James, and Dewey—not to mention Wittgenstein—suggests a rather more complicated philosophical genealogy for postmodernism than is sometimes assumed. As for Becker, it would be wrong to exaggerate the depth of his own philosophical formation, or to underestimate its eclecticism. Henry Adams and Benedetto Croce figure as often as James or Dewey as points of reference in his writing. Nevertheless, it seems clear that the sustained assault on notions of scientific "objectivity" in history led by Becker and his comrade-in-arms Beard—whose climax came with their successive presidential addresses to the AHA, "Everyman His Own Historian" (1931) and "Written History as an Act of Faith" (1933)—can only be understood in the context of the philosophical tradition of American pragmatism.[12]

Becker in fact adhered to a remarkably consistent set of beliefs in this regard, from his first exercise in the philosophy of history, the essay "Detachment and the Writing of History" (1910), down at least to his presidential address. Its hallmark was an emphasis on the "relativity" of all historical knowledge and narrative—relative, that is, to the multiple needs and purposes of historians and their audiences —such as to render the Rankean ideal of "objective" knowledge of the past an absurd illusion. The expression that these beliefs found in "Everyman His Own Historian" in particular have a strikingly contemporary ring. All historical narratives, Becker argued, are "in part . . . true, in part false; as a whole perhaps neither true nor false, but only the most convenient form of error." "It should be a relief to us to renounce omniscience, to recognize that every generation, our own included, will, must inevitably, understand the past and anticipate the future in the light of its own restricted experience, must inevitably play on the dead whatever tricks it finds necessary for its own peace of mind."[13] We are at the threshold, here, of the historical pragmatics of Hayden White's *Metahistory*, with its privileging of "ironic" historiography above all. It was, in any case, convictions such as these that supplied the philosophical underpinnings for *The Heavenly City*, from its opening presentation of incommensurate "climates of opinion"—which contemporary readers are liable to identify as either Kuhnian "paradigms" or Foucauldian *epistemes*, according to taste—to its portrait of both the naturalism of the Enlightenment and its theories of historical progress as comforting illusions, at best. Jameson suggests that the deepest goal of philosophical postmodernism is simply to complete what was already the modernist project of "traveling light"—of doing without "foundations" and "essences" altogether, of throwing one piece of inherited baggage after another overboard.[14] The scandal of what might be termed Becker's "pre-postmodernism" in *The Heavenly City* was that he proposed that the Enlightenment itself, now exposed as embarrassingly old-fashioned, should be among the first items to go.

At the same time, these philosophical affinities were no doubt reinforced by political convictions. Here too Becker seems to have arrived at a postmodern destination well ahead of his time. The second condition of possibility for the postmodern turn is often held to be a specific political experience within the Left-leaning Western intelligentsia—the massive inflation of revolutionary and even millenarian hopes in the 1960s, followed by their rapid deflation and dispersal in the 1970s. The result, on this account, was a new *trahison des clercs* on the Left, as active politics of any kind was abandoned in favor of rarefied forms of cultural critique, which prolonged and even intensified the apocalyptic tone of the 1960s while also embracing every variety of antiutopian thought, including a belief in the finality of capitalism—all punctuated and confirmed by the collapse of communism at the end of the 1980s. There are elements of caricature in such an account, of course.[15] But it is difficult to deny it a certain accuracy, given the biographical records of the leading postmodern theorists or the actual political content of their work—including the new repudiation of the Enlightenment. As for Becker's own politics, meanwhile, unlike Beard's, his liberalism never inclined to the Left. But it was consistently and genuinely progressive, born of a sincere attachment to the American constitutional order, about whose prospects Becker was capable of expressing, on occasion, considerable optimism. As for so many of his generation, the great political drama of his lifetime was of course the First World War and its denouement. This cut particularly close to home for Becker, who spent the summer of 1918 in Washington working on behalf of Creel's Committee on Public Information, for which he produced three publications—a patriotic history, *The United States: An Experiment in Democracy*, and two pamphlets promoting Wilson's war aims.

The settlement at Versailles, and Wilson's subsequent self-destruction—glimpses of which Becker saw firsthand—were profoundly, and apparently permanently, demoralizing.[16] This is certainly what lay behind a fallow period for Becker, in terms of scholarly production, in the 1920s.[17] This was over by the time of *The Heavenly City* and "Everyman His Own Historian." But no attentive reader will deny that the basic horizon of these texts, written at the height of the Great Depression, was political. The opening paragraphs of the first conjure up the ghost of Dante to debate the League of Nations; its closing pages survey two centuries of political history, in order to draw up a balance sheet on the revolutionary hopes descending from the eighteenth century. Becker looked on this panorama with more good humor than Tocqueville, the guiding spirit of his last lecture, but his conclusions were even bleaker. "The great Revolution, as an accomplished fact, betrayed the hopes of its prophets, the Rousseaus and Condorcets, the Robespierres and the Rolands, the Mazzinis and the Kossuths. . . . Before the end of the nineteenth century, at all events, it was obvious that the abolition of old oppressions and inequalities had done little more than make room for new ones; and when men realized that democratic government as a reality, as it actually functioned in that besmirched age of iron, was, after all, only another way of being indifferently governed, those once glamorous words, *liberté, égalité, fraternité*, lost their prophetic power for the contented, and the eighteenth-century religion of humanity, suffering the fate of all successful religions, fell to the level of a conventional and perfunctory creed for the many."[18] Given this, it was not difficult to foretell the fate of the "social religion" now attempting to succeed democratic liberalism, with its ominous talk of "planning" and "regulation": the melancholy Stoic emperor, last of the Antonines, sees us out of the lecture hall. Becker's liberalism was essentially generous and forward-looking. But here, having lost its moorings, it seems to drift in another direction. It is possible to discern examples of each of the chief figures of Hirschman's rhetoric of reaction in *The Heavenly City*: perversity (the effort to create a heaven on earth instead ushering in an age of blood and iron), jeopardy (the threat to liberty posed by "planning"), but above all, futility—which, on some accounts, at least, is the reigning political trope of postmodernism as well.

3.

Adapting Richard Rorty's celebrated phrase, then, Becker might properly be seen as a "pre-postmodern North Atlantic bourgeois liberal." If *The Heavenly City* strikes us, in certain respects, as an uncanny premonition of the postmodern critique of the Enlightenment, the reasons for it are perfectly intelligible. Becker's philosophical roots lay squarely in the tradition of American pragmatism, which has enjoyed so remarkable a renaissance at the end of the twentieth century; and he suffered just the kind of political disenchantment that seems to have been a central prompting for the postmodern turn. It remains, however, for us to reverse our perspective and look at the new critique of the Enlightenment through the lens of *The Heavenly City*. Does our glance backward at Becker's classic text have anything to teach us about postmodernism? Two lessons suggest themselves.

The first is that the *Heavenly City* affords us a certain perspective on the claims to novelty sometimes made on behalf of the postmodern critique of the Enlightenment. It would of course be absurd to deny the originality of the different works that, intentionally or otherwise, have helped form the latter in recent years; these would include, in addition to Rorty's revision of the history of philosophy and Lyotard's of the philosophy of history, contributions as various as Derrida's and DeMan's writing on Rousseau, Condillac, and Kant, and Foucault's archeologies of knowledge and genealogies of subjectivity, not to mention a dense undergrowth of writing on gender, race, and colonialism. The various postmodernisms have inspired a remarkable flowering of interest in eighteenth-century thought, and produced scholarship of great stimulation and insight, for which we can all be grateful. At the same time, the example of *The Heavenly City* suggests that the Enlightenment is yet another case in which it proves difficult to distinguish a specifically *post*modernist from a more generally modernist position. For Becker had no need of the category of "postmodernity" to reveal the Enlightenment as illusory. All that it took was the combination of a thoroughly modernist philosophical outlook, the American variation on a wider "Continental" tradition, and what might seem to be the defining political experience of modernity, a specific kind of political demoralization. Nor is Becker the only mid-century thinker in whom it is possible to discern the early arrival of postmodern motifs: in his extended essay on Fukuyama, for example, Perry Anderson points out how many of these are to be found in the Franco-German figures surveyed in Niethammer's *Posthistoire*.[19] In regard to the Enlightenment proper, there is, of course, also the example of *Dialectic of Enlightenment* to consider. It would not be an idle exercise at all, were there more space, to pursue an extended comparison between Becker's and Horkheimer's and Adorno's understandings of the eighteenth century. Indeed, the central assertion of *The Heavenly City*—"that the *Philosophes* demolished the Heavenly City of St. Augustine only to rebuild it with more up-to-date materials"—is plainly a variant of the second of the chief theses of *Dialectic of Enlightenment*, the claim that "enlightenment reverts to mythology." The *first* of Horkheimer's and Adorno's theses, on the other hand—that "myth is already enlightenment"[20]—is clearly missing or attenuated in *The Heavenly City*, which lacks the former's dialectical sympathy for premodern forms of thought, just as it is without the utopianism, a belief in a future qualitatively different from the present, that persists in *Dialectic of Enlightenment*. In other words, of these two great modernist meditations on the meaning of the eighteenth century, Becker's is actually the more pessimistic. This is precisely its distinction in any attempt to place the postmodern critique of the Enlightenment in a larger context. With *The Heavenly City*, perhaps for the first time, a self-aware liberalism found it necessary, and possible, to abandon its own "foundational" myth, together with hopes for a different and freer future. It is this move, far more than the anguished negative dialectics of Horkheimer and Adorno, that has become widely generalized with the postmodern turn.

A second lesson has to do not so much with the novelty as the *specificity* of the postmodern analysis of the Enlightenment. *The Heavenly City* makes manifest a certain claim that tends to appear in postmodernist accounts as well, yet typically in a latent or occluded form. This is the thesis of *secularization*: the assertion that the chief components of Enlightenment thought, a naturalist metaphysic and a progressive philosophy of history, were merely "translations" of fundamentally religious or theological beliefs into secular convictions. This is the real crux of *The Heavenly City*, the grounds for its exclusion of the Enlightenment from modernity. At first glance, the concerns of a good deal of postmodernist comment on the eighteenth century would seem to lie elsewhere—focused not so much on the sources of its thought as its consequences. Despite appearances, however, it would not be particularly difficult to show that the major works of the postmodern critique nearly all rely on one version or another of a "secularization" thesis, even if only as tacit presupposition. In the case of Lyotard, no demonstration is necessary. From *Rudiments païens* (1977) onward, his key works made explicit appeals to a claim that, for all intents and purposes, is identical to Becker's—that modern "metanarratives" of emancipation are merely secularized versions of theological narratives of redemption. As their antidotes, Lyotard consistently trumpeted the virtues of, first, "modern," then "postmodern," "paganism."[21] The critique of Enlightenment "foundationalism" rarely makes its reliance on the notion of secularization quite so manifest as this; but a case could be made, for example, that the analysis set forth in a text as fundamental as Rorty's *Philosophy and the Mirror of Nature* depends on a background narrative of just this kind—in which the eighteenth-century foundationalisms, whose demolition is now to be completed, were originally constructed out of materials supplied by the older Greco-Christian "essentialisms" that they themselves had replaced.

If this is true, it becomes relatively easy to identify the "grand narrative" on which—as is frequently suggested by critics—the postmodern critique of metanarratives secretly relies. Far from being particularly novel or heterodox, it is in fact one of the most familiar figures of the modern social imaginary, indeed touching at its deepest structures. The thesis of secularization is at the core of intellectual traditions as various as Hegelian idealism and Weberian sociology; among other mid-twentieth-century expressions to set alongside Becker's, there is Karl Löwith's *Meaning in History* (1949), one of the central texts in the modern speculative philosophy of history. Indeed, it is strange that Löwith should not be mentioned more frequently in connection with *The Heavenly City*, since his version of the secularization thesis is nearly identical to that of Becker. This points, in any case, to perhaps the chief lesson of the latter for contemporary discussion—that the problematic of secularization should be placed far more explicitly at the center of debates over postmodernism and the Enlightenment. Apart from every other consideration, this could certainly be expected to foster the kind of dialogue that is needed between the proponents and critics of postmodernism.

For there are not one but two different kinds of response to be made to the standard version of the secularization thesis, each with a long history and its own relevance to an understanding of the Enlightenment. The first is of course to meet the thesis head-on, rejecting it in favor of some alternative account of the foundations of philosophical modernity. The supreme example here, which should perhaps figure more centrally in debates over postmodernism than it has to this point, is Blumenberg's massive rejoinder to Löwith in *The Legitimacy of the Modern Age*—which has the further advantage, for amateurs of irony, of back-dating the break with premodern thought precisely to the Middle Ages. On Blumenberg's account, the Enlightenment was infinitely closer than we imagine to the *fourteenth* century, when the nominalist critique of neo-Aristotelianism gave us our first glimpse of a fully, and *legitimately*, disenchanted thought-world.[22] Other important attempts to meet the secularization argument in this fashion, on the terrain of the Enlightenment itself, would include Gay's *The Enlightenment* and Reinhart Koselleck's various analyses in *Futures Past: On the Semantics of Historical Time*—the latter very close in spirit to Habermas's own defense of the legitimacy of the modern age. The other response to the secularization thesis is virtually the opposite—to accept it as substantially true, while rejecting or even reversing the charge of illegitimacy that nearly always accompanies it. This move has been perfected by Jameson, who tirelessly points out that the accusation that Marxism is "really" or "merely" a religion is a double-edged sword, easily reversed—it is just as convincing to see religious belief and theological system as distorted *anticipations* of historical materialism. Extended to the Enlightenment, this maneuver would return us to Horkerheimer's and Adorno's assertion that "myth is already enlightenment." That is, the same evidence that suggests the Enlightenment might be a *residual* phenomenon, involving the illegitimate persistence of premodern modes of thought, might just as easily be read the other way around: the various narratives of redemption of the salvation religions become *emergent* figures pointing forward to some threshold of full maturity and legitimate self-awareness, otherwise known as the Enlightenment. Whether it is possible for a "secularization" theory of this kind to project utopian hopes to the *future* is, of course, another question. But such an account would at least help to explain an otherwise paradoxical feature of *The Heavenly City*—the fact that the text does retain the hint of a utopian moment after all, and its own conception of historical progress, revealed in the well-nigh Voltairean zeal and passion with which Becker, who was routinely described by contemporaries as a twentieth-century *philosophe*, pursued "superstition" into the heart of the Enlightenment itself.

The Heavenly City of the Eighteenth-Century Philosophers, then, points us toward some alternate, perhaps less polarizing ways of looking at the postmodern critique of the Enlightenment—suggesting avenues for tracing its sources to anterior traditions of philosophical modernism, as well as means of connecting its themes with wider debates about the origins of modernity. Lest this be thought an invitation to return to the sort of old-fashioned philosophy of history forbidden by postmodernism, it is worth adding that we are, in fact, better placed than ever before to supersede the distinction between speculative philosophies of history and more empirically grounded *theories* of historical change and development. Neither the postmodernist prohibition of "grand narratives" nor the "end of history" itself have been able to prevent a great flowering of the grandest historical sociology—neo-Weberian, neo-Marxist, neo-liberal—in recent years, a sociology of unprecedented analytical power and empirical range, much of it full of relevance for the Enlightenment. Paul de Man apparently once averred that "the trouble with Marxism is that it has no way of understanding the eighteenth century"[23]—Marxism, and everyone else, one is tempted to add. The Enlightenment remains the crux of modern intellectual history, as the intensity of the renewed debate over its meaning at the end of the twentieth century attests. But this is a good time for making still another effort to grapple with its mysteries. Even or perhaps especially for those who are more inclined than Becker or his postmodernist successors to argue for the actuality of the Enlightenment, *The Heavenly City* is likely to remain an indispensable reference.

NOTES

1. I would like to thank Dan Gordon for his invitation to contribute to the issue of *Historical Reflections* from which this collection originated; and Robert Wokler, for his inspiration and encouragement to write on this topic.
2. Carl L. Becker, *The Heavenly City of the Eighteenth-Century Philosophers* (New Haven, 1932), p. 31.
3. Ibid., p. 69.
4. Ibid., pp. 102–103.
5. Ibid., pp. 167–68.
6. Cited in Charlotte Watkins Smith, *Carl Becker: On History & the Climate of Opinion* (Ithaca, 1956), p. 212.
7. Peter Gay, "Carl Becker's Heavenly City," in Raymond O. Lockwood, ed., *Carl Becker's Heavenly City Revisited* (Ithaca, 1958), p. 51.
8. Ernst Cassirer, *The Philosophy of the Enlightenment*, trans. Fritz C. A. Koelln and James P. Pettegrove (Princeton, 1951), p. xii.
9. For Gay's homage to Cassirer, see *The Enlightenment: An Interpretation*, Vol. 1: *The Rise of Modern Paganism* (New York, 1966), pp. 423–25, 426; for the dismissal of Becker, p. 427.
10. See Fredric Jameson, "The Antinomies of Postmodernity," in *The Seeds of Time* (New York, 1994), pp. 44–52.
11. Jean-François Lyotard, *The Postmodern Condition: A Report on Knowledge*, trans. Geoff Bennington and Brian Massumi (Minneapolis, 1984), p. xxiv.
12. For this episode, see, of course, Peter Novick's marvelous reconstruction in *That Noble Dream: The "Objectivity Question" and the American Historical Profession* (Cambridge, 1988), especially chapters 7 and 8.
13. Carl Becker, "Everyman His Own Historian" in *Everyman His Own Historian* (New York, 1935), pp. 245, 253.
14. Jameson, "The Antinomies of Postmodernity," pp. 35–39.
15. The most caustic version of which can probably be found in Alex Callinicos, *Against Postmodernism* (New York, 1990), especially chapter 5.
16. The best evidence for which is Becker's correspondence, above all to his fellow historian William Dodd: "The war and what has come out of it has carried me very

rapidly along certain lines of thought which have always been more congenial to my temperament than to yours. I have always been susceptible to the impression of the futility of life, and always easily persuaded to regard history as no more than the meaningless resolution of blind forces which struggling men—good men and bad—do not understand and cannot control, although they amuse themselves with the pleasing illusion that they do. The war and the peace (God save the mark!) have only immensely deepened this illusion. . . . The war is inexplicable on any ground of reason, or common sense, or decent aspiration, or even of intelligent self interest; on the contrary it was as a whole the most futile and aimless, the most desolating and repulsive exhibition of human power and cruelty without compensating advantage that has ever been on earth. This is the result of some thousands of years of what men like to speak of as 'political, economic, intellectual, and moral Progress.' If this is progress, what in Heaven's name would retardation be!" Letter to William E. Dodd, 17 June 1920, in *"What Is the Good of History?" Selected Letters of Carl L. Becker, 1900–1945*, ed. Michael Kammen (Ithaca, 1973), pp. 71–72.

17. Wilkins characterized the subject of his intellectual biography as a "tired liberal" in the 1920s: Burleigh Taylor Wilkins, *Carl Becker: A Biographical Study in American Intellectual History* (Cambridge, MA., 1961), chapter 8.

18. Becker, *The Heavenly City*, pp. 160–61.

19. See in particular his remarks on Alexandre Kojève: Perry Anderson, "The Ends of History" in *A Zone of Engagement* (London, 1992), pp. 326–27.

20. For these theses, see Max Horkheimer and Theodor W. Adorno, *Dialectic of Enlightenment*, trans. John Cumming (New York, 1988), p. xvi.

21. For a shrewd analysis of the surprising convergences between Lyotard and Peter Gay in this regard, see Martin Jay, "Modern and Postmodern Paganism: Peter Gay and Jean-François Lyotard," *Cultural Semantics* (Amherst, 1998), pp. 181–96.

22. *The Legitimacy of the Modern Age* was first published in 1966; the English translation (Cambridge, MA., 1983), was of the second edition, revised to respond to the criticisms of Löwith, Gadamer, and others. Blumenberg's privileging of late-medieval philosophy, and nominalism in particular, makes it less surprising that historians have on occasion found it possible to turn Becker completely insideout, by tracing the origins of postmodernism itself to the Enlightenment. For a stimulating example, see Emmet Kennedy, "Anticipations of Postmodernist Enlightenment Epistemology" in Sven-Eric Liedman, ed., *The Postmodernist Critique of the Project of Enlightenment* (Amsterdam, 1997), pp. 105–21.

23. Reported in Fredric Jameson, "Immanence and Nominalism in Postmodern Theoretical Discourse," *Postmodernism, or, The Cultural Logic of Late Capitalism* (Durham, 1991), p. 221.

FOUCAULT, NIETZSCHE, ENLIGHTENMENT

Some Historical Considerations

LOUIS MILLER

I.

A declaration of allegiance to the French Enlightenment marks a decisive turning point in Nietzsche's development.[1] In 1878 the young professor of philology, who until then had made himself known, through *The Birth of Tragedy* (1872) and four *Untimely Meditations* (1873–1876), as a disciple of Schopenhauer and of Wagner, published a work entitled *Human, All Too Human,* with a motto from Descartes and a dedication to Voltaire. The attempt to situate this dramatic moment in Nietzsche's development as a whole encounters difficulties. On the one hand, Nietzsche's demonstrative repudiation of Schopenhauer and Wagner is comparable in important respects to Marx's break from Hegel and from Young Hegelianism in 1844–45. It is a break that defines Nietzsche's entrance into his own as a thinker, in that Nietzsche in 1878 ceased to be anyone's disciple and embarked on an independent project of thought which displays a recognizable continuity extending at least to his late work, *On the Genealogy of Morals* (1888). It is a break that seems to define the landscape of nineteenth-century German intellectual history: again like Marx's break from Hegel, Nietzsche's turn against Schopenhauer represents a momentous antimetaphysical and antitheological turn against a major representative of post-Kantian idealism. On the other hand, while Nietzsche's preoccupation with the French Enlightenment does not cease with *Human, All Too Human,* it does notably recede, so that the identification with Voltaire, the affiliation with the self-styled freethinkers Paul Ree and Lou Salome, and the emphasis on the contributions of natural science and especially Darwinism to philosophical method mark merely an episode, a "middle period" (often termed "positivistic" or "skeptical") in Nietzsche's development which he passed through before arriving at his "own" thought.

In the following I will offer a tentative interpretation of what I take to be some important aspects of the "Enlightenment moment" in Nietzsche's career: its emblematic significance as a passing episode, the deeper roots of this episode in his prior development and in the intellectual context on which he drew, and the more enduring significance for Nietzsche's thought of a turn toward a genealogy of morals, which was to survive his identification with Voltaire. I will use this account to frame an examination of some key points in Michel Foucault's "Nietzsche, Genealogy, History." Foucault's is a famous and in many ways representative postmodern evocation of Nietzsche, which is exceptional in offering arguments of a roughly traditional kind about where and when properly "genealogical" techniques appear in Nietzsche's writings. By entering into a micrological engagement with Foucault I hope to make a small contribution not only to addressing the general theme of this volume, but to bridging the gap between scholarship of a traditional kind and postmodern intellectual activity in an area where it happens to be particularly wide: in Nietzsche studies.

II.

The literature stimulated by the question of Marx's relationship to Hegel has made familiar the difficulties of "coming after Hegel": of finding oneself, an adherent of Hegelianism after Hegel's death in 1831, at the end of Spirit's journey, but confronted with a Prussian state which refused to fully shoulder its assigned world-historical task of embodying a successful Protestant modernity. Yet to be sorted out in a comparably satisfactory way by historians are the difficulties relevant to Nietzsche's early development, namely those which attended coming after Hegel's antipode, Schopenhauer. The blossoming of Schopenhauer's reputation after 1848; the campaign directed by Schopenhauer himself until his death in 1859 to vindicate his claim to be Kant's true successor; the rise of a generation of thinkers inspired by Schopenhauer, such as Eugen Dühring and Eduard von Hartmann: within and between each of these branches of "Schopenhauerianism" lived tensions for which even most Nietzsche specialists lack basic points of orientation.

These tensions are prefigured in Schopenhauer's own work and career, in the division between the masterpiece of his youth, *The World as Will and Representation* (1819), and his best-seller of the post-1848 period, *Parerga and Paralipomena* (1851).[2] Schopenhauer presented the first as the uniquely true continuation of Kant's transcendental turn, as the discursive presentation of a single irrefragable aperçu accessible only to kindred spirits, and as the culmination of all human philosophical endeavor.[3] The second formed Schopenhauer's contribution to the postrevolutionary Schopenhauer hagiography. It retailed a somber, but worldly and urbane *Lebensweisheit* which Schopenhauer offered as a frankly subphilosophical condescension to the needs of a humanity incapable, in its mass, of attaining to or sustaining the world-denying vision. Finally, Schopenhauer complicated the tension that already existed between these two dispensations of his wisdom, by seeking to bring the *Zeitgeist* on his side—an incongruous enterprise when viewed from within the suppositions of his own system, which derived from Kant the doctrine that time is illusory. He sought from contemporary developments in the natural sciences a confirmation of his views on will, causality, and teleology in nature,[4] and speculated that the public "victory" of his philosophy could play a critical role in an age in which the Christian religion was dissolving once and for all and the illusions of Protestant liberalism were being laid bare. One of his key polemical motifs had prophetic or revolutionary implications, and it was indissolubly linked to the heart of his philosophy: Schopenhauer uncoupled transcendental idealism from historical, "Jewish-optimistic" Christianity. He recast Kant's philosophy of practical reason to deny free will, moral accountability, and the possibility of a philosophical doctrine of moral repentance. To these doctrines, which formed the basis of Kant's philosophical translation of the Pauline theology of justification, Schopenhauer opposed his own violent reading of Paul, of Augustine's anti-Pelagian writings, and of Luther's *de servo arbitrio*. He argued that true philosophy coincided not with the pseudo-Christian, really Jewish, notion of repentance toward a transcendent God, but with non-Judaic, that is quietist Christianity; and that this philosophical-religious truth in turn ultimately coincided with Hindu and Buddhist wisdom.[5] Schopenhauer's linkage of this animus against Jewish "optimism" and "judaized"-Pelagian Christianity to a polemic against modern liberal and democratic tendencies, and especially against the Hegelian project of achieving a Christian modernity, didn't lead him to work out an anti-Hegelian genealogy of modernity, but it would seem to lie at the root of later efforts in this direction by Eugen Dühring and Nietzsche.[6]

No one branch of Schopenhauer's postrevolutionary following seems to have been able to sustain within itself the tensions which the force of Schopenhauer's personality held together. Schopenhauer's immediate disciples, the "school" proper, produced a hagiography which highlighted the theme of genius, dramatized Schopenhauer's lonely quest for recognition as Kant's true successor, stylized the "sage of

Frankfurt" as the authentic living representative of the *Goethezeit* against the historicization of that period by the postrevolutionary heirs to middle Hegelianism, and presented Schopenhauerianism as a kind of conventicle. There was no substantive continuation or criticism of Schopenhauer's thinking: the mystique with which Schopenhauer himself surrounded his teaching was invoked against all technical criticisms.[7]

A markedly different line of Schopenhauer's influence was represented above all by Eugen Dühring and Eduard von Hartmann,[8] who did not belong to the Schopenhauer conventicle proper and did not consider themselves primarily Schopenhauerians. This group of thinkers took up the most timely aspects of his philosophizing, such as the opening he provided to naturalism through his conception of the Kantian *a priori* as rooted in brain physiology, his general emphasis on the animality of humanity, and the invitation Schopenhauer's pessimism provided to recast the liberal history of progress, with the help of Malthusian considerations, as a history of disillusionment. But they were able to activate these motifs only at the cost of abandoning the cult of genius, more especially Schopenhauer's orientation of the concept of genius toward world-denying sainthood, and the technical doctrines in which Schopenhauer rooted this ideal. On this fundamental point they accepted the central standing criticism of Schopenhauer's system: that his idea of a cessation of willing in the saint, supposed to follow from perfect intellectual insight into the meaninglessness of the will's striving, was incompatible with his basic teaching that intellect is entirely accidental to will and entirely its instrument. Both thinkers referred the question of the relationship between will and intellect not as Schopenhauer had to the saint and to his transcendence of the ordinary world of social life and of space and time altogether[9]—a transcendence experienced at a remove by philosopher and artist—but to the cumulative and collective disillusionment of humanity in the course of a civilizational history which itself emerged from an animal prehistory. This new plateau of consciousness could be interpreted, as by von Hartmann, as preparatory to a collective euthanasia-suicide of humanity; or, as by Dühring, as an achievement of enlightenment about the roots of the phenomena of world-affirmation and world-rejection, which would permit a new scientific and philosophical endeavor to systematically enhance the "value of life."

At this point we may make some preliminary observations about Nietzsche's turn toward a positive estimation of the Anglo-French Enlightenment and certain nineteenth-century currents of thought, especially those identified with Darwin and Spencer, and a range of literature in anthropology and the history of religion associated with the continuation of the Enlightenment. It is often overlooked that Nietzsche's turn toward the Enlightenment was among other things a turn toward a certain region of Schopenhauer's own thought. It was a turn, first, toward the eudaemonistic world-wisdom and the French moralists' hermeneutic of moral suspicion which Schopenhauer deployed in the *Parerga and Paralipomena;* then, toward Schopenhauer's prophecy of Christianity's demise; and perhaps most important, toward his insistence on the philosophical invalidity of the Christian account of moral accountability. There are many precedents in the Schopenhauer literature for Nietzsche's decision to bring these aspects of Schopenhauer's thought to the foreground, while rejecting the ideal of world-denial. *Parerga and Paralipomena* provided a stylistic model—the aphoristic form—and a partial topical template for Nietzsche's work from *Human, All Too Human* on, excepting *Zarathustra* and the last works but including even *Beyond Good and Evil:* the roster of topics comprehending 'the world,' the individual in relationship to himself, to women, to society, to the state, and also Nietzsche's posing as a "good European," go back to the disposition of Schopenhauer's work of world-wisdom. Paul Ree, who has often been represented in the Nietzsche literature in the way in which he was seen by Nietzsche's friends, as the man who helped to turn Nietzsche toward a corrosive Voltairean skepticism, may in fact be seen as a Schopenhauerian in this sense. A look at the French motto and at the table of contents of his *Psychologische Beobachtungen,* the first work of Ree's that Nietzsche read, shows a clear imitation of the *Parerga and Paralipomena.* In his later works, such as *Die Illusion der Willensfreiheit: Ihre Ursachen und ihre Folgen* (1885), Ree labored central Schopenhauerian topics. Even the distinctly optimistic turn in Ree and Nietzsche, the affirmation of civilizational progress, of the role of science in furthering it, and the linkage of these two aspects of progress to the overcoming of the Judaeo-Christian "illusion of free will" and cognate pseudo-concepts in favor of scientific (especially Darwinian and Spencerian) eudaemonistic analysis, had parallels in Dühring—whom Nietzsche studied intensively. It fits with these considerations that Nietzsche, once he had given dramatic profile to his anti-Wagnerian turn by publicly celebrating Voltaire and rejecting Schopenhauer's pessimism,' at a later stage of his thinking declared his fundamental loyalty to the Schopenhauer "who lived and died a 'Voltairean'," that is, an anti-Christian such as no German philosopher had been.[10]

Reflection on the Schopenhauerian background, then, reveals a large potential within Schopenhauerian thought for a turn toward the Anglo-French—loosely, anti-Christian, skeptical, and positivistic—Enlightenment,[11] and on the valence which that turn might carry. The importance of Dühring and von Hartmann for Nietzsche deserves more extended notice here, since they are as little read today as the Young Hegelians would be were it not that Karl Marx was at one time one of them.[12] Meticulous scholarship has demonstrated just how intensive was Nietzsche's preoccupation with these thinkers, and how lasting was their imprint on Nietzsche's work.[13] Nietzsche's public reckoning with von Hartmann in the second *Untimely Meditation* makes evident that it was first von Hartmann who conjured up for Nietzsche the specter of the last man, and Nietzsche first encountered the analysis of *ressentiment* in Dühring. These are only two indices of the underlying importance of these two thinkers: no other philosophical writers did more to transpose Schopenhauer's analysis of the human condition into a project of enlightenment involving a genealogy of morals. Schopenhauer treats all philosophical cognition as derivative from the saintly cognition of the meaninglessness of human striving, and the identity of all human wills in Will. The saints see through and beyond the realm of moral account-ability, the realm of good and evil and of Kant's "Sollen," and transcend it in the sense of escaping altogether from motivated action. Dühring and von Hartmann, in accordance with their development of Schopenhauer's thought, treat the realm of moral accountability as an historically evolved complex. The philosopher sees through and beyond moral accountability by reconstructing its prehistorical origin and his-torical evolution, and points toward a transcendence of the realm of good and evil not in the quietism of the saints, but in the collective future of humanity. The immediate historical roots of Nietzsche's ver-sion of the hermeneutics of suspicion[14] lie here.

The fundamental significance of their innovations may be brought out by a more systematic comparison with Schopenhauer.[15] According to Schopenhauer, Will utterly transcends the realm of time and individ-uation; the doctrine of individual free will and its concomitants, includ-ing the Kantian "thou shalt," are falsifications of this truth which derive from the contamination of philosophy by Jewish revelation; the process of disillusionment in the individual is prelude either, as one's predeter-mined character has it, to a wise adoption of a policy of temperance or a real denial of self-will, complete only in the saint, in accordance with one's degree of insight into the truth of the unicity of all wills in Will. Valuations of good and evil, just and unjust, are epiphenomenal in rela-tion to this more fundamental process of disillusionment-enlightenment at work in humanity's spiritual avatars. Von Hartmann and Dühring, following Schopenhauer's program, sought out the graduated expres-sion of Will in nature, force, instinct, drive, and motivated action, and followed the science of their day in detecting a universal unilinear tem-poral unfolding and potentiation of this expression in the evolution of species. Accordingly they ceased to separate Will from its expressions and to regard time and individuation as illusion; the intrinsically tem-poral activity of Will became the ultimate reality revealed by the collective process of disillusionment. Science, alerted to the basic explanatory importance of the concept of Will and applying it to the all-significant process of evolution, could take over from metaphysics. And this science would no longer reproduce, as Schopenhauer's metaphysics had, the religious insight of spiritual avatars. The "self-denial of the will" would now be classed, along with "free will" and repentance, among fictions. Schopenhauer's "saints" could no longer be seen as citizens of the noumenal world, and so their mystical self-understanding could no longer be taken as an accurate rendition of ultimate reality. In the new, scientific, evolutionary and historical perspective, Schopenhauer's saints, and the whole body of religious phenomena, were enigmatic signposts on humanity's evolution toward an unprecedented collective self-awareness and an unprecedented moment of decision concerning human happiness. The philosopher, for Dühring and von Hartmann, was no longer, as with Schopenhauer, a kind of saint *manqué*. Rather, the philosopher's task was to provide a critical genealogy of the moral and religious past of humanity in order to help bring the ultimate stage of human self-awareness and historical decision into its own.

III.

As far-reaching as Nietzsche's affinities with these large developments in Schopenhauerianism are, as great as the actual influence of Dühring and von Hartmann upon him, as illuminating as is this entire context for the understanding of the mutations of the project of enlightenment in the nineteenth century, it would be wrong to suppose that one can explain either the dramatic turn in Nietzsche's development or the special character of the project of a genealogy of morals which runs through his mature work as a result of the influence of these two thinkers, any more than one could predict from a knowledge of the context Marx's unique solution to the dilemmas faced by the Young Hegelians. In the brief space available I will try to sketch one historically informed view, my own, of the formation of Nietzsche's distinctive project.[16]

It is of fundamental importance that Nietzsche, a pastor's son, took seriously the deepest theological or antitheological stratum in Schopenhauer's thought in a way that would allow him to be content neither with adhering to Schopenhauer as a *Bildungsreligion*, nor with evacuating the problem of the saint in the way Dühring or von Hartmann did. Schopenhauer's interpretation of the difference between the man by nature enslaved to the realm of respectable purposelessness, or *Vorstellung*, and the philosopher, artist, or saint delivered from this servitude in varying degrees, as the difference between the realm of works and the realm of grace, as the alternative hell or heaven,[17] seems to have struck Nietzsche with predestinarian force and allowed him no rest from doubts about his own genius and vocation.[18] It was this exigency that brought about his passionate commitment to Wagner, and it was Wagner's introduction of revolutionary activism into Schopenhauer's scheme of the relationship between genius and ordinary man, visible in the 1870 essay *Beethoven*, that inspired Nietzsche's first essay in a Schopenhauerian vision of history, *The Birth of Tragedy*. In *Beethoven* Wagner dynamized the theme central to Schopenhauer hagiography, the delayed vindication of genius. He located Beethoven on a continuum of musical geniuses who had in varying degrees succumbed to their philistine environments and compromised their art, made him precursor to Wagner himself, and prophesied, perhaps without the full seriousness that animated his manifestos of the 1848 period, the coming redemption of the world through music. In *The Birth of Tragedy* Nietzsche, reaching back to Wagner's *Art and the Revolution* of 1849, identified the coming "Baireuther Culturperiode"[19] with the annihilation of the respectable world and the rebirth of tragedy. He treated the interval of history since the decline of tragedy as the triumph and ultimate shipwreck of a Socratic-Alexandrian optimism from which, in Kant and Schopenhauer and the existential experience of his generation, was arising a "tragische Erkenntnis" and renewed longing for art.[20] Casting himself and his spiritual kin as a diaspora of Greece in its tragic age, he made of the longings, sufferings, and self-doubt of his generation's "dragon slayers"[21] a world-historical portent of tragedy's rebirth. When Wagner failed to bring that rebirth about, Nietzsche was left struggling in the vicissitudes of history. Only at this moment did he turn in the direction pointed out by Dühring, and later by Paul Ree; but he infused the project of a new, collective eudaemonism with hopes and tensions unknown to them.

Nietzsche's new orientation emerged in two ways following the publication of *The Birth of Tragedy*. Publicly, Nietzsche signaled a new stance in the subtext of the *Untimely Meditations*; he did so by quietly granting independent significance to the epochs and features of posttragic history which in *The Birth of Tragedy* figured only as privative and preparatory to the rebirth of tragedy. Nietzsche consciously embraced a radically new starting point by transferring his apocalyptic hopes from Wagner to the advent of a new post-Christian, postmetaphysical epoch in human history.[22] It is impossible to give here even a compressed account of these complex developments. I can only try to indicate the marks they left on *Human, All Too Human*.

First, the field of history remains, for Nietzsche, marked by the phenomenon of epigonal struggle, that is, by a residual orientation toward the ideal of genius and a longing retrospection upon Greek culture. In the *Untimely Meditations* all of the features that marked "so-called world history" either as fall from the tragic age into futility, or else as prelude to the rebirth of tragedy, come into their own both as an ideal form of existence and as the basic texture of historical life. *On the Use and Abuse of History for Life* urges an activist epigonality against the resignation inculcated by German historical education and by von Hartmann, and emphasizes the origination of Greek culture from a prior condition of epigonal emulation and assimilation of heteronomous elements.[23] *Richard Wagner in Bayreuth* applies to Wagner the analyses of struggle with temptation that he had applied to Haydn and Mozart. It stresses the epigonal and Alexandrian qualities of his art, while clearly signaling that the *tragische Gesinnung* of the young Wagnerian dragon slayers is coming into its own and is no longer attached unconditionally to Wagner's endeavor.[24] The emergence of this ideal gives a special inflection to Nietzsche's opposition to historical Christianity, which hadn't figured at all in *The Birth of Tragedy*: Christianity is attacked for inculcating historical resignation; it is the enemy of all rejuvenations and renaissances.[25] When Nietzsche embraces the view that science, by demonstrating the erroneous character of religion and therefore all previous culture, has created a new caesura in history, a new level of ambiguity is introduced into the affirmation of activist epigonality. Is the scientific life itself an entirely new form of human existence, a new ideal? Or is it a means to better understand and reproduce the conditions which allowed for the classic cultural attainments of human history? Nietzsche allows these questions to animate the "free spirit," the figure who replaces the struggling epigon in the pages of *Human, All Too Human*, and does not allow them to be quieted.

Second, Nietzsche's responsiveness to the religious exigency at the root of Schopenhauer's philosophy finds expression in his dramatization of the transition of humanity to the new epoch, as it plays itself out both on the stage of collective history and, above all, in the interior processes through which the "free spirits" recapitulate and overcome in themselves the entire human and animal past. Schopenhauer had adopted the Pauline language of the old and the new man, Adam and Christ, to express the difference between self-affirmation and self-denial of the will.[26] In his discussion of "critical history" in the second *Untimely Meditation*, Nietzsche already transferred this language to the identity-threatening self-dissection engaged in by the struggling epigon.[27] In *Human, All Too Human*, this language is transferred to the gestation of future humanity.[28] Even the title of that work may be taken as pointing to this basic theme. Nietzsche is aware that if "historical philosophizing" takes the realm of becoming disclosed by Darwin as the ultimate reality, and seeks to get behind the origin of all that makes up humanity, then humanity itself can no longer be objectively reflected upon as a stable entity. Humanity is not a generic quality or condition; rather the passage of this still undefined entity from its past to its future is eminently present in those few in whom it composes the personal drama of their own lives. To the extent that Nietzsche envisions a collective human future corresponding to the spiritual discoveries made by these few individuals, it is to be brought into existence by a class of spirits higher still who, having gained an unprecedented knowledge of the real conditions of culture, will set ecumenical goals for the deliberate organization of all aspects of human existence.[29]

These tensions, this drama, are unknown to von Hartmann and Dühring, and so is a third distinctive feature of Nietzsche's undertaking. Both von Hartmann and Dühring were generally satisfied to present their reflections as scientific, as effecting the introduction of nineteenth-century natural science into the domain of philosophy. As emphatically positivistic as he frequently sounds in *Human, All Too Human*, even here Nietzsche does not see human thought merely as progressing from metaphysics to science. Without philosophical precision or rigor, Nietzsche grasps better than Dühring and von Hartmann the consequences that follow from treating an intrinsically temporal reality as a philosophical ultimate. He understands that the disclosure of human evolution entirely upsets Schopenhauer's particular scheme of how essence and appearance meet in human willing and action, thereby delivering the ultimate secrets of Being to the philosopher, Schopenhauer. Because he identifies Schopenhauer with metaphysics (just as Marx did Hegel), Nietzsche sees the new evolutionary standpoint not merely as an abstraction or leave-taking from metaphysics, but as the advent of an antimetaphysics which divides the history of human thought in two: humanity's essence was thought to be eternal; now that it can be seen as having evolved, we understand that, contrary to what the philosophers have always thought, becoming precedes being.[30] This is the pathos that underlies Nietzsche's "historical philosophy," even when he declares its method to be inseparable from that of natural science.[31]

Nietzsche's breakthrough to *Human, All Too Human* should be seen not as the abandonment of Schopenhauerian or Wagnerian pessimistic idealism for a positivistic Enlightenment, but as a transformation of a pre-existing project, to unite two basic motivating concerns of Schopenhauerianism: its proclamation of a perennial human ideal of sainthood-genius transcending the common human social order, and indeed transcending space and time, and its prophecy, reinforced by excursions into natural science, of a post-Christian phase of European humanity. This transformation can usefully be understood in terms of the gradual transformation leading from the "dragon slayers" of *The Birth of Tragedy*, to the struggling epigons of the *Untimely Meditations*, to the free spirits of *Human, All Too Human*. Nietzsche's adoption of the banner of Enlightenment served him both to dramatize his break with Wagner and to mark a new set of transhistorical and personal affiliations, which for a time seemed to him to embody his concerns. But the positivistic stance and the air of serene wistfulness Nietzsche forced upon himself in *Human, All Too Human* through *The Gay Science* cannot disguise quite different undertones, and his affiliation with Paul Ree and Lou Salome, with whom he read Voltaire, was not to survive his "discovery" of the *Übermensch*. It seems to me implicit in the basic stance of *Human, All Too Human* that the era of transition to a new humanity should more and more contract into a moment of decision: the project to which Nietzsche wished to rally the free spirits, of overcoming in themselves the human, all too human, would eventually have to do without the providential sponsorship still implicit in the notion that humanity was heading somewhere. It would also have to do without such tools of analysis as utility, which still appealed to a generic human nature, and abstracted from the tensions responsible for making man the animal full of problematic futurity. As Nietzsche went down this path the Anglo-French Enlightenment ceased to be emblematic of his vision. The last thread connecting him with Voltaire would seem to be the issue of Christianity. For the Nietzsche of *Zarathusthra*, the passage of Christianity and its interpretations of human action could no longer be seen merely in terms of the natural death of an error: whoever was not fully alerted to its insidious aftereffects would succumb to them and become another impediment to the new humanity; the battle against Christianity would have to lie at the center of the decisive battle for the future. These general considerations seem to me to capture some of the main features of the trajectory that leads from *Human, All Too Human* to *On the Genealogy of Morals*.

IV.

Foucault's "Nietzsche, Genealogy, History"[32] is better known as a classic postmodern appropriation of Nietzsche and as an illustration of Foucault's own Nietzscheanism than as a study of Nietzsche's development from *Human, All Too Human* to *On the Genealogy of Morals*. Even appreciative Nietzsche scholars remark on its shortcomings in this regard.[33] In the following I shall nevertheless engage Foucault on just this point, not to pick on a weakness, but to demonstrate that postmodern Nietzscheology cannot satisfy its own ambitions without taking seriously the kind of historical questioning to which I devoted the first part of this paper: without it, postmodern claims for what Nietzsche accomplished, or for what was accomplished in him, risk being hopelessly ambiguous or simply wrong. The argument needs making. To get a sense of the situation created in Nietzsche studies by the divide between traditional modes of scholarship and postmodern sensibility, one would have to imagine Georg Lukacs or Herbert Marcuse being entirely uninterested in the discovery of Marx's Paris Manuscripts. It has been the postmodern Nietzsche who has been gaining a notable presence in academic intellectual life in the years (since 1967) in which the Colli-Montinari edition of Nietzsche's works and notebooks made possible, for the first time, a detailed reconstruction of the genesis of his works and his intellectual biography. It is from postmodernists that one might have expected an infusion of larger questions into this scholarship such as would help significant debates to crystallize. But the most notable heralds of this "new Nietzsche" have shown virtually no interest in using these new philological and historical resources to articulate or substantiate their understanding of Nietzsche's work and his historical importance.[34] As a result, common statements such as that Nietzsche "overcame metaphysics" continue to hover between apocalyptic pronouncement and debatable historical assertion.

Foucault's essay has its share of extravagant Nietzscheology, and his characterizations of the "traditional history in its dependence on metaphysics" (89), which Nietzsche is supposed to have exploded, do suffer from massive ambiguity. It is never very clear whether "traditional history" is beholden to metaphysics in the sense in which we all are when we use the verb "to be," or in the sense in which it tends toward Hegelianism; on either supposition Foucault seems to me not to supply enough meaningful differentiation in this part of his discussion to make his strictures of interest for the working historian. But his argument about Nietzsche's development is worth looking at more closely. Certainly it is only a sketch. But Foucault clearly does mean it to clarify and substantiate his claims about how Nietzsche "overcame metaphysics" in his own career. Clearly also, Foucault presents this achievement in terms of Nietzsche's progressive radicalization of the "historical philosophizing" on which he embarked in 1878. This part of Foucault's essay would seem, then, to offer a handhold for discussion which will illuminate from another point of view both Nietzsche's development beyond the Enlightenment and the strengths and weaknesses of postmodern attempts to claim the radicalization of Enlightenment strategies as their own.

The following outline of Foucault's argument is necessarily much simplified. First, Foucault supposes that one can identify "certain analyses that are characteristically Nietzschean," that these "begin with *Human, All Too Human*" and are especially characteristic of *On the Genealogy of Morals* (78). The footnotes he provides to his quotations from Nietzsche come almost entirely from the works of the middle period and from *On the Genealogy of Morals*.[35] Second, Foucault argues that Nietzschean genealogy or *wirkliche Historie*, and therefore the "effective history" (87) for which Foucault pleads, is recognizable by its preference for the quest of *Entstehung* or emergence and *Herkunft* or descent over the quest for *Ursprung* or origin. Foucault suggests that this is a distinction of which Nietzsche himself became more and more explicitly aware, and which comes fully into its own in *On the Genealogy of Morals*, although even in that work Nietzsche does not observe the terminological difference with full consistency. He sees the essential, genealogical Nietzsche emerging just when most people see the "classic" Nietzsche emerging, and it is this Nietzsche whom he sees as furnishing us with a "true historical sense" (89).

The categories of *Entstehung* and *Herkunft*, then, lie at the heart both of Foucault's argument about Nietzsche's method and its development, and of Foucault's positive methodological proposals. Before turning to more detailed analysis of his reading of key Nietzsche texts, I will attempt to sketch how these aspects of Foucault's argument fit together.

Foucault uses *Entstehung* and *Herkunft* to suggest those dimensions of events that continually solicit "traditional history in its dependence upon metaphysics" (without ever, in Foucault's eyes, justifying it). *Entstehung* pertains to the appearance, emergence, the coming about of things; *Herkunft* to the descent of things, that is, that they come from somewhere in the sense of ancestry or racial stock. It is doubtful that Foucault could rigorously define the relationship of these categories to those of the Western metaphysical tradition which he means to debunk,[36] but one can readily discern the work he means these words to do. They conjure up the Heraclitean realm of coming to be and passing away, and give to it a post-Hegelian signature: the realm of events as it appears after the attempt to rationally construct all of profane history as teleologically meaningful has decomposed. That is, instead of suggesting merely transience and alternation in opposition to perduring self-samehood, *Herkunft* and *Entstehung* suggest the recurrent accrual and dispersion of structures of legitimation, domination, and meaning in history. Nietzsche is accordingly seen as progressing toward an ever more self-aware practice of searches for *Herkunft* and *Entstehung* which, disparate themselves, continually "maintain passing events in their proper dispersion" (80), "disturb what was previously considered immobile," "fragment what was thought unified" (82), and disclose the "singular randomness of events," "series of subjugations," and the "hazardous play of dominations" (83) which make up history. This Nietzsche would be the great anti-Hegel of historical method.

My engagement with Foucault's presentation of Nietzsche will focus upon his reading of a critical passage near the beginning of *On the Genealogy of Morals*. The passage is *On the Genealogy of Morals*, I, 2. There, Nietzsche opposes his own ideas about how the idea of "the good" came about, to those of the "English genealogists"—chiefly Spencer and other authors favored by Paul Ree. In taking issue with this version of genealogy Nietzsche is of course in part reckoning with an earlier phase of his own development. It is natural, then, that Foucault should adduce this passage to illustrate just how Nietzsche's pursuit of genealogy has, in the course of Nietzsche's development since *Human, All Too Human*, disengaged itself from the metaphysically tinged quest of "origin" and substituted for that quest the disclosure of "emergence."

First, here is what Foucault says about this passage in the course of his discussion of how Nietzsche employs the concept of *Entstehung*:

> Emergence [*Entstehung*] is thus the entry of forces; it is their eruption, the leap from the wings to center stage, each in its youthful strength. What Nietzsche calls the *Entstehungsherd* of the concept of goodness is not specifically the energy of the strong or the reaction of the weak, but precisely this scene where they are displayed superimposed or face-to-face. It is nothing but the space that divides them, the void through which they exchange their threatening gestures and speeches. As descent [*Herkunft*] qualifies the strength or weakness of an instinct and its inscription on a body, emergence [*Entstehung*] designates a place of confrontation, but not as a closed field offering the spectacle of a struggle among equals. Rather, as Nietzsche demonstrates in his analysis of good and evil it is a "non-place," a pure distance, which indicates that the adversaries do not belong to a common space. Consequently, no one is responsible for an emergence; no one can glory in it, since it always occurs in the interstice. (84–85)

And here is an excerpt from *On the Genealogy of Morals* I, 2, to which Foucault's footnote to the above quotation refers us:

> "Originally [*ursprünglich*]"—so they [English psychologists] decree—"one approved unegoistic actions and called them good from the point of view of those to whom they were done, that is to say, those to whom they were *useful*; later one *forgot* how this approval originated and, simply because unegoistic actions were always *habitually* praised as good, one also felt them to be good— as if they were something good in themselves." [. . .] Now it is plain to me, first of all, that in this theory the source [*der eigentliche Entstehungsherd*] of the concept "good" has been sought and estab-

lished in the wrong place: the judgment "good" did *not* originate with those to whom "goodness" was shown! Rather it was "the good" themselves, that is to say, the noble, powerful, high-stationed and high-minded, who felt and established themselves and their actions as good, that is, of the first rank, in contradistinction to all the low, low-minded, common and plebeian. It was out of this *pathos of distance* that they first seized the right to create values and to coin names for values: what had they to do with utility! The viewpoint of utility is as remote and inappropriate as it possibly could be in face of such a burning eruption of the highest rank-ordering, rank-defining value judgments: for here feeling has attained the antithesis of that low degree of warmth which any calculating prudence, any calculus of utility, presupposes—and not for once only, not for an exceptional hour, but for good. The pathos of nobility and distance, as aforesaid, the protracted and domineering fundamental total feeling on the part of a higher ruling order in relation to a lower order, to a "below"—*that* is the origin [*Ursprung*] of the antithesis "good" and "bad." (The lordly right of giving names extends so far that one should allow oneself to conceive the origin of language itself as an expression of power on the part of the rulers: they say "this *is* this and this," they seal every thing and event with a sound and, as it were, take possession of it.) It follows from this origin that the word "good" was definitely *not* linked from the first and by necessity to "unegoistic" actions, as the superstition of these genealogists of morality would have it. Rather it was only when aristocratic value judgments *declined* that the whole antithesis "egoistic" "unegoistic" obtruded itself more and more on the human conscience—it is, to speak in my own language, the *herd instinct* that through this antithesis at last gets its word (and its *words*) in. And even then it was a long time before that instinct attained such dominion that moral evaluation was actually stuck and halted at this antithesis (as, for example, is the case in contemporary Europe: the prejudice that takes "moral," "unegoistic," *"désintéressé"* as concepts of equivalent value already rules today with the force of a "fixed idea" and brainsickness).[37]

When we take as a point of departure the particular arrangement Foucault has made of motifs and key terms to be found in the passage from *On the Genealogy of Morals*, we are compelled to notice that Nietzsche himself does with them something very different, in fact almost diametrically opposed. I will note the key disparities singly, with some overlap, before considering whether they follow a pattern or suggest a larger problem.

First, while Foucault speaks of a "confrontation" of groups—he rather casually mentions the strong and the weak, then the good and the bad—"superimposed or face to face," and presents this confrontation spatially, as stage, site or "non-place,"[38] Nietzsche himself connects the spatial concept of "distance" to a "pathos" which itself is ranged on a vertical scale of emotional temperature; and the relationship between groups is so emphatically a relationship of subordination that the term "confrontation" does not apply. A term with different connotations, *Gegensatz*, does occur. In one relevant instance, rendered by Kaufmann with "contradistinction," it characterizes the difference between groups as unilaterally experienced by the dominant group; in another, rendered by Kaufmann with "antithesis," it means the opposite end of the temperature scale from the low degree of warmth presupposed by the "calculus of utility."

Second, in the matter of "eruption" and its relationship to *Entstehung* and *Ursprung,* Foucault's attempt to disassociate "eruption" from *Ursprung* forces us to see that Nietzsche is doing no such thing in this passage. Nietzsche says quite clearly and emphatically not that the English genealogists seek "origins" rather than "emergences" or "eruptions," but that they *mislocate* the *Entstehungsherd* of the good; and very clearly, Nietzsche means the word *Entstehungsherd* to convey, if anything, a stronger notion of origin: the English genealogists' "origin" is not sufficiently originary. The good arose *not* among beneficiaries of goodness, *but* in a self-approbation and self-positing of "'the good' themselves"; the viewpoint of utility, which applies in a mild emotional climate, is inapplicable to this "burning eruption of the highest rank-ordering, rank-defining value judgments," an event which, Nietzsche stresses, is not to be thought of as unique or exceptional, but as *für die Dauer*—a phrase difficult to translate which Kaufmann renders as "for good." The "pathos of nobility and distance": *"that,"* Nietzsche insists, "is the origin [*Ursprung*] of the antithesis 'good' and 'bad'."

Third, while Foucault conjures up a hostile exchange of words between groups confronting each other over a void, Nietzsche lets the "noble, powerful, high-stationed and high-minded" not only "coin names for values" but "seal every thing and every event with a sound and, as it were, take possession of it" so that the "origin [*Ursprung*] of language itself" is to be understood as "an expression of power on the part of the rulers." The retort to this "lordly right of giving names" could come only later, when "aristocratic value judgments *declined,*" allowing the *"herd instinct"* to "get its word (and its *words*) in," precisely in and through the growing predominance of the opposition between "egoistic" and "unegoistic" actions with which the English genealogists operate.

Foucault has invited us to read this passage *On the Genealogy of Morals* closely, and we find that a close reading, attentive precisely to the motifs which he has selected, must draw at least the preliminary conclusion that Foucault has, by the traditional canons, read the passage quite incorrectly. The passage tends rather to disconfirm than to confirm a central point of Foucault's argument about how Nietzsche's escape from enthrallment to the metaphysical temptation is reflected in the way he conducts genealogical investigations.

When we take together the three aspects that Foucault emphasizes, we find that Nietzsche conjures up for the reader a primordial situation which unites in itself metaphysical origination, biblical Creation, and Adamic original rectitude, while being this-worldly, individuated in time and place, human, and civilizationally developed. The passage lives from these tensions. We are amid history, but the original and originating situation bears no traces of memory or suppressed trauma. We are in the realm of passibility (pathos) and of opposition (hot and cold), but under and precisely through these conditions comes about a maximum pitch of feeling which escapes the transitory and the episodic to become definitive, to attain *Dauer.* We are witnessing an aboriginal self-aggrandizement by individuals with no proper names, but there is no trace of the penury which self-aggrandizement implies. Rather these men do not merely enjoy higher privileges or a gift of transparent cognition but claim rights and give names in a way that collapses into a single act the Adamic privilege of naming things, the dominical *fiat* by which the world came into being, God's approval of what he had done as good, and the self-love eminently proper to God. The image of overflowing plenitude classic in Neoplatonism and gratefully adopted by Christian theologians as a symbol of divine generosity and omnipotence has been adapted, in the phrase *heisses Herausquellen,* the "eruption" of which Foucault makes so much, to express this innerworldly, intrahistorical demiurgic action. And the last part of this passage, in which Nietzsche speaks of the development that occurs only after aristocratic values have declined, adumbrates a general tendency of the arguments in the rest of the book: just as Nietzsche assigns dominical and transcendent attributes to the originators of aristocratic values, he will transfer to the reaction against these values all of the attributes which in Platonic and Christian theology attach to evil, to the devil: the reaction is entirely privative, no selfhood underlies it, it proceeds rather from a lack or privation of selfhood and has no other recourse than to invert and pervert the good which it hates: the "good" of master morality is the "evil" of slave morality.

If this account of what is going on in *On the Genealogy of Morals* I, 2 is basically correct, then we can be more specific about the shortcomings of Foucault's interpretation and reframe the larger questions with which he approached Nietzsche. Foucault's reading, it seems to me, is very responsive to one central aspect of this passage and systematically neglectful of another. Foucault brings out the way in which Nietzsche submerges that which is supposedly original and originating into the realm of relationality and difference; he entirely neglects the way in which Nietzsche, far from allowing originality to be entirely dispersed in a historicity composed of ever changing power configurations, strives to reconstitute the differences between transcendent and immanent, integrity and fallenness, creator and creature, original and originate, form and matter, *within* the realm of history. On Foucault's view, it seems, the overcoming of metaphysics ought to yield a world simply cut off from transcendence, whether toward heaven or toward the future: the people exchanging menacing gestures and words across a void are like St. Paul's pagans before redemption, "having no hope, and without God in the world" (Ephesians 2:12); or, they are like men who have never left and are destined never to leave a Hobbesian state of nature. As Foucault puts it: "only a single drama is ever staged in this 'non-place,' the endlessly repeated play of dominations" (85). It is a drama that is no drama at all, and it is not surprising that Foucault the genealogist seems to view it with detachment. But Nietzsche's vision quite emphatically says: "in the beginning." We are not then surprised to read near the very end of the first essay of *On the Genealogy of Morals*: "Must the ancient fire not some day flare up much more terribly, after much longer preparation? More: must one not desire *this*[39] with all one's might? even will it? even promote it?"[40]

This close reading of *On the Genealogy of Morals* I, 2, I think, begins to make the case that the kind of historical account of Nietzsche's development offered at the outset of this paper not only brings us closer to the texts, but also makes possible a more differentiated grasp of precisely those problems in which Foucault is interested. This key text tends to confirm that Nietzsche displaces and redirects theological and metaphysical exigencies in the complex ways which that history suggested, rather than banishing or dissipating them in the way suggested by Foucault.

V.

In conclusion I would like to bring the discussion back to the Enlightenment, drawing out some general considerations about what specialists in that period and specialists in Nietzsche might have to say to each other.

I am deeply sympathetic to the view that the internal tensions of the Enlightenment are still very much with us, and that this often goes underrecognized by self-consciously postmodern intellectuals. The case of Nietzsche usefully illustrates both the suggestiveness and the shortcomings of postmodern versions of the career of "Western rationality." Foucault's reading of Nietzsche drives at the problem of the relationship of philosophical rationality to the historicity of human existence, and sharpens our sense of what to look for. But ultimately his analytic categories suffer impoverishment from an overeagerness to claim Nietzsche as a precursor of modern academic sophistications, rather than to understand him as an eminent expression of the travails of the legacy of the Enlightenment in the century of revolution. The reader who approaches *On the Genealogy of Morals* with some understanding of the competing conceptions of and motivating forces behind the enterprise of philosophical history in the eighteenth century will, I think, be better prepared to understand what is specific to Nietzsche's enterprise of historical philosophy than the reader who approaches it with current sophistications in mind. Rousseau's transposition of the problem of original sin into the problem of the origins of society; the Protestant legacy of counterhistories of the Church; the battle of ancients and moderns and its aftermath; the attempts to found universal history on the concept of "civilization" or "society"; the development connecting sixteenth and seventeenth-century reflections on the Adamic language to eighteenth-century reflections on the original form of human self-expression; and, of course, the Enlightenment's various genealogies of morality and religion: these are just a few of the topics familiar to traditional Enlightenment scholars eminently relevant to situating Nietzsche in Western intellectual history. Postmodern advocates of Nietzsche who wish to clarify to themselves and others the ambiguities attaching to many versions of what Nietzsche is supposed to have brought about could only benefit from studying any of these topics.

Any rapprochement between self-consciously postmodern intellectuals and traditional scholars will involve many personal attempts by individuals who find themselves on either side of the divide to turn the estrangement into a productive tension. That demands not only conciliation but productive debate where something is at stake. Two recent contributions to Kant studies, one from a political scientist, Susan Meld Shell,[41] one from a professor of literature, Peter Fenves,[42] strike me as outstanding examples of what is required in a field directly relevant for our larger historical understanding of Nietzsche. These books evince a sophisticated awareness both of postmodern concerns and of eighteenth-century complexities, and through impressive erudition and compelling close readings bring to light dimensions of Kant which are absent from the classic renditions of Ernst Cassirer and others familiar to intellectual historians. Such rich works will help us to understand how Kant could give rise not only to the line of progressive Protestant thought which runs from Fichte to Hegel, but also to the Schopenhauerian and Nietzschean countermovement.

NOTES

1. A brief English-language orientation on this turning point in Nietzsche's development may now be found in the translator's afterword to Friedrich Nietzsche, *Human, All Too Human (I)*, trans. and afterword Gary Handwerk. *The Complete Works of Friedrich Nietzsche*, ed. Ernst Behler (Stanford, 1997), vol. III. This translation is the only one made from the Colli-Montinari critical edition, or rather from the *Studienausgabe*: Friedrich Nietzsche, *Sämtliche Werke, Kritische Studienausgabe in 15 Bänden*, ed. Giorgio Colli and Mazzino Montinari (Berlin, New York, Munich, 1980). References to Nietzsche's works will use section numbers uniform in all editions, or where that is not sufficient, will cite volume and page number of the *Kritische Studienausgabe*, hereafter *KSA*.

2. Throughout I have cited Schopenhauer's works only by section numbers, which are uniform in all editions.

3. These topoi, together with many of the others mentioned here, including the polemic against "Pelagian-judaized-optimistic" Christianity, can be conveniently garnered from the introductions to the first and second editions of *On the World as Will and Representation*.

4. Arthur Schopenhauer *Über den Willen in der Natur. Eine Erörterung der Bestätigungen, welche die Philosophie des Verfassers, seit ihrem Auftreten, durch die empirischen Wissenschaften erhalten hat* (1836).

5. The basic passage is at *The World as Will and Representation*, section 70.

6. A direct prophesy of the inevitable end of "judaized" Christianity, destined to decompose because only the *Weltlauf* has brought about the accidental amalgamation of Jewish and Indian elements, and of the transformation of European history by the influx of Indian wisdom, can be found already in *The World as Will and Representation*, sections 68 and 63, respectively. This theme was to break into the center of Nietzsche's work at the very end of his life, in the passages on the Book of Manu in *Twilight of the Idols* and *Antichrist*. The case of Dühring is notorious: see his *Der Ersatz der Religion durch Vollkommeneres und die Ausscheidung alles Judenthums durch den modernen Völkergeist* (1883). Schopenhauer speculates tantalizingly and at length about the relationship between the reception of his philosophy and the religious future of Europe in a dialogue at the beginning of the essay, "Über die Religion" in *Parerga und Paralipomena*.

7. Basic documents of the conventicle's activity include: Julius Frauenstädt, *Briefe über die Schopenhauersche Philosophie* (Leipzig, 1854); Julius Frauenstädt und Ernst Otto Lindner, *Arthur Schopenhauer. Von Ihm. Über Ihn* (Berlin, 1863); Wilhelm Gwinner, *Arthur Schopenhauer, aus persönlichem Umgang dargestellt* (Leipzig, 1862).

8. Chief among those of Dühring's works with which Nietzsche occupied himself are *Der Werth des Lebens* (1865) and *Cursus der Philosophie als streng wissenschaftlicher Weltanschauung und Lebensgestaltung* (Leipzig, 1875). A general introduction to von Hartmann can be found in the valuable article by Federico Gerratana, "Der Wahn jenseits des Menschen. Zur frühen Eduard von Hartmann-Rezeption Nietzsches (1869–1874)," *Nietzsche-Studien* 17 (1988): 391–433. Aspects of Dühring's influence on Nietzsche have been studied in the works by Peter Heller and Marco Brusotti on Nietzsche's middle period, cited below.

9. In Schopenhauer's usage, the "world as representation" means both the spatiotemporal world and the world of the ordinary man who, unlike the genius, remains entirely immured in spatiotemporality.

10. *The Gay Science*, section 99. Here too Nietzsche emphasizes the significance of those of Schopenhauer's doctrines which formed the foundation of his and Paul Ree's sceptical, antimetaphysical turn: "his immortal doctrines of the intellectuality of perception, the *a priori* nature of the law of causality, the instrumental nature of the intellect, and the unfreedom of the will."

11. My loose usage of "Anglo-French" here of course skips over some interesting questions, to which *Beyond Good and Evil*, sections 252–54 provide important clues.

12. Of course Dühring has some notoriety as the target of Engels's *Anti-Dühring*.

13. See the article by Federico Gerratana cited above for von Hartmann, and the works by Peter Heller and Marco Brusotti cited below for Dühring.

14. Since Paul Ricoeur made the link, Marx and Freud come to mind; I will therefore mention that, as Frank Sulloway and others have pointed out, Eduard von Hartmann was very important for Freud's intellectual development as well.

15. In the following I have lumped together innovations which chiefly characterize von Hartmann's work and innovations which chiefly characterize Dühring's work. Of course they are radically opposed in the direction each would impart to the new eudaemonistic project. Nietzsche was haunted and repelled by von Hartmann's notion of a deliberate, collective suicide of humanity, while Dühring in places points in the direction of Nietzsche's overman.

16. The following account draws on my dissertation, "The Revolution of Genius: Toward an Interpretation of Nietzsche's Early Development" (Ann Arbor, MI, 1995).

17. See *The World as Will and Representation*, sections 38, 53, 60.

18. This point of course cannot be argued here at length, but the reader may wish to look at the weighty testimony of Franz Overbeck in Sander Gilman, ed., *Begegnungen mit Nietzsche* (Bonn, 1981), pp. 203ff.

19. See Nietzsche's letter to Wagner of 2 January, 1872, in Friedrich Nietzsche, *Sämtliche Briefe. Kritische Studienausgabe*, vol. 3 (Berlin and New York, 1986), pp. 271–72.

20. See especially sections 15, 18, and 19 of *The Birth of Tragedy*. The expression *tragische Erkenntnis* comes at the end of section 15: *KSA* I, p. 101.

21. "Drachentödter": *KSA* I, p. 119.

22. The relevant manuscripts are collected in *KSA* VIII. Documents critical to the interpretation offered here include: manuscript 3, fragment 76 = *KSA* VIII, 37–38; and the extensive notes on Dühring which compose manuscript 9, including the long "mein Evangelium" at the end of fragment 1 = *KSA* VIII, 180–81. For a searching analysis of some of this material and of the first group of aphorisms in *Human, All Too Human*, see Peter Heller *"Von den ersten und letzten Dingen": Studien und Kommentar zu einer Aphorismenreihe von Friedrich Nietzsche* (Berlin/New York, 1972).

23. See especially sections 6 and 8.

24. See especially sections 3 and 4. *Tragische Gesinnung* is at the end of section 4 = *KSA* I, p. 453.

25. *On the Use and Abuse of History for Life*, section 8.

26. See *The World as Will and Representation*, section 70.

27. See section 3.

28. See above all section 107. There is a similar, even more striking passage on this theme in *The Gay Science*, section 337, entitled: "The Future 'Humanity'."

29. See section 25.

30. See especially sections 1, 2, and 16.

31. Section 1.

32. Parenthetical page numbers in the following passages refer to Michel Foucault, "Nietzsche, Genealogy, History," *The Foucault Reader*, ed. Paul Rabinow (New York, 1984), pp. 76–100. I have also consulted the French original: "Nietzsche, la généalogie, l'histoire," *Hommage à Jean Hyppolite*, ed. Suzanne Bachelard et al. (Paris, 1971), pp. 145–72.

33. Marco Brusotti, *Die Leidenschaft der Erkenntnis. Philosophie und ästhetische Lebensgestaltung bei Nietzsche von* Morgenröthe *bis* Also Sprach Zarathustra (Berlin/New York, 1997), p. 250, n. 78, notes that in Foucault's "important study" the difference between the genealogy of morals as practiced by Nietzsche in his

middle period and as practiced by him in *On the Genealogy of Morals* remains "very underexposed."

34. A convenient reference point for the postmodern Nietzsche in the English-speaking world is David Allison, *The New Nietzsche* (Cambridge, MA, [1977] 1985). Both this volume and a sequel volume, Keith Ansell-Pearson and Howard Caygill, eds., *The Fate of the New Nietzsche* (Aldershot, UK, and Brookfield, VT, 1991) illustrate the all but total absence of the new Nietzsche edition and scholarship from discussions of the New Nietzsche.

35. There are scattered references to *Twilight of the Idols* (cited five times), *Nietzsche contra Wagner* (once), *Beyond Good and Evil* (eight), and to the second *Untimely Meditation* (once).

36. See the incoherent indictment of the quest for origins on pp. 78–79: at the beginning of the paragraph the search for origin is blamed for locating the identities, the forms of things beyond the "external world of accident and succession"; at the end it is blamed for locating the identities of things at their "historical beginning," that is, within the world of accident and succession. This paragraph seems to be aimed at both Plato and Hegel but strikes neither.

37. Friedrich Nietzsche, *On the Genealogy of Morals,* trans. Walter Kaufmann and R. J. Hollingdale, and *Ecce Homo,* trans. Walter Kaufmann (New York, [1967] 1989), pp. 25–26.

38. It has been pointed out to me that "non-lieu," translated by Rabinow as "non-place," also has the meaning of "nonsuit." My remarks below also tell against this implication of the word, which Foucault seems to intend us to hear as well.

39. Nietzsche's original text emphasizes "das"; Kaufmann and Hollingdale render an unemphasized "it."

40. *On the Genealogy of Morals* I, 17; p. 54.

41. Susan Meld Shell, *The Embodiment of Reason. Kant on Spirit, Generation, Community* (Chicago, 1996).

42. Peter D. Fenves, *A Peculiar Fate. Metaphysics and World-History in Kant* (Ithaca, NY, 1991).

ON THE SUPPOSED OBSOLESCENCE
OF THE FRENCH ENLIGHTENMENT

DANIEL GORDON

As a means of commenting on the preceding essays and synthesizing some of their conclusions, it seems appropriate to address three key questions:

1. *What is postmodernism and what is the source of its bias against the Enlightenment?*

2. *What is essential to know in order to counteract postmodernism's misconceptions of the Enlightenment?*

3. *How can we redefine the "dialectic of the Enlightenment" so that the concept becomes free of the historical inaccuracies of postmodernism while continuing to play the role for which it was designed—to sponsor critical debate about the legacy of the Enlightenment?*

The questions are theoretical and the proposed answers must take on an abstract quality. But to ground the discussion, it will be useful to introduce Voltaire into the arguments in several places. Voltaire was a figure of such symbolic importance to his contemporaries that any characterization of the Enlightenment that does violence to his thought is open to question. Interpreting Voltaire thus becomes one method for establishing with precision what is wrong with postmodernism's conception of the Enlightenment and what must be included in any alternative interpretation.

1. WHAT IS POSTMODERNISM?

The most famous definition of postmodernism is Lyotard's: "I define *postmodern* as incredulity toward metanarratives."[1] According to Lyotard, the two metanarratives that prevailed from the Enlightenment to the late twentieth century were the myth of the progressive liberation of humanity and the myth of the progressive unfolding and unification of knowledge. To accept Lyotard's definition of postmodernism is to accept the premise that postmodernism is the first movement since the Enlightenment to think critically about such narratives.

This premise is questionable. To give but one example, Voltaire's *Candide* is not a metanarrative but rather what Jean Starobinski calls "the simulacrum of a narrative"—a parody "whose moral is to beware of all morals."[2] Candide appears to be like the hero of Homer's *Odyssey* who longs to bring his unwanted adventures to an end and return to the comfort of the woman he loves. But when he is finally reunited with Cunégonde, the symbol of joy that he encounters bears no resemblance to what he was seeking. Cunégonde has become horribly ugly. Possession of her proves to be as much a problem as separation from her.

Through Cunégonde's ugliness Voltaire communicates one of his central messages: the world does not remain stable during the time we take to master it. Hence, what we gain is never what we anticipated, and this holds true for philosophy as well as love. Long trains of thought designed to establish the ultimate causes of things blind us to the advent of new problems that arise during the period of our meditations. For this reason, thought always lags behind reality; only labor keeps us in touch with it. "We must work without theorizing" (chap. 30). Throughout the tale, whenever the characters indulge in metaphysics, basic physical processes overtake them. "While he was perfecting his logical proof, the ship broke into two and everyone perished" (chap. 5).

Lyotard's notion of "incredulity" does serve a useful purpose: it orients the reader in favor of skepticism. But the disadvantage of his rhetoric is that it leads the reader to perceive skepticism as a new form of self-consciousness rather than a literary and philosophical tradition that certain Enlightenment thinkers worked with. Skepticism about democracy and science is not in fact postmodern or even modern; it is ancient. What is particular about the incredulity of postmodernist thinkers is the historical consciousness in which it is embedded: postmodernists frequently simplify historical chronology, treating their own skepticism as if it were part of a recent and dramatic break with the past. Everything up to the Enlightenment tends to be ignored, while the period from the Enlightenment to the supposed advent of incredulity becomes the Old Regime against which postmodernism defines itself as a revolt. What is needed is a definition of postmodernism that is extricated from the revolutionary chronology in which it presents itself—a definition that will focus critically not so much on the principle of skepticism associated with postmodernism but on the historical perspective that accompanies it.

Since Jürgen Habermas is the most respected critic of postmodernism, we must consider his formulation. Yet Habermas shares some of the assumptions of his postmodernist opponents and does not really provide us with a different sense of historical time. According to Habermas, modern thought is characterized by a certain "dialectic" that consists in seeing the solution to every problem as internal to the very forces that produced the problem. "Enlightenment can only make good its deficits by radicalized enlightenment."[3] For example, in Marxism history is defined as a series of economic transformations. These produce inequality and exploitation. The solution, however, is nothing other than a complete working out of the process of economic change. History will produce communism through the same mechanism that it produced capitalism. Habermas refers to such visions as "the dialectic of enlightenment." He believes that this style of thought is one of the legacies that the eighteenth century passed on to the nineteenth. According to Habermas, postmodernism begins with Nietzsche because he bid "farewell to the dialectic of enlightenment."[4] Nietzsche refused to believe that time can transmute evil into good. Postmodern thinkers, in Habermas's scheme, construe modernity in terms of a *negative* dialectic of enlightenment: the supposedly progressive forces of rational thought and capitalist production engender unexpected problems that cannot be solved.

In this way, Habermas reinforces the postmodernist conception of the Enlightenment as a time in which people believed that reason and progress would resolve all the problems of society. He also supports postmodernism's self-image by defining it as a relatively recent break (beginning with Nietzsche) with the Enlightenment's assumptions about progress. He stands apart from postmodernism simply by virtue of his decision to side with the Enlightenment and to defend its belief in reason and progress with new ideas of his own. His philosophy is thus an effort to continue the Enlightenment in the limited sense in which he understands it—to iron out the problems of modernity and the skeptical objections of postmodernism through a systematic theory of communicative action in the public sphere.[5]

It is true that what Habermas calls the "dialectic" of the Enlightenment—the belief that the process of history will ultimately solve the very problems that it creates—can be found in some Enlightenment texts, notably Condorcet's *Sketch of the Progress of the Human Mind* (1793). Yet it is also true that as often as not, the major Enlightenment thinkers bring us to an impasse. Rousseau, for example, traces the degeneration of man in the Second Discourse and leaves us there. He theorizes on a possible solution in *The Social Contract*, but this text does not represent a faith in the historical process. It merely delineates a speculative solution to a set of problems that history only seems to aggravate. If one objects that Rousseau is not of the Enlightenment, we can turn instead to Montesquieu. In this context, Elena Russo's analysis is suggestive. She shows that Montesquieu was concerned about the decline of noble virtues in a commercial society and that this concern was a lasting source of tension for him. Montesquieu accepted the overall advantages of market culture but simultaneously yearned for the unmeasured generosity of premodern man. Unlike Hegel or Marx, he offered no synthesis in which the best spiritual traits of every historical epoch are fulfilled in one imagined regime. He labored to show that commerce should be promoted because it enhances peace and prosperity while also pointing out that commerce diminishes the magnanimous soul. The sense of loss and limits is built into his philosophy of history.

It is well known that most Enlightenment thinkers welcomed the advance of commercial society, which they called "civilization." But analyzing the irreparable damages of civilization was also in the program of some of the most ardent defenders of the free market. Turgot, who liberalized the grain trade and abolished guilds during his tenure as controller general, stressed the loss of poetic language in commercial societies. Voltaire, while praising luxury and trade, did not hesitate to take stock of its perversions. "It is at this price that you eat sugar in Europe," says the mutilated slave in *Candide* after telling how his master had deprived him of a hand and leg for trying to escape (chap. 19). Much of Enlightenment thought was designed not merely to convince people to regard commercial society as the best regime, but also to dramatize the personal qualities of courage, patriotism, and refinement that one should cultivate in opposition to the very same regime. This double-edged mentality produced much of the finesse and irony of Enlightenment writing. Instead of defining the "dialectic" of the Enlightenment as an absolute belief in history that led to a disenchantment in the late nineteenth and early twentieth centuries, we should see this dialectic as a process internal to the Enlightenment—a process in which a certain degree of historical optimism immediately produced doubts about the completeness of the society desired.

There is undoubtedly room for more nuance in this discussion of historical consciousness in Enlightenment thought. Yet enough has been said to suggest that the image of the Enlightenment within postmodernism is not one that can absorb any nuance at all. This in turn makes it impossible to adopt postmodernism's self-definition without reproducing its bias against the Enlightenment. How then to define postmodernism?

One could argue that it is futile to define it—that any general definition will dissolve in the diversity of ideas found in postmodernist thought. To refuse definitions, however, is to allow a term that is already very popular to circulate without precision. "Postmodernism" does in fact stand for a distinctive intellectual disposition characterized by a rejection of European thought up to the late nineteenth century, and a skepticism about all institutional claims to knowledge and authority. This disposition is present in the writings of most of the European theorists referred to throughout the essays in this volume. It is also, however, most influential among educators and students in the United States today. In fact, any definition of postmodernism must take into account that it has become a social force influencing all the humanistic disciplines and shaping the general tone of pedagogy. Postmodernism is now an institution, not just a set of critical texts. One way to define postmodernism is to approach it not only as a school of European theory but as social phenomenon emanating from this theory: a set of widespread suppositions, a mentality. From a historical perspective, it is clear that this mentality is more common in the United States than in Europe. With this irony in mind, we might try to define and explain postmodernism by emphasizing two points of tension between its rhetoric and its actual historical situation.

a. First, postmodernism confers upon itself a European genealogy going back to Nietzsche, but as a popular movement, it appears to be non-European: it has become most pervasive in former European colonies, such as the United States and Australia. Since the genealogy does not explain the history in this case, the project of defining postmodernism must distance itself from postmodernism's self-image; it must become critical.

As Louis Miller shows, the connection between postmodernism and Nietzsche is far looser than the connection between twentieth-century Marxism and Marx. In contrast to Marxism, postmodernism has no scholarly, exegetical relationship to the major thinkers it claims as predecessors. Miller himself has studied Nietzsche's evolution away from Schopenhauer with the care an earlier generation of Marxists devoted to the study of Marx's evolution away from Hegel. His analysis of Nietzsche, combined with his discussion of Foucault's questionable reading of him, suggests that postmodern thinkers have no intimate knowledge of their supposed ancestor. On the basis of Miller's essay, one could draw the conclusions that postmodernism is *sui generis* and has little affinity with Nietzsche's philosophical ambitions.

The same could be said about Horkheimer and Adorno as alleged founders of postmodernism. It is true that their *Dialectic of Enlightenment* is a key reservoir of postmodern epithets about the supposed evils of modernity in general and the Enlightenment in particular. Ronald Schechter thus makes an important contribution when he lays out the terms of Horkheimer and Adorno's interpretation of the Enlightenment and subjects them to exact scholarly revision. It does not nullify the force of Schechter's analysis to further note that Horkheimer and Adorno remained too attached to Marxism to be veritable forefathers of postmodernism. They have been used by postmodernism, but they were not postmodernist thinkers themselves. Their thought gropes toward a higher conception of reason—something beyond the limited instrumental logic they attribute to the Enlightenment—as well as toward a social utopia in which the problems of modernity are resolved. Horkheimer and Adorno were simply too visionary to be postmodernist.

The genealogy of postmodernism thus remains unclear and bears no direct relationship to the genealogies that postmodernism gives to itself. Postmodernism, in fact, is a very recent phenomenon, dating back only to the 1960s and gaining wide currency in the 1970s. The history of the term bears this out.[6] The word "postmodern" was used by Arnold Toynbee in the late 1940s to refer to the process of globalization that had occurred since 1875. In the 1950s, literary critics such as Irving Howe and Harry Levin used the term to refer to postwar writing, which they regarded as inferior to nineteenth- and early-twentieth-century literature. There is thus a fairly long tradition of using the term "postmodern" to highlight one's belief that an important cultural change has occurred in the recent past. The usages in the '40s and '50s, however, do not convey the assault upon the European legacy that is integral to postmodernism. It was in the 1960s that critics such as Leslie Fiedler, Ihab Hassan, and William Spanos reversed the judgments of Howe and Levin by idealizing the discontinuity between present and past and affirming that postwar culture could not be judged by previous standards because those standards were historically bounded and outdated.

It is worth stressing that postmodernism as a mode of literary and art criticism emerged in the United States independently of the influence of Foucault, Lyotard, and other French thinkers. Critics of postmodernism often treat it as a French import, but this is not the case. In his discussion of the "pre-postmodernism" of Carl Becker, Kent Wright shows that as early as the period between the two world wars, American progressivism took a cynical turn and produced at least one intellectual who anticipated some postmodern ideas. In the 1960s, as noted above, a whole American school of postmodernist literary criticism took shape, and by the mid-1970s, American postmodernism had moved, apparently on its own, from a theory of aesthetics to a critique of Western thought as a whole.[7]

This is not to deny that French postmodern thinkers—Lyotard, Foucault, Derrida—deepened the critique of modernity for American academics. Nor does it mean that these thinkers fail to offer, at times, profound insights. It does help to explain, however, why these thinkers have been so much more popular in the United States than in their own country. French academics continue to be surprised by Derrida's popularity in the United States Foucault is a thinker of great stature, but he never became the object of an academic cult in France to the degree that he did in the U.S. Lyotard began *The Postmodern Condition* by freely admitting that he had borrowed the term "postmodern" from American critics and sociologists.[8] His work reduces postmodernism to simple and comprehensible terms; it is a concise textbook of the kind that the French produce with great skill. But it was commissioned in Canada and it has become more canonical in the United States than in France.

What are the reasons for this popularity? The first is perhaps what Richard Hofstadter described as a widely shared "contempt for the past," a rejection of the idea that American society, in order to be complete, requires an added layer of culture borrowed from another epoch.[9] Thinkers such as Derrida, with their critique of European society and the canon of great books, confirm the lack of historical deference in America while turning the rejection of culture into a form of intellectualism in its own right. No other school of theory offers such a comfortable fit with the native American belief in self-reliance.

The popularity of postmodernism must also be understood in connection with the state of other disciplines in the United States, especially philosophy. Here it must be stressed that the influence of postmodernism has been entirely positive. Postmodernism, in other words, has been the primary counterweight against technical specialization. In a different era, students energized by grand questions about the fate of modern civilization might turn to the discipline of philosophy. But in the United States this discipline has become so removed from history that it operates without any concepts of cultural change at all. The impact of logical positivism (or logical empiricism) upon academic philosophy has been decisive. Contested from the start and ultimately rejected as a systematic theory of knowledge, it has nevertheless shaped the whole discipline of philosophy with its distaste not only for history but for literature, religion, and all other fields of discourse that are tied to everyday consciousness and do not express themselves as a formal series of unambiguous statements. A rejection of "psychologism," that is, an insistence that philosophy deal only with the logical classification of "propositions" and not explore "how human beings actually think," is indeed one of the central principles of contemporary logic and analytical philosophy (and also what most separates it from the Continental school of phenomenology).[10] On account of this principle, American analytical philosophers have not participated in the major debates about culture that have taken place in the late twentieth century. In contrast to German and French philosophers, they have written virtually nothing important about issues such as the Holocaust, the place of religion in an increasingly secular society, the merits and flaws of capitalism, and the effect of the subconscious upon behavior.

For the most part, American professors of philosophy ignore postmodernism and do not try to give alternative answers to the questions posed by it. But when they do respond, they have only revealed the limitations of their methods. For example, Hilary Putnam, a leading mathematical logician and analytical philosopher, has argued that Foucault is wrong to stress the socially constructed and subjective nature of values. In the classic style of his discipline, Putnam sets aside historical and cultural context. He takes the case of an individual's preference for chocolate ice cream over vanilla, arguing that the preference elicited by chocolate is intrinsic in the individual's taste and is thus physiologically idiosyncratic but not a matter of subjectivity.[11] In other words, since the pleasurable taste flows from one's physiological makeup and since the value of goodness we assign to a pleasurable taste is supposedly automatic, there is no space between the action of tasting and the judgment upon it for the willful invention of preference. Putnam does not consider the possibility that sensations, including even food preferences, can be shaped by the will of others: by advertising that overlays sensation with associations of status, or by the degree of socially dictated exposure. Beer tastes bad at first, but if one keeps drinking it because of peer pressure, it might begin to taste good. From a purely logical perspective, the same could be true of certain flavors of ice cream, which allows considerable room for contingency in the formation of taste. But perhaps the most important point regarding ice-cream flavors is that they are all very sweet, and that people have no innate preferences among all of them: one must simply invent preferences in response to situations that require it (such as ordering at a birthday party). Preference, in other words, is often a product of social situations requiring us to establish a clear order among things that are intrinsically about the same to us. The formation of preferences ultimately lies with those who have the power to ask us what we want.

One of the virtues of postmodernism is that it refuses to sever the bonds connecting philosophy to the sense of the social and historical grounds of experience. Its historical vision may be crude, but it at least sustains the concept of the historicity of human action. Academic philosophy in the United States has created a hole in the humanities that postmodernism alone has dared to fill.

If this account of the factors generating postmodernism as a wide movement is true, the same factors ought to be found in other places where postmodernism has become popular. The second home to postmodernism, it seems, is Australia.[12] The proper conditions do in fact obtain there: a former European colony with a tradition of the self-made man and hostility to the Old World, and a philosophical culture that is predominantly analytical and impervious to the philosophy of history, allowing postmodernism to take the lead in public intellectual debates.

b. The second point of tension in postmodernism is a matter of its political mystique. Postmodernist authors, educators, and students often adopt a radically critical stance toward the Enlightenment, the revolutions of the eighteenth century, and the institutions of liberal democratic society. Yet postmodernism itself seems to flourish within the framework of capitalism and to represent less a critique of democracy than its most subjectivist expression.

"I write in order to act," Voltaire said.[13] Writing meant intervention and risk—establishing a position against an opponent in power. Voltaire was a skeptic, but his was a skepticism designed to induce choice and action. He defended Protestants in a Catholic regime, mocked nobles in an aristocratic society and condemned slavery when Europeans took it for granted that Africans were fit only to receive orders. His writing was action because it established a point of difference with those in power. But what is the power against which postmodernism establishes its difference?

Postmodernist educators and students believe that spreading relativistic criticism can liberate individuals. Hence, they repeatedly call into question the claims of literature, art, and even science to truth and moral value. But is this skepticism a critique or confirmation of the regime in which it is located? In the 1970s, Gerald Graff addressed this question in "The Myth of the Postmodernist Breakthrough," a provocative article in which he suggested that postmodernism reinforces the ideology of late capitalism.[14]

Graff begins by denying the revolutionary character of postmodernism in relation to modern (in this context, Romantic) literature. He notes that while textbook descriptions of Romanticism present it as a confident secular religion, the Romantics often conceded that artistic meaning was self-created. They were haunted by the thought that the spirit in nature might not actually inhere in the external world and might instead be a creation of their own mind.[15] Postmodernism fails to acknowledge this ambivalence; it takes no stock of the long history of subjectivism which goes back, as Graff notes, to the late eighteenth century.[16]

Graff continues by observing that what is new is not subjectivism *per se* but the ease with which it is being assimilated. In the eighteenth and nineteenth centuries, it was a disorienting experience to ponder the contingency of one's own commitments. Today, the context has changed and Americans luxuriate in the lap of relativism. Advanced industrial society thrives on the idea that action is the expression of nothing more than individual preference. Postmodernism's emphasis on the impossibility of an objective point of view is highly congenial to the ideology of the marketplace, which offers goods to anyone who wants them without regard to judgments about their ultimate value.[17] Pluralism, Graff states, "is the reigning philosophy of the establishment."[18] Hatred of tradition is also assimilated into the capitalist trend which Graff (drawing on Lionel Trilling) calls "the acculturation of the anti-cultural, or the legitimization of the subversive."[19] The establishment itself prefers uneducated subjectivity to cultivated judgment. Graff writes:

> Advanced industrial society has outstripped the avant-garde by incorporating in its own form the avant-garde's main values—the worship of change, dynamic energy, and autonomous process, the contempt for tradition and critical norms. With the technocratic and bureaucratic transformation of the old bourgeois values into the values of the age of consumption, the arch antagonist against which the avant-garde revolted and against which it defined itself has all but disappeared. Yet cultural radicals continue to cling to the threadbare dialectic which opposes vital energy to the rigidities of reason and tradition.[20]

Perhaps Graff exaggerates the ease with which cultural iconoclasm (such as questioning traditional gender and ethnic stereotypes) is absorbed into capitalist society. His article, however, succeeds in establishing a challenge to postmodernism that is not usually engaged within postmodernist discourse. For example, postmodernist historiography, inspired largely by Foucault's *Discipline and Punish*, tends to define modern society in terms of a subtle tightening of supervision and control in all areas of life. It does not recognize the concurrent dynamic by which manners and rules have become looser and free choice enshrined as a principle of social organization. The historiography thus creates an ambience in which the central problem of modern times appears to be the invention of new kinds of power. But one could well argue that one of the most pressing problems of liberal democratic societies is the increasing difficulty they encounter, within the framework of their own principles, in justifying authority of any kind.

One way to think about Enlightenment political thought is that it was an effort to bring about a double institutionalization of liberty—to proclaim liberty as a basic human right and to set its limits in practice. In her article on censorship, Sophie Rosenfeld demonstrates with great nuance that Enlightenment thinkers were simultaneously concerned with liberating the written word and policing it. Among other things, she reveals that eighteenth-century attitudes toward censorship were considerably more complex than the standard postmodernist critique of "liberalism" suggests. This should not lead us to idealize the solutions that were proposed, but it does imply an approach that is concerned with both sides of governance—freedom, and order. Foucault, in contrast, advocates a radicalization of the Enlightenment's pursuit of freedom, which he calls "the art of not being governed,"[21] without a corresponding intensification of the Enlightenment's concern with the problem of how to reconcile one person's freedom with another's. If Foucault is an indication, it is evident that postmodernism refuses to ponder the social contract.

This may be the secret of its hostility to the Enlightenment. As Graff's analysis suggests, postmodernism thrives by presenting its own iconoclasm as a novelty within an intolerant and strictly governed regime. Postmodernist authors must constantly discover new rigidities and hierarchies in the world so that their own concern with autonomy, their refusal to take up the art of governing, does not appear to be one-sided. Then these complaints must be aggrandized, which is to say historicized, so that they appear to be constitutive of liberal modernity from beginning to end. The Enlightenment, at this point in the logic, becomes a useful reference point; it symbolizes the program of modernity, the source of all its horrors and inequalities.

2. MISCONCEPTIONS ABOUT THE ENLIGHTENMENT

The specific charges of postmodernism against the Enlightenment can be grouped under two headings: epistemological and political. In terms of the former, a revealing postmodernist description of the Enlightenment's conception of knowledge is the following:

> The Enlightenment project . . . took it as axiomatic that there was only one possible answer to any question. From this it followed that the world could be controlled and rationally ordered if we could only picture and represent it rightly. But this presumed that there existed a single correct mode of representation which, if we could uncover it (and this was what scientific and mathematical endeavors were all about), would provide the means to Enlightenment ends. This was a way of thinking that writers as diverse as Voltaire, d'Alembert, Diderot, Hume, Adam Smith, Saint-Simon, Auguste Comte, Matthew Arnold, Jeremy Bentham, and John Stuart Mill all had in common.[22]

Clearly, the author is uninformed and has combined thinkers from two centuries in a way that does justice to neither the eighteenth nor the nineteenth century. Not all postmodernist accounts of the Enlightenment are so crude. But postmodernism, especially in the United States, creates an ambience in which such unscholarly boldness is possible. How to cut through error on such a grand scale? Perhaps the most direct route of refutation is to return to Cassirer's distinction between the *esprit de système* of seventeenth-century philosophy and the *esprit systématique* of the Enlightenment.[23] The idea of a single vantage point from which everything can be seen objectively and all knowledge unified is precisely what the *philosophes* denied. Since postmodernism's historical perspective generally goes back no further than the eighteenth century, the moves the *philosophes* made *away* from the foundationalism of Descartes and Leibniz are beyond the limits of its comprehension. The seventeenth-century philosophers, however, must be brought into any general account of the history of reason in modern times—not only because they form part of the background out of which the Enlightenment emerged but also because philosophers such as Descartes and Leibniz managed to survive the Enlightenment critique; they continue to be important in the self-image of analytical philosophy today. The Enlightenment is thus in a state of tension both with its past and our present.

The renaissance of classical logic initiated by Russell and Frege in the early twentieth century has led to the canonization of the systematic thinkers of the seventeenth century. Classical logic is based on the supposition that all meaningful statements are either true or false, and that truth and falsehood are mutually exclusive. Hence the law of the excluded middle, which holds that there is no middle or third truth-value. Closely related is the law of identity, according to which an item either has or does not have certain attributes. On the basis of such principles, classical logicians believe that philosophy can perform a transcendental function (judging without reference to empirical contingencies) in relation to the arguments made by practitioners of specific disciplines. For example, they would point out that it is patently false to say that Louis XIV died in 1715 and that Louis XIV did not die in 1715. Moreover, the truth-value of this statement (its being false) is not contingent upon historical fact. It is a necessary truth, not only in this world but all possible worlds, that the statement is false because its terms are self-contradictory.

It is interesting to note that contemporary philosophers sometimes credit Leibniz for being the first to talk about possible worlds as a device for sharply distinguishing necessary and contingent truths.[24] Philosophy thus redeems the seventeenth century as positive historical ground. In contrast, French thinkers of the eighteenth century do not figure in the canon of the analytical tradition. They are either absent or reduced to third-rate status in various reference works for American and British philosophers, such as *The Oxford Companion to Philosophy* (1995), *The Cambridge Dictionary of Philosophy* (1995), and *The Blackwell Companion to Philosophy* (1996). The analytical tradition thus disowns the eighteenth century as philosophically irrelevant at the same time that it embraces the seventeenth century as an era of creativity.

But there is good reason for this: the *philosophes* repudiated the binary concepts of truth and falsehood. Voltaire's rejection of Leibniz is crucial in this context. I have elsewhere tried to explain in detail that the character of Pangloss, far from representing a caricature of Leibniz's ideas, was based on a very precise understanding of the problems inherent in Leibniz's philosophy.[25] The key problem was the inability of Leibniz's philosophy to keep pace with contingencies that, as he himself admitted, constituted *prima facie* refutations of his conviction that the world operates according to the principles of logic. Unable to account for concrete events within the terms of his conceptual system, Leibniz repeatedly reverted to religious faith, asserting that we must trust in God's existence and have confidence that from the divine perspective everything that happens must do so for a logical reason. The most extreme rationalism thus coexisted with, and in fact generated, the most extreme religious passivity. Voltaire refused to enter this space, where systematic reasoning and reliance on God were different faces of the same coin.

This rejection of Leibniz's concept of intelligence accounts for the style of writing that Starobinski has noted in Voltaire's *contes*, a style based on the "incongruous pairing" of terms and the representation of "contrary emotions."[26] Voltaire brings us into adventures that acquire meaning not through the logical consistency of facts but through the characters' painful confrontation with states of being that fall between the terms of binary description. As Starobinski writes:

> The Voltairean tale offers us an accelerated, caricatural image of this constant motion, of this oscillation between nature and culture, vice and virtue, laughter and tears, pessimism and optimism, and leaves us in a state of overall confusion despite all the clarity of the individual details.[27]

Once the terms of representation change in this way, the central technique of philosophy becomes not formal logic but *esprit*, or descriptive irony.[28] The use of oxymorons becomes common and acquires the deepest philosophical significance. *Candide* is filled with them. Voltaire writes "His Miserable Highness" (chap. 27) instead of "His Royal Highness" to show that kings are ordinary people subject to the same afflictions as the rest of humanity. He says that Admiral Byng was "ceremoniously murdered" (chap. 23) instead of "ceremoniously executed" in order to break down the distinction between crime and justice. He describes a battle as a scene of "heroic butchery" (chap. 3) to suggest that military virtue and unregulated bloodlust are inseparable. After the battle, each side thanks God for its victory with a *Te Deum*—a logical absurdity, but who is to say who really lost? If the winner is he who celebrates afterward, then nothing prevents both sides from winning. Voltaire uses oxymorons to force readers to see that from a Leibnizian perspective, the world in which we live is an impossible one. What lies between the terms of mutual exclusion is simply everything important that we experience in historical time.

Voltaire makes no effort to set all knowledge upon a single foundation. "*Les fondements se dispersent,*" he writes in *Candide:* "The foundations disintegrated" (chap. 5). The reference is literally to the homes of Lisbon during the earthquake, but the word *fondements* in the Enlightenment plays an epistemological role too. Voltaire himself uses it in such phrases as "the foundations of religion," "the foundations of history," and "the foundations of reason" (all used, for example, in his *Essai sur l'histoire générale,* published in 1756, three years before *Candide*). Postmodernist scholars have been insensitive to this kind of language and have tended to identify Enlightenment thinkers with the very rationalism that they tried to avoid.

Daniel Rosenberg makes a similar argument in his essay on the *Encyclopédie.* Dismissing the views of those who assert that the Enlightenment regarded language as ahistorical and knowledge as static, he shows that the *Encyclopédie* publicizes a tension between truth and time, between thought which seeks to represent the enduring nature of things and thought whose own representations are ever changing. The periodical form of the *Encyclopédie*—the constant updating of knowledge—is not an accident related to the massive scale of the enterprise but is rather a result of a philosophy riveted by the evanescence of its own ideas.

Needless to say, not all Enlightenment thinkers had the subtle sense of limits possessed by Diderot, the central character in Rosenberg's fine article. A recent book, *Telling the Truth about History,* even implies that Diderot was unique. The coauthors of this work are all experts in eighteenth-century history. One of the themes of their text—similar to the theme of the present volume—is the relationship between postmodernist skepticism and the Enlightenment legacy. In their introduction, they note that "some degree of skepticism" was already evident in the Enlightenment, and they cite Diderot as someone who called for the questioning of all traditions, including the Bible and the Church. Yet, at the very beginning of chapter 1, the authors assert that Enlightenment thinkers believed in "a granite-like platform upon which all knowledge could rest." And they add: "The absolute character of their truth mimicked the older Christian truth upon which Westerners since late Roman times had come to rely." From here to the end of the book, the authors sarcastically refer to the Enlightenment as a "heroic" faith in science. The thinkers of the Enlightenment, they say, were "true believers," in contrast to today's historians of science who recognize the "more provisional, less absolute" character of science. At one point, they describe the Enlightenment as a naive belief in "neutral and passionless" investigation. They also claim that this "absolutism" was properly "dethroned" in the 1960s.[29]

What happened to Diderot? While the introduction of *Telling the Truth* hints at a nuanced image of the Enlightenment grounded in the interpretation of major thinkers, this image quickly gives way to a stock notion of the Enlightenment as the Old Regime against which a recent generation of pioneers has revolted. The authors do try to temper this revolt. They are the Girondins of postmodernism. Much of their book is a critique of the excesses of postmodernist "nihilism" and a call for a "moderate skepticism." But because the authors deny that the Enlightenment is a source for their own project, they become theorists without a tradition— moderates without a precedent to guide their thinking. The result is that they situate themselves in Year One of philosophy, and since they are not themselves trained as philosophers, they never manage to make their epistemological position clear. They reject the radical skepticism of postmodernism but without refuting it by means of logic or by means of a biographical example of a philosophical life well lived.[30]

These intelligent and well-intentioned critics of postmodernism are thus an example of the hold that postmodernism has over the imagination even of its opponents. As specialists of the eighteenth century, the authors of *Telling the Truth* have all the information needed to integrate the eighteenth century into a variety of narratives about modern history. Yet they stick to the narrative of their opponents—a narrative about the necessity of a break with the Enlightenment conception of knowledge— because they are committed, like their opponents, to a rhetoric of new beginnings.

Diderot was not in fact unique. Several of the essays in this volume draw attention to the epistemological sophistication of Enlightenment thinkers. As regards the "heroic" model of science, it is true that for Voltaire, Newton was a hero and Newtonian physics a model of rational inquiry. But Voltaire presented Newton as an alternative to the epistemological excesses of his time. Newton, for him, was the middle ground between religious existentialism (God willed the world for no rationally demonstrable reasons) and scientific essentialism (science can show us exactly how and why the world is constructed). Newton's genius, according to Voltaire, was to explain the "effects" of gravity while openly confessing his inability to explain its ultimate "principle." In this way, Voltaire stressed that the rigor of science is primarily at the level of experiment and description; it is not a matter of first causes. "The anatomist who first declared that the motion of the arm is owing to the contraction of the muscles taught mankind an indisputable truth. But are we less obliged to him because he did not know the reason why the muscles contract?" The ultimate reason for things, says Voltaire, "is among the Arcana of the Almighty." And he adds the motto: "Thus far shalt thou go, and no farther." In this way, Voltaire combined human reason and cosmic inscrutability—a sense of progress and a sense of the absurd—into a single framework.[31]

Turning from postmodernism's epistemological critique of the Enlightenment to its political critique, we must begin by noting that the two are interconnected. Postmodernist thinkers take pride in their ability to analyze the relations between knowledge and power. Their political accusations against the Enlightenment are therefore grounded in their own stereotypes about Enlightenment epistemology. Thomas Docherty, the editor of *Postmodernism: A Reader*, writes:

> Enlightenment's "emancipatory" knowledge turns out to involve itself with a question of power, which complicates and perhaps even restricts its emancipatory quality. Knowledge, conceived as absract and utilitarian, as a mastery over recalcitrant nature, becomes characterized by power; as a result, "Enlightenment behaves toward things as a dictator toward man. He knows them insofar as he can manipulate them."[32]

The citation at the end is to Horkheimer and Adorno, and after quoting them at greater length, Docherty concludes:

> Knowledge thus becomes caught up in a dialectic of mastery and slavery in which the mastered or overcome is not nature but rather other human individuals; it is therefore not purely characterized by disenchantment and emancipation. From now on, to know is to be in a position to enslave.[33]

Finally, Docherty affirms that "the Enlightenment project" led to the Holocaust.[34]

Since the primary target of the Holocaust was the Jews, Ronald Schechter's essay on Enlightenment anti-Semitism directly engages the thesis that the Enlightenment produced the Holocaust. Schechter brings out some important ironies. First, the Jews of eighteenth-century France sometimes identified with the Enlightenment and used forms of discourse characteristic of the Enlightenment to defend themselves against anti-Semites. Second, philosophical anti-Semitism in the eighteenth century did not emerge in the context of "abstract" and "utilitarian" philosophy; on the contrary, anti-Semitic thinkers spoke the language of feeling and accused the Jews of being unsentimental and excessively calculating. Finally, Schechter deepens and supports Peter Gay's classic argument that anti-Semitism in the Enlightenment was subordinate to a larger liberal aim: the undermining of Christian bigotry.

To attack Judaism was rarely an end in itself but was principally a means to attack Christianity through its historical and theological sources.

Schechter also notes an affinity between some Zionists and post-modernism. Both are suspicious of the ideal of assimilation; both maintain that the universalism of the Enlightenment is intolerant of diversity and minority traditions. The essays by Malick Ghachem, Alessa Johns, and Arthur Goldhammer, however, do much to correct this most common of anti-Enlightenment charges.

Focusing on Enlightenment visions of utopia and economic reform, Johns suggests that feminism and the Enlightenment are not antithetical terms. Debates about agricultural improvement and population growth created a space in which women could cultivate a cosmopolitan voice and advance reforms on behalf of their sex. This argument is consistent with the views of other feminist historians who are disenchanted with postmodernist feminist theory because it fails to acknowledge the full history of feminist thought. "A return to the sources," writes Karen Offen, "demonstrates unequivocally that the European Enlightenment is far richer in content and scope on gender issues, indeed far more explicitly 'feminist' in its claims and aspirations than has been generally acknowledged."[35] Some feminists have also doubted that postmodernism, with its tendency to dissolve the category of "women"—that is, to deny that there are any inherent differences between male and female—can really advance the interests of women.[36]

Ghachem, for his part, treats the subject of the Enlightenment's influence on colonial law. Postmodern thinkers, he observes, have neglected the study of law and legal theory precisely because their concept of power is designed to draw attention away from government and toward the diffuse "sites" of discipline. Ghachem exposes the resulting lack of balance in postmodernist assessments of the Enlightenment's impact on colonialism. In his study of the debates surrounding the incorporation of Saint-Domingue into the French legal system, he finds no lack of sensitivity to the particular and the concrete. Under the influence of Montesquieu, "local knowledge" was considered essential to the formulation of law and policy. Indeed, one of the implications of Ghachem's work is that the inhabitants of Saint-Domingue became aware of their specific identity, of their difference vis-à-vis France, *through* the categories of French jurisprudence.

Goldhammer's essay does not deal with the theme of universalism and difference in terms of racial, ethnic, or sexual identity. But that is appropriate since the *philosophes* themselves were not preoccupied with these categories to the same degree as their postmodernist critics. The type of difference that most concerned them, Goldhammer suggests, is that which an individual establishes through style. Style, he suggests, is the form of distinction that the Enlightenment saw as necessary in an increasingly homogenized society. The forces of commerce, transportation, urbanization, and state centralization tended toward the breaking down of barriers, the elimination of corporate identities. The Enlightenment was characterized by an anxiety about confronting others in a context of unstructured and disorienting uniformity. Far from being the instrument of homogenization that postmodernist thinkers claim, language in the Enlightenment was construed as a therapy for the alienating effects of sameness. As Goldhammer writes:

> Human language . . . must therefore not only express difference, it must create it; it must be not just conceptual language "constative" of difference but a "performative" instrument, a carillon of the self. . . .What is distinctively human about language, then, is not just the capacity to ascribe universal denominations to concepts but the ability to project the movement, the passions, the velleities of the self that each speaker's unique utterances enfold.

3. THE "DIALECTIC OF THE ENLIGHTENMENT"

In a recent study of Kant, Susan Meld Shell notes that much that passes today for a postmodernist critique of "Western metaphysics" is in fact part of the forgotten legacy of the Enlightenment. "The central difficulty with the new historicist attack upon philosophy," she states, "may be that it is insufficiently historical."[37] The essays in this volume confirm that the deeper one looks into the Enlightenment, the more one finds thoughtful answers to the very questions posed by postmodernism. But the purpose of this volume is not simply to break down the polarity of postmodernism/Enlightenment by demonstrating that the Enlightenment foreshadows the concerns of postmodernism. Such a conclusion, even though it negates postmodernism's image of the Enlightenment, would be a triumph for postmodernism—a triumph, because it implies that at best the former is an anticipation of the latter.

In the end, we must acknowledge that the two terms, Enlightenment and postmodernism, remain distinct. On the one hand, the Enlightenment surpasses postmodernism, and to return to the eighteenth century is to move forward in the seasons of thought. The Enlightenment was a more mature movement because the individuals comprising it confronted more realities. The *philosophes* were more active in politics and business than postmodernist theorists, almost all of whom have passed their lives entirely in the university. The *philosophes* also endured greater risks and had more contact with the extremes of life. They faced prison and exile. They rose at times to advise rulers, and sometimes even ruled themselves. As social beings they had more attachments and knew more types of people, not only because they were more convivial but because in a corporate society there are more kinds of people to know. They had more ties to a multiplicity of institutions—government, church, banks, academies, salons, theaters, publishers. Philosophically, they were attuned to skepticism and its implications. But they recognized that authority is necessary in the world and that responsible intellectuals must theorize not only about how to defy power but also about how to establish it.

They produced a complex culture that is still hard to understand. Voltaire's tragic and critical irony, Diderot's refined and half-crazed dialogues, Montesquieu's synthetic and chatty treatises—the high points of the French Enlightenment represent a unity of abstraction and personality, philosophy and living, anxiety and generosity not yet equaled in postmodernist thought.

On the other hand, postmodernism has one supreme advantage, the advantage of hindsight and of knowing two more centuries of history. The French Revolution, world wars, the genocides of totalitarian regimes, and the degenerations of mass democracies were outside the purview of the Enlightenment. Postmodernism has oversimplified matters by blaming the Enlightenment directly for what it regards as history's worst disasters. But it would be equally simplistic to maintain that the Enlightenment is entirely disconnected from the contradictions and calamities of modern history. Peter Gay, the Enlightenment's greatest champion, was reluctant to link it with anything bad, even with the Revolution that was continguous to it in time. More recently, Robert Darnton has linked the Enlightenment with the Terror, but as a champion of the Revolution, he sees nothing deeply wrong with the latter.[38] Each has been the leader of a generation of Enlightenment scholars, but neither has a sense of a paradoxical connection between good and evil.[39]

What is in question here is not the documentary scope of contemporary scholarship (which has certainly become very broad) but the philosophical spirit in which it is carried out. Perhaps the scholarship of the future will combine the critical vision of postmodernism with an understanding of the Enlightenment that is appreciative enough to bring out the full pathos of modern history. Then one might begin to explore how the Enlightenment tried, with only partial success, to temper its own dangerous logic. How it tried to mitigate the principle of skepticism that tends toward nihilistic cruelty and turn it into a generous code of tolerance. How it tried to circumscribe the principle of equality that tends toward mutual indifference and turn it into an inclusive code of sociability. How it tried to soften the ideal of universal citizenship that tends to efface minority traditions and turn it into a flexible code of law.[40]

The sense of dialectic requires a critical perspective on the Enlightenment; the sense of responsibility requires admiration for it. To deny either of these terms is to risk sinking into superficial veneration or shallow hatred. Every age wishes to construct a new ideal. But to be an insurgent, one must also be an heir. The Enlightenment is the inheritance one must accept in order to revolt against the present.

NOTES

1. Jean-François Lyotard, *The Postmodern Condition: A Report on Knowledge* (Minneapolis, 1984; first published in French in 1979), p. xxiv.
2. Jean Starobinski, "Voltaire's Double-Barreled Musket" in *Blessings in Disguise; Or, the Morality of Evil*, trans. Arthur Goldhammer (Cambridge, MA, 1993), p. 84. The quotations by Voltaire that follow come from my translation of *Candide* (Boston, 1999).
3. Jürgen Habermas, *The Philosophical Discourse of Modernity* (Cambridge, MA, 1990; first published in German in 1985), p. 84.
4. Ibid., p. 86.
5. See especially Habermas's *Theory of Communicative Action*, 2 vols. (Boston, 1984–87).
6. The following discussion is based on Michael Köhler, "'Postmodernismus': Ein begriffsgeschichtlicher Überblick," *Amerikastudien* 22 (1977): 8–18.
7. See Köhler's discussion of William Spanos, pp. 14–15.
8. Lyotard, p. xiii.
9. Richard Hofstadter, *Anti-Intellectualism in American Life* (New York, 1962), esp. pp. 238–39.
10. See the textbook by Raymond Bradley and Norman Swartz, *Possible Worlds: An Introduction to Logic and Its Philosophy* (Indianapolis, 1979) for a typical Anglophone discussion of the difference between philosophy and psychology. On the relationship between philosophy and psychology in phenomenology, see Emmanuel Levinas, *The Theory of Intuition in Husserl's Phenomenology* (Evanston, IL, 1973), pp. 97–102.
11. Hilary Putnam, *Reason, Truth, and History* (Cambridge, 1981), pp. 152–54.
12. Keith Windschuttle, *The Killing of History* (New York, 1996) was originally written as a commentary on academic conditions in Australia. While the author's criticism of theory is at times superficial, the book amply illustrates the popularity of postmodernism in that country.
13. Letter to Vernes, 15 April 1767; *Correspondence and Related Documents*, ed. Theodore Besterman (Geneva, 1968–77), pp. 116: 53.
14. Gerald Graff, "The Myth of the Postmodernist Breakthrough," *Triquarterly* 26 (1973): 385.
15. Ibid., pp. 388–89.
16. Ibid., p. 389. Of course, one could argue that skepticism goes back even further than Graff acknowledges.
17. Ibid., p. 415.
18. Ibid., p. 410.
19. Ibid., p. 416.
20. Ibid., p. 415.
21. Michel Foucault, "Qu'est-ce que la critique/Critique et Aufklärung," *Bulletin de la Société française de Philosophie* 84 (1990): 35–63.
22. David Harvey, *The Condition of Postmodernity* (Oxford, 1989), pp. 27–28.
23. Cassirer, *The Philosophy of the Enlightenment*, pp. 8–9. One cannot overestimate the importance of Cassirer's distinction as a corrective of the postmodernist view of the Enlightenment. Cassirer formulated this distinction in order to refute Heidegger's vision of Kant and the Enlightenment. Like the postmodernist thinkers of today, Heidegger argued that the Enlightenment failed to confront the limits of knowledge

and needed to be replaced with a new kind of philosophy (his own). Cassirer's reaction consisted in showing that the Enlightenment was a move in the direction of limits and that consequently it was an indispensable legacy. See Gordon, "Ernst Cassirer."

24. Bradley and Swartz, *Possible Worlds*, p. 63.
25. Introduction to *Candide*, pp. 18–24.
26. Starobinski, *Voltaire's Double-Barreled Musket*, p. 106.
27. Ibid., p. 117.
28. Voltaire defined *esprit* as "sometimes a new comparison, sometimes a subtle allusion; here the misuse of a word that one presents with one meaning while hinting that it may have another; there a delicate connection between two uncommon ideas; a striking metaphor; the search for what an object does not initially suggest but still effectively contains; the art of uniting two distant things or of dividing two things that seem to be united, or of opposing one to another." *Dictionnaire philosophique* in *Oeuvres complètes*, ed. Moland (Paris, 1879), p. 3.
29. Joyce Appleby, Lynn Hunt, Margaret Jacob, *Telling the Truth About History* (New York, 1994), pp. 6, 15, 17, 241, 243.
30. See the critique by Raymond Martin in the *Forum* devoted to the book in *History and Theory* (vol. 34, no. 4, 1995), especially, pp. 320–21, 327.
31. See *Lettres philosophiques*, 1734, Letters XIV and XV. See also Voltaire's *Eléments de la philosophie de Newton* (first published 1738 but supplemented with new epistemological reflections in the 1741 version; the essential edition is that of the Voltaire Foundation, Oxford, 1992, ed. Robert L. Walters and W. H. Barber). Both in the text and in the editors' introduction, there is ample material for refuting the supposed "absolutism" of Enlightenment conceptions of science. See especially pp. 15–16, 23, 26–27, 101, 113, 209.
32. *Postmodernism: A Reader*, ed. Thomas Docherty (New York, 1993), p. 6.
33. Ibid.
34. Ibid., p. 12.
35. Karen Offen, "Reclaiming the European Enlightenment for Feminism: Or Prolegomena to any Future History of Eighteenth-Century Europe," in *Perspectives on Feminist Political Thought in European History: From the Middle Ages to the Present*, ed. Tjitske Akkerman and Siep Stuurman (London, 1998), p. 99.
36. For the debate on this issue, see Karen Offen, "Defining Feminism: A Comparative Historical Approach," *Signs* 14 (1988), pp. 119–57 (but especially pp. 150–53); and Karen Offen, "Feminism and Sexual Difference in Historical Perspective," in *Theoretical Perspectives on Sexual Difference*, ed. Deborah L. Rhode (New Haven, 1990), pp. 13–20 (especially p. 15).
37. Susan Meld Shell, *The Embodiment of Reason: Kant on Spirit, Generation, and Community* (Chicago, 1996), p. 8.
38. Robert Darnton, *The Kiss of Lamourette* (New York, 1990), pp. 3–20.
39. Many other scholars, such Reinhart Koselleck, Eric Voegelin, J. L. Talmon, and Keith Baker argue that the Enlightenment helped make the Terror possible. Unlike Darnton, these scholars abhor the Terror, but they show no warmth for the Enlightenment precisely because they regard it as the Terror's cause. Hence, they do not think dialectically either.
40. The idea that different "codes" can be derived from the same philosophical "principle" and that the crucial difference between codes is whether they are based on a spirit of human solidarity or not comes from Albert Camus, "Letters to a German Friend" in *Resistance, Rebellion, and Death* (New York, 1988); *Lettres à un Allemand* was originally written in 1943–44.

CONTRIBUTORS

Malick W. Ghachem is a doctoral candidate in history at Stanford University and a student at Harvard Law School.

Arthur Goldhammer is a Senior Associate of the Center for European Studies at Harvard, co-editor of *French Politics and Society*, and the translator of more than seventy works from the French.

Daniel Gordon is associate professor of History at the University of Massachusetts at Amherst and has been visiting professor at Stanford University and the Collège de France.

Alessa Johns is an Assistant Professor in the Department of English at the University of California, Davis.

Louis Miller is a member of the faculty at St. John's College, Annapolis.

Daniel Rosenberg is Assistant Professor of History in the Robert D. Clark Honors College at the University of Oregon.

Sophia Rosenfeld is Assistant Professor of History at the University of Virginia.

Elena Russo is Professor of French at the Johns Hopkins University.

Ronald Schechter is an Assistant Professor of History at the College of William and Mary.

Johnson Kent Wright is Associate Professor of Interdisciplinary Humanities at Arizona State University.

INDEX